CONSIDERING DRAMA

CONSIDERING DRAMA

Andrew Mayne & John Shuttleworth

Hodder & Stoughton

A MEMBER OF THE HODDER HEADLINE GROUP

By the same authors:

Considering Prose

British Library Cataloguing in Publication Data

Mayne, Andrew
Considering drama.
1. Drama — Study and teaching
I. Title II. Shuttleworth, John
792'07'1 PN1701

ISBN 0 340 38194 9

First published 1986
Impression number 14 13 12 11 10 9 8 7 6 5
Year 1998 1997 1996 1995 1994 1993

Typeset by Macmillan India Ltd, Bangalore.
Printed in Great Britain for Hodder & Stoughton Educational, a division of Hodder Headline Plc, Mill Road, Dunton Green, Sevenoaks, Kent TN13 2YA by Athenæum Press Ltd, Newcastle upon Tyne.

Contents

Preface

This book on the criticism of drama is designed to meet the needs of both the student (and teacher) in the classroom and the individual reader who is working through the material on his or her own. In the first situation, teachers may wish the members of the class to read through and prepare particular sections of the book before they designate exercises to be covered in class. As far as possible we have tried to devise questions that can form the basis for either written work or oral discussion. We have also included a number of ideas and suggestions throughout the book which are designed to encourage students to involve themselves actively in the *practice* of drama.

1

What is 'dramatic'?

Perhaps you have read of the Prime Minister making 'a *dramatic* intervention in a debate in the House of Commons' or heard about somebody arriving at a party 'wearing a *dramatic* yellow silk suit and maroon tie'. We bandy around this word 'dramatic' all the time, but what exactly do we mean by it? In the first example, the word seems to suggest the suddenness, the unexpected nature of the intervention, whereas in the second, the reference appears to be to a flamboyant or striking style of dress.

Now, when we speak of the 'dramatic' elements that go to make up a play, are we simply referring to some idea of 'suddenness' or 'flamboyancy'? Or will it be necessary to make some distinction between the word's everyday usage and what it might mean to a playwright or an audience watching a play? And in connection with the 'dramatic' as we experience it in a play, is it possible to say that certain ingredients will always make good drama? Are certain events or experiences inherently 'dramatic'—and others inevitably 'undramatic'?

These are the questions which we wish to consider in this introduction, and to get you thinking along the lines which might lead to some possible answers, we would like you to read the following outline of a day in the life (or part of it) of a student. We would like you to imagine that you have been commissioned to write a play for the stage which dramatises this material. We do not actually want you to write the play (though that could come later, if you wish!); we want you to consider carefully the following questions in relation to this plot outline.

(i) In terms of their potential impact as part of a play on stage, do any of these episodes seem to you to be inherently 'dramatic' or 'undramatic'? Say why.

(ii) Bearing in mind adaptation of this material to the stage, would any of these episodes present particular problems? Would you leave out any of this material?
(Be prepared to justify your decisions.)

One word before you begin: if you are using this book as a member of a class, we suggest that you split up into pairs or small groups to work on this exercise. Make notes on the conclusions you come to, in response to the questions above, and then report back to the class on your findings.

We will frequently suggest you adopt this method of approach as a way of generating initial discussion and of sharpening and clarifying your response. It is important when you are studying literature to share your ideas with other people, and at the same time to listen to what they have to say.

If you are working through this book on your own, it is still important for you to jot down some response to the questions we set before reading on.

A PLOT OUTLINE

1. On your way to the last class of the day, a friend Jake, who is a year older than you, stops you in the corridor to invite you to a party at his house that evening. His parents are away from home and he and his girlfriend, Jane Caprice, with whom he has been going out for a year, plan to invite all their friends. Before rushing off, Jake describes in glowing terms the delights that will be on offer.

2. Halfway through the lesson, in which all the time is spent working through maths problems while the teacher reads *New Society*, another friend, Spike, passes you a note. The note reads: 'Are you coming to Jake's party? Guess what? I'm going with Jane C!' You are thrown into quite a frenzy of curiosity at this—has Jane left Jake?—but the teacher keeps you back at the end of the lesson to try to persuade you to join a steel-drum band that he is forming, and you have no chance to talk to Spike.

3. On the way home on the bus you witness the aftermath of a bad road accident. An injured motorcyclist is lying on the pavement being attended to by ambulancemen; two police cars screech to a halt, their lights flashing and their sirens wailing. A crowd has gathered. As the bus pulls past the scene, all the passengers crane their necks to see what is going on. A woman next to you mutters 'Poor man' and you find yourself touched by the pathos of the scene and yet annoyed that, just like everyone else, you experience a morbid fascination when confronted with such scenes. The rest of the journey passes in silence.

4. Over tea at home you tell your parents that you intend going to a party at Jake's that evening. Your father objects at once: he reminds you that examinations are near and that your last report was highly critical. How can you hope to pass your exams and get a job, your father says, when you go out nearly every night? Your mother supports this view. Moreover, she does not approve at all of Jake: he is a 'bad influence' and his parents have no control over him. An argument soon develops. You accuse your parents of treating you like a child. Only when you promise to spend the next three evenings working in your room do your parents relent and reluctantly agree to your going to the party.

5. On your way to Jake's house you meet Jane Caprice. When you ask her whether she is planning to meet Spike she looks surprised and says that Spike did ask to take her, but she dislikes him intensely. She confides in you, however, that Jake is wildly jealous of Spike—so much so that she has decided to tell Jake this evening that their relationship has 'got far too serious' and must come to an end. Just as you are beginning to grasp the situation, you arrive at Jake's house and Jane takes you by the arm. With a beseeching look she says: 'Would you tell Jake about this? It's all so difficult. And then perhaps we could escape. I know where there's going to be a much better party tonight . . . ' At this moment a smiling Jake opens the door and welcomes you in.

Our thoughts on the questions we posed follow shortly, but we want to emphasise again the importance of making some notes of your own *before* you read on. While we cannot, of course, stop you 'cheating'—and while we do not claim to offer definitive answers—we do assure you that you will gain much greater benefits if you try exercises of this kind for yourself before you turn to our suggestions.

It is very important to underline the point that we are considering the potential dramatic impact of these episodes from the point of view of (i) their representation in *a play on stage*; and (ii) their *unity* as an unfolding sequence of events.

Episode 1, therefore, while in itself not containing very much in the way of immediate excitement or tension is nevertheless indispensable. The success of this scene of necessary exposition—the introduction of the characters and their situation—would depend very much on the quality and economy of the writing. We stress the importance of economy here because any scene of mere exposition which does not develop impetus fairly quickly, by extending the play's opening situation, is liable to lose an audience's attention.

Episode 2 contains drama certainly: it derives from the quandary in which the note places our main character (the protagonist); the scene might work very effectively in a film (close up on the passing of the note—perusal of its contents—pan to the reaction of the protagonist etc.), but as the 'drama' essentially takes place inside the protagonist's head and the situation gives him no opportunity to voice his feelings or share his thoughts, this scene would probably present insoluble problems to any dramatist who wished to present it on stage. Words and actions are virtually the *sine qua non* of drama on a stage, and it is likely that any adaptation to this medium would involve re-casting this material.

Episode 3 might superficially appear to be strongly dramatic, but closer inspection would probably force us to the conclusion that this material was purely contingent to the protagonist and his essential concerns in these scenes: he has no vital connection with either the people on the bus or in the accident and these events do not have any meaningful relation to the rest of the dramatic material in this sequence. Possibly if the protagonist were to be made to talk to the woman beside him on the bus, he might be made to reveal some interesting facets of his character, but any extended treatment of this scene would end up as an excrescence of melodrama and throw the developing sequence of events out of balance (to say nothing of the problems of presenting a realistic staging of these events). For these reasons, this scene would best be jettisoned from our dramatisation.

Episode 4 exhibits one element which is generally felt to be at the centre of the 'dramatic'—*conflict*. This is potentially a lively scene involving as it does the clash of opposing wills—and, perhaps, of values too, across the generation gap. Moreover, this scene is at the hinge of the action: an earlier episode has prepared us for the protagonist's request to his parents, and on the outcome of this quarrel the rest of the action depends. The shape of the material, too, would allow for a clean-cut dramatic structure, involving an argument for three voices which moves to a climax and then a negotiated peace.

Episode 5, too, contains potentially rich sources for dramatic action on stage. This potential derives from the revelation of character through dialogue and the way in which the situation is shown to be growing increasingly, and interestingly, more complex. Our interest as spectators of this scene would be likely to be involved because we are clearly at a point—or drawing near to it—of possible changes in the lives of several people. Elements of suspence are involved ('How will Jake react to the news he is shortly to hear?') and as we have been given access to privileged information which will not be known to certain characters who must figure in the next scene (Jake and Spike) our appetite for the sequel is whetted. We know that Jake is probably in for an unpleasant surprise, but a lot of unanswered questions are hanging in the air. For instance, 'Will the protagonist act on Jane's request?' and 'What are Jane's motives? Are we to believe she is genuinely interested in our hero, or is she simply attempting to use him?'. And so on. Questions of this kind create the potential for a kind of dramatic momentum.

Episodes 4 and 5 certainly, as raw material, have strong dramatic *potential*, but the realisation of that potential would depend entirely on the skill which the dramatist brought to bear on his material. This is a point we will return to later (see page 13).

SOME IDEAS FOR WRITING AND DISCUSSION

1. Perhaps you could continue (or even complete) the plot outline we gave you on page 2. Or maybe you have some ideas of your own for material you think suitable for dramatisation. When you have produced your outlines, subject them to a scene by scene analysis of their dramatic potential.

2. One of our students was reluctant to write a plot outline. He argued that to do this, 'would kill stone dead any play I was about to write'. He

was sure that the best dramatists 'would not plan a play out in such an unnatural, methodical way—they would simply let the play grow scene by scene as their inspiration caught fire'. What do you think?

3. Now try our first idea in reverse. That is, take some play you know well, summarise its plot and then comment on the dramatic effectiveness of the skeletal shape you have laid bare. This exercise led some of our students into interesting discussions concerning the differences between 'simple' and 'complex' plots and a consideration of such matters as the use of subplots and the patterning effect that can be produced by the parallelling or balancing of one scene against another. We should add, however, that a couple of our students who chose to summarise and comment on the plot outlines of comedies—*A Midsummer Night's Dream* was one example—did exhibit some signs of strain.

We wish to explore in a little more depth the question of 'What is dramatic?'—and this time not in terms of the dramatic potential of a mere plot outline. There follow three extracts which are set out in dialogue form. Again, we suggest you work initially in groups, each group concentrating on one of the extracts and working out a response to these two questions.

(i) What elements in the passage's subject matter and the way in which the situation is presented might be considered to be 'dramatic'?
(ii) Assess the extent to which the language at work in the passage is 'dramatic'.

Share your thoughts on these questions with the whole class and then consider together this final question:

(iii) Are all the extracts equally 'dramatic'? How would you arrange them on a scale which recorded your estimate of the maximum potential dramatic impact of each passage?

When you have completed this exercise, read on to see the extent to which your general impressions are in accord with those of a group of our students whose conclusions we have summarised.

A. *Miss Moffat, a schoolteacher in a small Welsh mining village in the latter part of the last century, is giving tuition to her promising pupil, Morgan Evans.*

MISS MOFFAT: (*Opening another book.*) By the way, next Tuesday I'm starting you on Greek.
MORGAN (*looking up, feigning interest*): Oh yes?
He writes again.
MISS MOFFAT (*subduing her excitement*): I am going to put you in for a scholarship to Oxford. 5
A pause. He looks up at her, arrested.

MORGAN: Oxford? Where the lords go?
MISS MOFFAT (*amused*): The same. I've made a simplified alphabet to begin with. It's jolly interesting after Latin . . . 10

She searches among her papers. The matter of factness with which she is (typically) controlling her excitement over the scholarship seems to gall him more and more; he watches her, bitterly.

Have a look at it by Tuesday, so we can make a good start—oh, and before we go on with the lesson, I've found the nail-file I mentioned— 15

In his mood, this is the last straw. He flings his pen savagely down on the table.

(*Without noticing, rummaging briskly.*) I'll show you how to use it. I had them both here somewhere—
MORGAN (*quietly*): I shall not need a nail-file in the coal-mine. 20
MISS MOFFAT (*mechanically, still intent at the desk*): In the what?
MORGAN: I am going back to the coal-mine.

She turns and looks at him. He rises, breathing fast. They look at each other. A pause.

MISS MOFFAT (*perplexed*): I don't understand you. Explain yourself. 25
MORGAN: I do not want to learn Greek, nor to pronounce any long English words, nor to keep my hands clean.
MISS MOFFAT (*staggered*): What's the matter with you? Why not?
MORGAN: Because . . . (*plunging*) . . . because I was born in a Welsh hayfield when my mother was helpin' with the harvest— and I always 30 lived in a little house with no stairs only a ladder—and no water—and until my brothers was killed I never sleep except three in a bed. I know that is terrible grammar but it is true.
MISS MOFFAT: What on earth has three in a bed got to do with learning Greek? 35
MORGAN: It has—a lot! The last two years I have not had no proper talk with English chaps in the mine because I was so busy keepin' this old grammar in its place. Tryin' to better myself . . . (*his voice rising*) . . . tryin' to better myself, the day and the night! . . . You cannot take a nail-file into the 'Gwesmor Arms' public bar! 40
MISS MOFFAT: My dear boy, file your nails at home! I never heard anything so ridiculous. Besides, you don't go to the Gwesmor Arms!
MORGAN: Yes I do, I have been there every afternoon for a week, spendin' your pocket-money, and I have been there now, and that is why I can speak my mind! 45

She looks at him, alarmed and puzzled.

MISS MOFFAT: I had no idea that you felt like this.
MORGAN: Because you are not interested in me.
MISS MOFFAT (*incredulously*): Not interested in you?
MORGAN (*losing control*): How can you be interested in a machine that you 50 put a penny in and if nothing comes out you give it a good shake? 'Evans, write me an essay, Evans, get up and bow, Evans, what is a subjunctive'! My name is Morgan Evans, and all my friends call me Morgan, and if there is anything gets on the wrong side of me it is callin' me Evans! . . . And do you know what they call me in the village? Ci bach yr 55 ysgol! The schoolmistress's little dog. What has it got to do with you if my nails are dirty? Mind your own business!

He bursts into sobs and buries his head in his hands on the end of the sofa. She turns away from him, instinctively shying from the spectacle of his grief. A pause. She is extremely upset, but tries hard not to show it. She waits for him to recover, and takes a step towards him. 60

MISS MOFFAT: I never meant you to know this. I have spent money on you—(*as he winces quickly*)—I don't mind that, money ought to be spent. But time is different. Your life has not yet begun, mine is half over. And when you're a middle-aged spinster, some folk say it's pretty near finished. Two years is valuable currency. I have spent two years on you. (*As he raises his head and stares before him, trying not to listen to her.*) Ever since that first day, the mainspring of this school has been your career. Sometimes, in the middle of the night, when I have been desperately tired, I have lain awake, making plans. Large and small. Sensible and silly. Plans, for you. And you tell me I have no interest in you. If I say any more I shall start to cry; and I haven't cried since I was younger than you are, and I'd never forgive you for that. (*Walking brusquely to the front door and throwing on her cloak.*) I am going for a walk. I don't like this sort of conversation, please never mention it again. If you want to go on, be at school to-morrow (*Going.*) If not, don't. 65 70 75

MORGAN (*muttering, fiercely*): I don't want your money, and I don't want your time! . . . I don't want to be thankful to no strange woman—for anything! 80

A pause.

MISS MOFFAT (*shaking her head, helplessly*): I don't understand you. I don't understand you at all.

She goes out by the front door.

Emlyn Williams: *The Corn is Green* (1938)

B. *Naval law requires that William, a sailor, be sentenced to death after he has wounded his captain, Crosstree—albeit in the defence of the virtue of William's wife, Susan. Both William and Susan have also suffered injustice at the hands of Susan's uncle.*

SUSAN *shrieks without—rushes in,* L., *and throws herself in* WILLIAM'S *arms.*

WILLIAM: Oh, Susan! Well, my poor wench, how fares it?

SUSAN: Oh, William! and I have watched, prayed for your return—smiled in the face of poverty, stopped my ears to the reproaches of the selfish, the worst pity of the thoughtless—and all, all for this! 5

WILLIAM: Ay, Sue, it's hard; but that's all over—to grieve is useless. Susan, I might have died disgraced—have left you the widow of a bad, black-hearted man; I know 'twill not be so—and in this, whilst you remain behind me, there is at least some comfort. I died in a good cause; I died in defence of the virtue of a wife—her tears will fall like spring rain on the grass that covers me. 10

SUSAN: Talk not so—your grave! I feel it is a place where my heart must throw down its heavy load of life.

WILLIAM: Come, Susan, shake off your tears. There, now, smile a bit—we'll not talk again of graves. Think, Susan, that I am a going on a long 15 foreign station—think so. Now, what would you ask—have you nothing, nothing to say?

SUSAN: Nothing! oh, when at home, hoping, yet trembling for this meeting, thoughts crowded on me. I felt as if I could have talked to you for days. 20 Stopping for want of power, not words. Now the terrible time is come—now I am almost tongue-tied—my heart swells to my throat, I can but look and weep. [*Gun fires.*] That gun! oh, William! husband! is it so near!—You speak not—tremble.

WILLIAM: Susan, be calm. If you love your husband, do not send him on 25 the deck a white-faced coward. Be still my poor girl, I have something to say—until you are calm, I will not utter it; now Susan—

SUSAN: I am cold, motionless as ice.

WILLIAM: Susan! you know the old aspen that grows near to the church porch; you and I, when children, almost before we could speak plainly, 30 have sat and watched, and wondered at its shaking leaves—I grew up, and that tree seemed to me a friend that loved me, yet had not the tongue to tell me so. Beneath its boughs our little arms have been locked together—beneath its boughs I took the last kiss of your white lips when hard fortune made me turn sailor. I cut from the tree this little branch. 35 [*Produces it.*] Many a summer's day aboard, I've lain in the top and looked at these few leaves, until I saw green meadows in the salt sea, and heard the bleating of the sheep. When I am dead, Susan, let me be laid under that tree—let me—

[*Gun is fired*—SUSAN *falls—at this moment a voice without cries* A 40 body overboard! PETER *and* SAILORS *come in, with* MASTER-AT-ARMS *and* MARINE OFFICER—*Music*—WILLIAM *gives* SUSAN *into charge of* SAILORS, *and she is borne off.*]

WILLIAM: What cry was that?—a shipmate overboard?

PETER: No, William—but as the gun was fired, a body rose up just at the 45 port-hole; they have taken it aboard; it is the body of Susan's uncle—a packet, directed to the captain, was taken from it.

WILLIAM: What, Susan's uncle! villain, may the greatest—[*bell tolls*]—no, no,—I shall soon be like him; why should the dying triumph over the dead? [*after a moment*] I forgive him. [*Music-Exeunt,* L.] 50

The Forecastle of the ship—Procession along the starboard gangway; minute bell tolls.—MASTER-AT-ARMS *with a drawn sword under his arm, point next to the prisoner;* WILLIAM *follows without his neckcloth and jacket, a* MARINE *on each side;* OFFICER OF MARINES *next;* ADMIRAL, CAPTAIN, LIEUTENANT, *and* MIDSHIPMEN, *following.* WILLIAM 55 *kneels; and all aboard appear to join in prayer with him. The procession then marches on and halts at the gangway;* MARINE OFFICER *delivers up prisoner to the* MASTER-AT-ARMS *and* BOATSWAIN, *a* SAILOR *standing at one of the forecastle guns, with the lock-string in his hand.—A platform extends from the cat-head to the fore-rigging. Yellow flag flying at the fore.* 60 *Colours half-mast down—Music—*WILLIAM *embraces the union jack—shakes the* ADMIRAL'S *hand.*

MASTER-AT-ARMS: Prisoner, are you prepared?

WILLIAM: Bless you! bless you all—

[*Mounts the platform.*] 65

CAPTAIN CROSSTREE *rushes on from gangway.*

CROSSTREE: Hold! Hold!
ADMIRAL: Captain Crosstree—retire, sir, retire.
CROSSTREE: Never! if the prisoner be executed, he is a murdered man. I alone am the culprit—'twas I who would have dishonoured him. 70
ADMIRAL: This cannot plead here—he struck a superior officer.
CROSSTREE: No!
ALL: No?
CROSSTREE: He saved my life; I had written for his discharge, villainy has kept back the document—'tis here dated back; when William struck me 75 he was not the king's sailor—I was not his officer.
ADMIRAL [*taking the paper—Music*]: He is free!
[*The* SEAMEN *give three cheers;* WILLIAM *leaps from the platform.* SUSAN *is brought on by* CAPTAIN CROSSTREE.]

CURTAIN 80

Douglas Jerrold: *Black Ey'd Susan* (1829)

C. *Socrates, imprisoned at Athens in 399 BC and facing a sentence of death, is visited by Crito who tries to persuade Socrates to escape. Crito argues that failure to follow his advice will leave both Socrates and his friends open to the criticism of public opinion.*

SOCRATES: Serious thinkers, I believe, have always held some such view as the one which I mentioned just now: that some of the opinions which people entertain should be respected, and others should not. Now I ask you, Crito, don't you think that this is a sound principle?—You are safe from the prospect of dying to-morrow, in all human probability; and you 5 are not likely to have your judgement upset by this impending calamity. Consider, then; don't you think that this is a sound enough principle, that one should not regard all the opinions that people hold, but only some and not others? What do you say? Isn't that a fair statement?
CRITO: Yes, it is. 10
SOCRATES: In other words, one should regard the good ones and not the bad?
CRITO: Yes.
SOCRATES: The opinions of the wise being good, and the opinions of the foolish bad? 15
CRITO: Naturally.
SOCRATES: To pass on, then: what do you think of the sort of illustration that I used to employ? When a man is in training, and taking it seriously, does he pay attention to all praise and criticism and opinion indiscriminately, or only when it comes from the one qualified person, the 20 actual doctor or trainer?
CRITO: Only when it comes from the one qualified person.
SOCRATES: Then he should be afraid of the criticism and welcome the praise of the one qualified person, but not those of the general public.
CRITO: Obviously. 25
SOCRATES: So he ought to regulate his actions and exercises and eating and drinking by the judgement of his instructor, who has expert knowledge, rather than by the opinions of the rest of the public.

CRITO: Yes, that is so.

SOCRATES: Very well. Now if he disobeys the one man and disregards his opinion and commendations, and pays attention to the advice of the many who have no expert knowledge, surely he will suffer some bad effect? 30

CRITO: Certainly.

SOCRATES: And what is this bad effect? Where is it produced?—I mean, in what part of the disobedient person? 35

CRITO: His body, obviously; that is what suffers.

SOCRATES: Very good. Well now, tell me, Crito—we don't want to go through all the examples one by one—does this apply as a general rule, and above all to the sort of actions which we are trying to decide about: just and unjust, honourable and dishonourable, good and bad? Ought we to be guided and intimidated by the opinion of the many or by that of the one—assuming that there is someone with expert knowledge? Is it true that we ought to respect and fear this person more than all the rest put together; and that if we do not follow his guidance we shall spoil and mutilate that part of us which, as we used to say, is improved by right conduct and destroyed by wrong? Or is this all nonsense? 40 45

CRITO: No, I think it is true, Socrates.

SOCRATES: Then consider the next step. There is a part of us which is improved by healthy actions and ruined by unhealthy ones. If we spoil it by taking the advice of nonexperts, will life be worth living when this part is once ruined? The part I mean is the body; do you accept this? 50

CRITO: Yes.

SOCRATES: Well, is life worth living with a body which is worn out and ruined in health? 55

CRITO: Certainly not.

SOCRATES: What about the part of us which is mutilated by wrong actions and benefited by right ones? Is life worth living with this part ruined? Or do we believe that this part of us, whatever it may be, in which right and wrong operate, is of less importance than the body? 60

CRITO: Certainly not.

SOCRATES: It is really more precious?

CRITO: Much more.

SOCRATES: In that case, my dear fellow, what we ought to consider is not so much what people in general will say about us but how we stand with the expert in right and wrong, the one authority, who represents the actual truth. So in the first place your proposition is not correct when you say that we should consider popular opinion in questions of what is right and honourable and good, or the opposite. Of course one might object 'All the same, the people have the power to put us to death.' 65 70

CRITO: No doubt about that! Quite true, Socrates; it is a possible objection.

SOCRATES: But so far as I can see, my dear fellow, the argument which we have just been through is quite unaffected by it. At the same time I should like you to consider whether we are still satisfied on this point: that the really important thing is not to live, but to live well. 75

CRITO: Why, yes.

SOCRATES: And that to live well means the same thing as to live honourably or rightly?

CRITO: Yes.
SOCRATES: Then in the light of this agreement we must consider whether or not it is right for me to try to get away without an official discharge. If it turns out to be right, we must make the attempt; if not, we must let it drop. 80

Plato: *Crito* (trans. H. Tredennick) (c. 370 BC)

One group of our students studying these extracts came to these conclusions, which we have summarised.

(i) There are elements in all three passages which might be considered to be dramatic.

In passage A Miss Moffatt and Morgan have clearly reached a turning-point in their relationship; there is conflict between them and the future of both of them seems to hang in the balance. In passages B and C we are presented with characters who face imminent death—something which, it was felt, offered the most extreme and potentially tense of all 'dramatic' situations. It was observed that in passage B the dramatist was obviously hoping to produce a very striking effect by means of the last-minute reprieve of a man on the brink of an unjust execution, though in passage C, while the matter of Socrates' fate was the starting-point of the discussion, the possible drama of the situation—a prisoner's fear of death, his anxiety and so on—was not fully exploited (perhaps because this was not the real interest of the writer).

(ii) The language of passage A, with its climaxes and the contrasts between the speakers, was felt to be dramatically successful in bringing to the surface the nature of the conflict between the two characters. Most members of the group, however, were critical of the language of passage B: it was described as being 'artificial', 'stilted' or 'too high-flown', and in connection with passage C it was felt that the dialogue form was not really used to create drama because the language suggested that Socrates was too obviously in charge, had probably already made up his mind that he was not going to escape and that the author was simply using the format of a discussion to define certain philosophical views rather than to impress upon us any overpowering urgency in the situation. Certain members of the group also felt that while the language of passage B was in some way 'puerile'—it was said 'people would not really speak like that in this situation'—the language of passage C was in places difficult and an audience in the theatre would have trouble grasping the point.

(iii) There was criticism of the artificial way in which the 'happy ending' was brought about in passage B; it was described as 'incredibly pat', 'too good to be true', 'too sudden and manufactured'. It was felt, however, that while extract B strove (perhaps too hard) for a dramatic effect, passage C—for reasons previously stated—had no such apparent intentions and would register low on any scale of potential dramatic impact.

Crito was described as 'simply a stooge'—somebody Socrates could be made to bounce his ideas off to show that he knew best all along.

There was general agreement that passage A would be likely to 'work' best on stage, and the following factors were singled out as being of importance:

(a) conflict between characters—both are given a fair chance to articulate their feelings;
(b) the scene moves to moments of climax and ultimatum;
(c) the deeper motives and feelings of both characters are gradually revealed;
(d) the audience's sympathies would probably be somewhat divided between the two characters;
(e) there was an effective contrast in the language of the two characters—most notably when Morgan reverted to his 'native speech' as a way of rejecting Miss Moffat's social and educational values; the language also registered strong feelings finally breaking through Miss Moffat's at first schoolmistressly and buttoned down manner of speaking;
(f) some thought had been given to the reactions, moves and gestures of characters (though the point was made that the mere insertion of stage directions could not, *in itself,* make a scene dramatic) and significant details, such as the nail file, were made to take on quite a wide significance;
(g) finally, the scene would produce in most spectators a desire to find out what happened next. Any audience would want to see if—and how—the conflict would be resolved.

By drawing together some of the points we have made so far, it should now be possible to arrive at some general conclusions concerning the questions we posed at the outset:

(i) Is there a difference between our everyday usage of the word 'dramatic' and what it means in the criticism of writing for the stage?
(ii) Can it be said that, with a view to stage presentation, some raw material is inherently 'dramatic' or 'undramatic'?

First, we have to bear in mind that what is 'dramatic' in a play must be an integral part of an unfolding sequence of events. Of course, surprise and 'suddenness' are often essential ingredients in a play, but whereas in everyday life we may say that an event is 'dramatic' which suddenly appears out of the blue to shock or horrify us, when an unexpected incident is suddenly sprung on an audience in the theatre, it must have some vital, causal connection with what has gone before or what will occur after. Simply to introduce into a play an event such as a road accident—certainly a 'dramatic' enough incident according to everyday experience—will *not* be dramatically effective unless this occurence has an organic relation to the play's main characters and its plot.

Secondly, we must recognise that, even though there have been great advances in modern techniques of staging and lighting, there are physical limitations on the kind of action it is possible to represent in the theatre. So, to stay with our previous example, if it was thought to be integral to a play's action, it might be straightforward enough to show on stage the aftermath of a road accident, but any playwright who required a totally convincing head-on crash between two juggernauts to be represented in the theatre would undoubtedly be asking for the impossible.

Thirdly, it is obviously the case that dramatists down the ages have been drawn to dramatise stories which give them the opportunity of showing human beings 'on the stretch'—that is, facing moments of crisis and tension in their lives, the greatest of which is perhaps a struggle for identity when threatened with the imminence of death. Yet we have already seen that dramatic potential in the selection of material is no necessary guarantee of the achievement of excellence in the form of a play. Simply to include a life and death struggle in a drama will not ensure that an audience is gripped by the action in the theatre. In passage B, the extract from Douglas Jerrold's *Black-Ey'd Susan,* the way in which a sudden reprieve from death by hanging was presented will strike most modern audiences as being over-melodramatic—that is vulgarly extravagant, implausible and over-sentimental. On the other hand we will see later that what appears to be the most sketchy material—perhaps two tramps making conversation on a country road in an effort to avoid facing the futility of their lives (see page 94)—can produce the very stuff of drama. It is, of course, the skill and experience that the playwright brings to his material which dictate the success of a play: what counts is, for instance, his ability to construct dialogue and to shape individual scenes so that they dovetail into the design of the whole play. The analogy we might use here is that of cooking a meal. Having the right ingredients certainly helps, but a bad cook's faulty technique can render inedible the most delicate of ingredients, while the great chef who can show his mastery of *haute cuisine* will also be able to produce something which is wholly satisfying from the simplest of raw materials. In this book we will be considering a range of recipes for good drama.

GENERAL DISCUSSION POINTS

It will probably be useful at this stage to develop in discussion some of the points we have just outlined—and to introduce some new ideas. The following questions are designed to direct your attention to some of the wider ramifications of the question we started with—what is 'dramatic'?—and to prompt some further thinking, in preparation for the next chapters on the strengths and limitations of dramatic form.

1. What are the elements of the 'dramatic' in the following: a political rally; Prime Minister's question time in the House of Commons; a great

state occasion such as a royal wedding or coronation; a circus; a religious service; a cup final at Wembley; a rock music concert; a fancy dress party?

2. In daily discourse we constantly use metaphors drawn from the stage. For instance, we may speak of somebody 'playing a role' or 'putting on a performance'; of someone who 'seeks the limelight' or 'remains in the wings'. Think of other examples, and say why these kinds of comparison are so prevalent.

3. Young children often 'improvise' scenes in which they take part in fantasy games, play at 'cops and robbers' or pretend they are acting as parents or carrying out certain adult jobs or 'roles'. What does this widespread practice indicate about both the nature of drama and of children? Consider, for instance, the value of these activities in the development of the child.

4. Discuss the following statements:
(a) 'In its ability to express character and relationships vividly, drama is the most concrete and expressive of all art forms.'
(b) 'A play about the problems of unemployment or drug-taking is far more likely to make us think about the issues (because our feelings are directly involved) than a government report or a straightforward documentary.'

5. What sort of material do you think it is either difficult or impossible to portray effectively on the stage because of the limitations of the form? Consider, for instance, the presentation of battles, sporting events, travel through a wide range of different countries. How successfully can the natural landscapes or changes in weather be shown in the theatre? Include other examples. What are some of the methods that playwrights have made use of to get round the difficulty of showing certain events on stage?

6. Are there also—or should there be—limitations imposed on what may be portrayed in drama as a result of what is felt to be 'good taste' or 'generally accepted morality'? What particular areas of human experience might be involved here? Does the practice of playwrights differ much, in these areas, from one period or culture to another?

2

The conventions of drama

All art uses conventions. They act as a convenient shorthand which allows instant communication by means of a mutually recognised system, the meaning of which can be readily appreciated by those who are presented with the medium of art in question. For instance, you are watching a film, and one character is talking to another about some incident from his past life; suddenly the image of the character's face on the screen dissolves and you see this same character now dramatically participating in the scene which a moment earlier he was simply describing. This is, of course, a 'flash-back', and because the members of the audience in the cinema have grown up with this convention, they will have no difficulty in following what is happening: indeed the convention is now so well established that it has virtually become a cinematic cliché.

Conventions can be a way of overcoming some of the given limitations of an art form. For instance, at the end of the last chapter we were discussing the type of material it is difficult to portray on stage. Imagine, for instance, that like Shakespeare in *Henry V* you are dealing with material which requires warfare to be shown on stage. How are you to deal with Agincourt? In his Prologue to Act V Shakespeare informs his audience of the difficulties:

> And so our scene must to the battle fly;
> Where—O for pity,—we shall much disgrace,
> With four or five most vile and ragged foils,
> Right ill disposed in brawl ridiculous,
> The name of Agincourt. Yet sit and see;
> Minding true things by what their mockeries be.

Nevertheless, through the intensity of his language, Shakespeare will convey the excitement and fear of battle. We *will* 'sit and see' because the language of the play enlists our visual imagination. Moreover, we will accept the convention that battles on stage may be represented in a stylised manner: four or five 'ragged foils', some banners and crests, a king addressing a few men in battle dress, skirmishes between the two sides rapidly depicting various parts of the battlefield—all this is a perfectly acceptable set of conventions for dealing with this material.

Again, let us imagine that a dramatist finds it essential to convey to an audience some information concerning a vital event which takes place in the world 'beyond' that in which the play is set: it might concern the outcome of a battle or a debate in the House of Commons. Technical or artistic reasons make it impossible or undesirable to portray this action in dramatic terms as it actually occurs. What is the dramatist to do? In fact, there is a range of ready-made conventions for getting around this problem and allowing events which have occurred 'off stage' to be incorporated into the main action. Two characters, for instance, may be made to discuss what has taken place somewhere else in a way in which they would hardly be likely to do in real life. Or a messenger may enter to give a report, a letter may be read, the telephone may ring . . . and so on. Such devices are part of the conventional stock-in-trade of the dramatist.

However, the use of dramatic conventions may present problems. Used clumsily, they can appear ridiculous; they can easily harden into stage clichés. But perhaps the main problem presented by conventions occurs when we are considering plays from the past. Unlike the cinema, its relatively new offspring, the history of drama goes back a long way and the conventions the drama has adopted, therefore, have differed greatly from one culture to the next, and from one period of time to another. This means that what was once a readily understood shorthand, a widely recognised convention, may leave a twentieth century reader with a sense of bewilderment, a feeling that there is an unbridgeable gap between some apparently artificial dramatic device and the kind of theatrical vocabulary with which he is familiar.

Conventions in the drama dictate the nature of what is to be shown on stage, the kind of theatrical techniques that operate and the language that is to be used. In the following pages we will be considering some of the specific implications of this statement in relation to a series of brief glances at a number of different periods of the history of drama. Let us, for instance, imagine that it might be possible for us to attend a performance of a Greek tragedy, presented at one of the essentially religious festivals held in Ancient Greece in the fifth century BC. Greek drama has had a profound influence on the whole of the following tradition of western European drama, and yet the reaction of a twentieth century 'time-traveller' at the original staging of, say, Sophocles' great masterpiece, *Oedipus Rex,* would undoubtedly be one of puzzlement. He would notice, for instance, that the actors all wore masks made of linen, cork or wood; he would hear a chorus of fifteen speak in unison at intervals throughout the drama, sometimes conversing with the actors, sometimes commenting on the events of the play; he would observe that scenes of violence were never portrayed on stage—they were reported to the audience by a messenger. (Something of the flavour of the language of the play, admittedly in translation, may be sampled later in the passage taken from *Oedipus Rex*—see page 65).

The beginnings of English drama are also to be found in religious festivals and rituals. By the thirteenth century the trade guilds in many medieval towns were presenting sequences of plays known as 'Mystery

Cycles': in a cyclical form these plays portrayed virtually the whole Biblical span of history, beginning with God in Heaven banishing Lucifer and then creating the world, portraying stories from the Old Testament and then from Christ's ministry and concluding with the Last Judgement. Each scene from the cycle was presented on a moveable stage wagon, as is described by David Rogers in the *Breviary of Chester History* (1609):

> They (the Chester pageants) were divided into twenty-four pageants or parts, according to the number of the Companies of the City, and every Company brought forth their pageants, which was the carriage or place which they played in.
>
> They were played upon Monday, Tuesday and Wednesday in Whitsun week. And they first began at the Abbey gates, then it was wheeled from thence to the Prentice at the High Cross before the Mayor; and before that was done, the second came, and the first went into the Watergate Street, and from thence unto the Bridge Street, and so all, one after another, till all the pageants were played appointed for the first day, and so likewise for the second and the third day. This pageant or carriage was a high place made like a house with two rooms, being open on the top; in the lower room they apparelled and dressed themselves, and in the higher rooms they played; and they stood upon six wheels.

Here is a section from the Chester Pageant—'Noah's Flood'—which was presented appropriately by the Water-Leaders and Drawers in Dee. The manuscript dates from the late sixteenth or early seventeenth century, though the material itself is much older than that.

The questions which follow the passage are designed to prompt you to think about the conventions which operate in this extract.

God has just told Noah to build a ship so he and his family may be saved from the Flood which will destroy the rest of mankind.

NOAH: Ah, Lord, I thank thee loud and still, — *at all times*
That to me art in such will,
And sparest me and my house to spill,
As now I soothly find.
Thy bidding, Lord, I shall fulfil, 5
And never more thee grieve ne grill, — *nor offend*
That such grace has sent me till — *to me*
Among all mankind. — *above*
[*To his family:*
Have done, you men and women all! 10
Help, for aught that may befall, — *whatever happens*
To work this ship, chamber and hall, — *build*
As God hath bidden us do.
SHEM: Father, I am all ready boun: — *prepared*
An axe I have, by my crown, 15
As sharp as any in all this town,
For to go thereto. — *to it*

HAM: I have a hatchet wondrous keen
To bite well, as may be seen; *cut*
A better grounden, as I ween, *sharpened; think* 20
Is not in all this town.
JAPHETH: And I can well make a pin, *peg*
And with this hammer knock it in;
Go and work without more din,
And I am ready boun. 25
N'S WIFE: And we shall bring timber to, *to this place*
For we mun nothing else do; *may*
Women be weak to underfo *undertake*
Any great travail. *labour*
S'S WIFE: Here is a good hackstock; *chopping-block* 30
On this you may hew and knock;
Shall none be idle in this flock,
Ne now may no man fail.
H'S WIFE: And I will go to gather slitch, *pitch*
The ship for to caulk and pitch; 35
Anointed it must be every stitch, *part*
Board, tree, and pin. *beam*
J'S WIFE: And I will gather chips here
To make a fire for you in fere, *you all*
And for to dight your dinner, *prepare* 40
Against you come in.

Then they make signs as if they were working with different tools.

NOAH: Now, in the name of God, I will begin
To make the ship that we shall in, *live in*
That we be ready for to swim *float* 45
At the coming of the flood.
These boards I join here together,
To keep us safe from the weather,
That we may row both hither and thither,
And safe be from this flood. 50
Of this tree will I make the mast,
Tied with cables that will last,
With a sail-yard for each blast, *yard-arm*
And each thing in their kind;
With topcastle and bowsprit, 55
With cords and ropes, I have all meet *fit*
To sail forth at the next wet; *downpour*
This ship is at an end. *finished*

Then Noah with all his family again make signs of working with different tools. 60

Wife, in this castle we shall be kept; *kept safe*
My children and thou, I would, in leapt.
N'S WIFE: In faith, Noah, I had as lief thou slept.
For all thy frankish fare,
I will not do after thy rede. 65

NOAH: Good wife, do now as I thee bid.
N'S WIFE: By Christ, not ere I see more need,
Though thou stand all the day and stare.
NOAH: Lord, that women be crabbed ay, *always perverse*
And never are meek, that dare I say. 70
This is well seen by me to-day,
In witness of you each one.
Good wife, let be all this bere *clamour*
That thou makes in this place here;
For all they ween thou art master— 75
And so thou art, by St John!

A. C. Cawley (ed.): *Everyman and Medieval Miracle Plays*

(i) Two conventions operate here in connection with the presentation in the scene of (a) the building of the ark, and (b) the passing of time. Explain the nature of each of these conventions.
(ii) Do these conventions seem to you at all 'clumsy'? Why (not)?
(iii) 'Primitive and crude—hardly a drama as we understand the term.' 'Contains excellent dramatic material—and even some good touches of humour.'
'The language gets in the way and would have to be modernised.' Taking these statements into account and also bearing in mind what you have already stated about the use of convention here, how would you rate the 'dramatic potential' of this scene?

Whether or not you think this scene makes good dramatic material, it could certainly be staged quite easily in nearly any kind of modern theatre. But remember the way in which the play would have been presented in mediaeval times (see page 17). In our own period many of these cycles of mystery or miracle plays—of those which have come down to us in manuscript the Chester, York and Towneley plays (from Wakefield) are the most notable—have been revived and presented as 'street theatre' with the backs of lorries perhaps serving in the place of the old guild wagons. This leads to one final general question. If you wished to present one of these cycles of plays in a *theatre*, can you think of some suitable ways of staging them so as to maintain something of the original 'moveable feast' element of a pageant, but in a manner which a modern audience would find acceptable?

[2–3] That are so minded towards me, and refrainest from destroying me and my household.
[15] *by my crown*, an asseveration.
[33] Nor may any one now fail [to do his part].
[54] And every kind of thing [needed].
[55] *topcastle*, a fortified platform at the mast-head.
[61] *castle*, a raised structure on the deck of a ship.
[62] I would like my children and you to hurry in.
[63–65] I would as soon you slept. For all your polite behaviour I won't do as you advise.
[72] As each of you (i.e. the audience) has witnessed.
[75] *they*, i.e. the audience.

Let us imagine that our modern theatre-goer could enter his time-machine for one final trip and witness a performance in the late Elizabethan or Jacobean period when giants such as Marlowe, Shakespeare and Ben Jonson were creating the first, and probably the greatest, period of English drama. The illustrations (on pages 161–2) give some idea of the kind of theatre in London on the South Bank of the Thames that our spectator would enter—a 'wooden O', an octagonal structure, open to the sky and to the elements. Standing in the pit (entrance fee, one penny) and looking up at an apron or thrust stage of considerable dimensions—probably about forty feet wide—he would witness a continual unfolding of the action of the play: there would be no curtain to end a scene, no lighting to create special effects, and a minimum of scenery and props. (Some further details are given later about the nature of this theatre (see page 161)).

The physical structure of the theatre for which a dramatist writes determines in a number of important ways the nature of the plays he produces. On the face of it, it might seem that Shakespeare's playhouse would have imposed severe limitations on him. This is hardly so. Like all great dramatists he turned possible limitations to his own creative advantage, and in fact the nature of the acting arena for which he wrote—where language was king—suited his purposes. The scene which follows from *Macbeth* (1606) illustrates, for instance, the way in which Shakespeare makes use of the close physical (and mental?) proximity of actors and audience. This allows a certain convention to operate which in the kind of theatre favoured, for instance, by the Victorians—a proscenium arch stage with an orchestra pit and a considerable distance separating the audience from the action—tends to look and sound very odd. The questions that follow this passage are designed to lead you into a discussion of the use to which Shakespeare puts this convention—which we will leave you to discover for yourselves.

After victory in battle, Macbeth, who is Thane (Lord) of Glamis, and his fellow general, Banquo, have met three witches who have prophesied that Macbeth will become Thane of Cawdor and 'king hereafter'. The witches also foretell that Banquo will be the father of a line of kings. Now Rosse and Angus enter with a message from King Duncan.

ANGUS: We are sent,
To give thee from our royal master thanks;
Only to herald thee into his sight,
Not pay thee.
ROSSE: And, for an earnest of a greater honour, 5
He bade me, from him, call thee Thane of Cawdor:
In which addition, hail, most worthy Thane,
For it is thine.
BANQUO: What! can the Devil speak true?
MACBETH: The Thane of Cawdor lives: why do you dress me 10
In borrow'd robes?

ANGUS: Who was the Thane, lives yet;
But under heavy judgment bears that life
Which he deserves to lose. Whether he was combin'd
With those of Norway, or did line the rebel 15
With hidden help and vantage, or that with both
He labour'd in his country's wrack, I know not;
But treasons capital, confess'd and prov'd,
Have overthrown him.
MACBETH [*Aside.*]: Glamis, and Thane of Cawdor: 20
The greatest is behind. [*To Rosse and Angus*] Thanks for your pains.—
[*To Banquo*] Do you not hope your children shall be kings,
When those that gave the Thane of Cawdor to me
Promis'd no less to them?
BANQUO: That, trusted home, 25
Might yet enkindle you unto the crown,
Besides the Thane of Cawdor. But 'tis strange:
And oftentimes, to win us to our harm,
The instruments of Darkness tell us truths;
Win us with honest trifles, to betray's 30
In deepest consequence.—
Cousins, a word, I pray you.
MACBETH: [*Aside.*] Two truths are told,
As happy prologues to the swelling act
Of the imperial theme.—I thank you, gentlemen.— 35
[*Aside.*] This supernatural soliciting
Cannot be ill; cannot be good:—
If ill, why hath it given me earnest of success,
Commencing in a truth? I am Thane of Cawdor:
If good, why do I yield to that suggestion 40
Whose horrid image doth unfix my hair,
And make my seated heart knock at my ribs,
Against the use of nature? Present fears
Are less than horrible imaginings.
My thought, whose murther yet is but fantastical, 45
Shakes so my single state of man,
That function is smother'd in surmise,
And nothing is, but what is not.
BANQUO: Look, how our partner's rapt.
MACBETH [*Aside.*]: If Chance will have me King, why, Chance may crown me, 50
Without my stir.
BANQUO: New honours come upon him,
Like our strange garments, cleave not to their mould,
But with the aid of use. 55
MACBETH: [*Aside.*] Come what come may,
Time and the hour runs through the roughest day.
BANQUO: Worthy Macbeth, we stay upon your leisure.
MACBETH: Give me your favour: my dull brain was wrought
With things forgotten. Kind gentlemen, your pains 60
Are register'd where every day I turn

The leaf to read them.—Let us toward the King.—
[*To Banquo*] Think upon what hath chanc'd; and
at more time.
The Interim having weigh'd it, let us speak 65
Our free hearts each to other.
BANQUO: Very gladly.
MACBETH: Till then, enough.—Come, friends. [*Exeunt.*]

(i) What convention does Shakespeare draw on here to give us access to Macbeth's thoughts and feelings?
(ii) What does the extensive use of this convention tell us about Macbeth's character and mood at this point in the play's action?
(iii) Explain why the use of this convention suggests an extremely close relationship between actor and audience.

GENERAL DISCUSSION TOPICS

1. It is interesting that in our own period many directors have seen the advantages of a theatre design which makes it possible to stage a play with an audience seated on three sides of the acting area—or even surrounding it completely ('theatre in the round'). Have you seen any plays presented in these ways? What special advantages—or disadvantages—did you observe? Are there some types of play which benefit from—or even demand—one particular design of theatre or one definite method of stage arrangement? (We will return to some of these questions in a later chapter—see page 168.)

2. We observed earlier, in connection with the theatre of Ancient Greece and the English mystery cycles, that drama often has its roots in religious rituals and festivals. Why do you think this is a feature of the early development of the drama in so many different cultures?

The conventions of the drama at any given period embody, by definition, what audiences are accustomed to seeing on stage—both the subject matter and the way in which it is presented. Fortunately, in performance the greatest drama is not tied to the conventions of a definite place or time: witness the protean forms Shakespeare's plays have taken on since they left the Globe. Yet there must be a sense in which plays from the past—in the form of a text—can only speak to us clearly if we, as readers, at least have some familiarity with the dramatic conventions that underpinned their original composition. So, a director who wishes to make, for instance, Sophocles' *Oedipus Rex* live in the modern theatre must grapple not only with a play translated from a dead language; he must also find ways in which the conventions of the theatre of Ancient Greece may be transposed to the contemporary stage. This will frequently involve finding some acceptable equivalent for what is now perhaps an alien dramatic mode of communication—a task we invited you to embark on in connection with a consideration of the question of how you would stage a cycle of mediaeval mystery plays in a modern theatre.

In certain periods and places during the course of the history of drama, convention has ruled with an iron hand. For example, during the great neoclassical age of the French seventeenth century a whole set of critical dicta, which were rigidly enforced, laid down the stylistic mode of tragic drama—the rhyming couplet of the alexandrine with its most exacting rules of metre and diction—and the manner in which plot and subject matter were to be presented: a convention such as the 'Three Unities', for instance, required the plot of a play to be set in one single location, in a timespan of not more than one day, and developed as a clearly concentrated piece of dramatic action, unhindered by any diversions, comic relief or subplots.

These rules, for such they were, produced some plays, the tragedies of Corneille and Racine, for instance (see *Phèdre*, 1677), which blended formal control with the most concentrated expression of dramatic intensity; yet 'rules' for the writing of plays is an odd notion and, even for the highly logical French, at some point the rules had to be made to bend. However, the strength of an audience's expectations, deriving from established conventions, may be judged at precisely the moment when there is some striking innovation or experiment attempted: audiences presented with something on stage which does not accord with its sense of what should go to make up an evening's entertainment will often react with emotions ranging from bemused rejection to complete outrage. When Victor Hugo's play *Hernani* was first presented on the stage of the Comédie Française in 1830, the curtain rose and an old woman responded to a knock at the door with the apparently innocuous line *Serait-ce déjà lui?* (Can that be him already?); but instantly a near riot broke out in the theatre with boos and counter cheers from rival factions. Why? Quite simply this line was not an alexandrine, the perfectly balanced rhyming couplet with its six iambic feet that nearly all French drama since the seventeenth century had adopted. The prevailing orthodoxy of convention had been threatened—and perhaps not before time, for some dramatic conventions can after a while turn into straitjackets. Our own period, too, provides examples of considerable controversy—when, for example, in the 1950s plays such as Beckett's *Waiting for Godot* (1955) and Osborne's *Look Back in Anger* (1956) signalled in their very different ways that drama was about to take a new direction.

Should our very sketchy look at some aspects of the history of drama send us back to reconsider the passage from Douglas Jerrold's play *Black-Ey'd Susan* (see page 7)? Did we perhaps dismiss the extract too glibly? This play and many like it were once very popular on the nineteenth-century English stage. Is it simply intolerance on our part—and an unfamiliarity with the dramatic conventions of the time—which made us reject the play almost out of hand? Read the extract from the play again and consider which of the following statements you are in general agreement with before you read on.

(a) If we know the conventions of melodrama, this piece can be seen as potentially successful on the stage.
(b) Even allowing for different dramatic conventions, this material represents an appeal to the lowest common denominator of taste—rather like the modern television 'soap opera'.
(c) You have to remember that this kind of play was written for a new popular audience which demanded escapism—thrilling action, sudden reverses and exaggerated emotions.
(d) Moreover, the play was written for the kind of large proscenium arch theatre in which striking effects and high-flown rhetoric were the only possible medium.

We feel that points (c) and (d) help to explain why the extract is as it is; we also believe that the passage might still be performed with some success on stage, even today; and yet our literary judgement is that, even allowing for these points, the writing of Douglas Jerrold is third rate. Let us explain the contradiction we seem to have got ourselves into!

It is often said that a comedian is only as good as his material; but this is not entirely true. A great comedian, by means of his timing and his stage manner, *can* 'get away' with poor material (and equally, excellent material can be ruined by a poor performer). And so it is with an actor in performance. Words on the page may appear dull and flat, but all playwrights rely on the fact that an actor can, in performance, add something of his physical presence and theatrical skill, thus breathing the breath of life into the most unpromising material. We have all seen good actors in television soap opera bring a character to life, perhaps through a touch of original characterisation—a gesture, a look, a sense of innate histrionic ability—whereas to a reader of the script from which the actor is working, the lines on offer seem to be only a rehashing of cliché. And there is nothing new in this. The great Victorian actor, Henry Irving, established his reputation through what was by all accounts a continuously riveting performance as Mathias in the melodrama *The Bells*; contemporary reports from many reputable sources reveal that the charismatic Irving could make an action such as the mere removal of his boots an overwhelming *coup de théâtre*.

The point is that the critic in his study will find it very difficult to judge what a great actor will bring to the material that is given to him. It is possible that *Black-Ey'd Susan* might still be made to be viable on the modern stage—though how would an actor cope with the moribund language and heavy-handedly moral gesturings of such lines as 'I died in defence of the virtue of a wife—her tears will fall like spring rain on the grass that covers me'? A purely literary judgement on the text must find it lacking, and as this book will be primarily concerned with dramatic literature in which language is used in fresh and dynamic ways and the conventions (of any period of theatrical development) extended and developed, the play will probably remain for us principally an example of historically interesting but dramatically inferior writing.

There is, however, an important tailpiece to add here. What we have suggested is that there is a world of difference between coming to a text cold and the experience of living theatre. The theatre can be a place of magic; we often speak of a great actor or production 'casting a spell over the audience'—and the audience, too, is an agent in this alchemy. Remember that unlike other art forms—think of reading a novel or even watching television drama—the performance of a play *demands* the active response of a group of spectators at a 'live' event. The corporate response of an audience adds so much to a play in the theatre; it provides not only a sense of occasion (these people have left their homes on a cold winter's evening and paid good money to see this show) and excitement (not least because things can go disastrously wrong in a performance); it also affects in a positive (or negative) way the very nature and quality of what happens in the theatre. This is perhaps easiest to appreciate when a comedy is performed: audience response in the form of laughter and obvious enjoyment add to the warmth and pleasure of the occasion; lack of reaction can kill a comedy stone dead. But in other ways, too, that are more difficult to define objectively, the 'vibrations' sent out by an audience establish a two-way contact with the actors on stage. And no two audiences are ever quite the same. If you have ever yourself acted in a play you will know how differently audiences can respond and the extent to which this affects the nature of the performance. Any study of the drama, therefore, which is cut off from experiencing a wide variety of plays in the theatre is arid, and for this reason—as well as the obvious pleasures of play-going—we would urge you to link your reading of dramatic texts with as many visits to the theatre as your pocket and geographical considerations allow.

THE STRENGTHS AND LIMITATIONS OF DRAMATIC FORM

Our last point brings us to the most basic of all dramatic conventions, and one which we have not so far considered. Behind all experience of living drama lies this notion: we agree, as an audience, to sit in a theatre for anything up to three hours, watching people we know to be actors speaking lines we know have been written for them; yet we 'suspend our disbelief' and 'pretend', as it were, that what we are watching is something like an actual representation of human life. The extent to which we ever can, or should, totally 'suspend our disbelief' and become completely emotionally involved in what we see happening on stage is a complex and much-debated point of dramatic theory (and practice—see page 175). It is likely, perhaps, that even at our most intense moments of identification with the action of the play, we never totally forget that what we are witnessing is, after all, a piece of artifice. It could be that one of the pleasures that drama offers us is emotional involvement combined with (what is usually denied us in real life) a certain final detachment from any direct need to take personal responsibility or to commit ourselves to any definite response or course of action. Watching a play can involve a number of contradictory responses of this kind. So, when we witness a performance of Shakespeare's *Othello* (1602–04), for instance, we will no doubt be horrified by Iago's deception of Othello into believing that his wife, Desdemona, has been unfaithful to him; yet at the same time we may not be able to resist admiring Iago's amazingly inventive power—this while we condemn Iago morally and are desolated that Desdemona should be the innocent victim of such diabolical ingenuity. And this mixture of response goes hand in hand with what we have previously described as a certain final detachment from events which, while moving us most powerfully, we know to be fundamentally part of a cleverly sustained theatrical illusion.

To assist us, however, in considering at a more basic level both the strengths and limitations of drama as an art form, we would like you to read the following two extracts. The first is taken from the beginning of a novel, *Billy Liar* (1959) by Keith Waterhouse; the second passage is the stage version of the same material which Waterhouse adapted in 1960 with Willis Hall.

Write answers to these two questions before you read on:

(i) What different kinds of reaction do you have to meeting much the same material in two different forms? Try to compare your response to these two different media—dialogue from a play and a passage from a novel.

(ii) Bearing in mind particularly that these two extracts are taken from the *opening* of the works in question, which one is more likely to win your immediate interest?

A. I slopped down into the hall, took the *Stradhoughton Echo* out of the letter-box, where it would have remained all day if the rest of the family had anything to do with it, and went into the lounge. It was a day for big decisions.

The breakfast ceremony at Hillcrest had never been my idea of fun. I had made one disastrous attempt to break the monotony of it, entering the room one day with my eyes shut and my arms outstretched like a sleep-walker, announcing in a shaky, echo-chamber voice: 'Ay York-shire breakfast scene. Ay polished table, one leaf out, covahed diagonally by ay white tablecloth, damask, with grrreen strip bordah. Sauce-stain to the right, blackberry stain to the centre. Kellogg's corn flakes, Pyrex dishes, plate of fried bread. Around the table, the following personnel: fathah, mothah, grandmothah, one vacant place.' None of this had gone down well. I entered discreetly now, almost shiftily, taking in with a dull eye the old man's pint mug disfigured by a crack that was no longer mistaken for a hair, and the radio warming up for Yesterday in Parliament. It was a choice example of the hygienic family circle, but to me it had taken on the glazed familiarity of some old print such as When Did You Last See Your Father? I was greeted by the usual breathing noises.

'You decided to get up, then,' my mother said, slipping easily into the second series of conversations of the day. My stock replies were 'Yes,' 'No, I'm still in bed' and a snarled 'What does it look like?' according to mood. Today I chose 'Yes' and sat down to my boiled egg, stone cold as threatened. This made it a quarter to nine. 20

The old man looked up from some invoices and said: 'And you can start getting bloody well dressed before you come down in a morning.' So far the dialogue was taking a fairly conventional route and I was tempted to throw in one of the old stand-bys, 'Why do you always begin your sentences with an "And"?' Gran, another dress fanatic who always seemed to be fully and even elaborately attired even at two in the morning when she slunk downstairs after the soda-water, chipped in: 'He wants to burn that raincoat, then he'll have to get dressed of a morning.' One of Gran's peculiarities, and she had many, was that she would never address anyone directly but always went through an intermediary, if necessary some static object such as a cupboard. Doing the usual decoding I gathered that she was addressing my mother and that he who should burn the raincoat was the old man, and he who would have to get dressed of a morning was me. 'I gather,' I began, 'that he who should burn the raincoat—' but the old man interrupted: 25 30 35

'And what bloody time did you get in *last* night? If you can call it last night. This bloody morning, more like.' 40

I sliced the top off my boiled egg, which in a centre favouring tapping the top with a spoon and peeling the bits off was always calculated to annoy, and said lightly: '*I* don't know. 'Bout half-past eleven, quarter to twelve.'

The old man said: 'More like one o'clock, with your half-past bloody eleven! Well you can bloody well and start coming in of a night-time. I'm not having *you* gallivanting round at all hours, not at your bloody age.' 45

'Who *are* you having gallivanting round, then?' I asked, the wit rising for the day like a pale and watery sun.

My mother took over, assuming the clipped, metallic voice of the morning interrogation. '*What were you doing down Foley Bottoms at nine o'clock last night?*' 50

I said belligerently: 'Who says I was down at Foley Bottoms?'

'Never mind who says, or who doesn't say. You *were* there, and it wasn't that Barbara you were with, neither.' 55

'He wants to make up his mind who he *is* going with,' Gran said.

There was a rich field of speculation for me here. Since my mother had never even met the Witch—the one to whom she referred by her given name of Barbara—or Rita either—the one involved in the Foley Bottoms episode, that is—I wondered how she managed to get her hands on so many facts without actually hiring detectives. 60

I said: 'Well you want to tell whoever saw me to mind their own fizzing business.'

'It *is* our business,' my mother said. 'And don't you be so cheeky!' I pondered over the absent friend who had supplied the Foley Bottoms bulletin. Mrs Olmonroyd? Ma Walker? Stamp? *The Witch herself?* I had a 65 sudden, hideous notion that the Witch was in league with my mother and that they were to spring some dreadful coup upon me the following day when, with a baptism of lettuce and pineapple chunks, the Witch was due to be introduced to the family at Sunday tea. 70

Gran said: 'If she's coming for her tea tomorrow she wants to tell her. If she doesn't, I will.' My mother interpreted this fairly intelligently and said: 'I'm *going* to tell her, don't you fret yourself.' She slid off down a chuntering landslide of recrimination until the old man, reverting to the main theme, came back with the heavy artillery. 75

'He's not bloody well old enough to stay out half the night, I've told him before. He can start coming in of a night, or else go and live somewhere else.'

This brought me beautifully to what I intended to be the text for the day, but now that the moment had come I felt curiously shy and even a little sick 80 at the idea of my big decisions. I allowed my mother to pour me a grudging cup of tea. I picked up the sugar with the tongs so as to fall in with house rules. I fingered the used envelope in my raincoat pocket, see S. re job. I cleared my throat and felt again the urge to yawn that had been with me like a disease for as long as I could remember, and that for all I knew *was* a 85 disease and a deadly one at that. The need to yawn took over from all the other considerations and I began to make the familiar Channel-swimmer mouthings, fishing for the ball of air at the back of my throat. The family returned to rummage among their breakfast plates and, aware that the moment had gone by, I said: 90

'I've been *offered* that job in London.'

B. (BILLY FISHER *begins to come down the bedroom stairs. He is nineteen years old and slightly built. He is wearing an old raincoat over his pyjamas. He is smoking a cigarette.*)

ALICE: Is that him? He's stirred himself at last, then. I'll see what his breakfast is doing. 5

(ALICE *exits to the kitchen as* BILLY *reaches the foot of the stairs.* BILLY *takes the morning paper from behind the door and enters the living-room.*)

FLORENCE: She lets him do just as he likes.

BILLY (*reading aloud from the paper*): Cabinet Changes Imminent. 10

GEOFFREY: Yes, and you'll be bloody imminent if you don't start getting up on a morning.

BILLY: Good morning, Father.

GEOFFREY: Never mind bloody good mornings. It's bloody afternoon more like. If you think your mother's got nothing better to do than go 15 round cooking six breakfasts every morning you've got another think coming.

FLORENCE: She lets him do what he wants.

BILLY (*ignoring his father he turns and bows, acting out the situation to his grandmother*): Your servant, ma'am. 20

GEOFFREY: And you stop that bloody game. I'm talking to you. You're bloody hopeless. And you can start getting bloody well dressed before you come down in the morning.

FLORENCE: He wants to burn that raincoat. He wants to burn it. Sling it on the fire-back. Then he'll have to get dressed whether or no. 25

BILLY: I gather that he who would burn the raincoat is Father and he who should get dressed of a morning is my good self. Why do you always address all your remarks to the sideboard, Grandmother?

GEOFFREY (*almost rising from his chair*): Here, here, here! Who do you think you're bloody talking to? You're not out with your daft mates now. And what time did you get in last night? If it was night. This bloody morning, more like. 30

(ALICE *enters from the kitchen.*)

BILLY: I really couldn't say. 'Bout half-past eleven, quarter to twelve. Good morning, Mother. 35

GEOFFREY: More like one o'clock, with your bloody half-past eleven! Well, you can bloody well start coming in of a night-time. I'm not having you gallivanting round at all hours, not at your bloody age.

BILLY: Who are you having gallivanting around, then?

GEOFFREY: And I'm not having any of your bloody lip. I'll tell you that, for a start. 40

ALICE: What were you doing down at Foley Bottoms at nine o'clock last night?

BILLY: Who says I was down at Foley Bottoms?

ALICE: Never mind who says, or who doesn't say. That's got nothing to do with it. You were there — somebody saw you. And it wasn't that Barbara you were with, either. 45

FLORENCE: He wants to make up his mind who he is going with.

GEOFFREY; He knocks about with too many lasses. He's out with a different one every night. He's like a bloody lass himself. 50

BILLY: Well, you want to tell whoever saw me to mind their own fizzing business.

ALICE: It is our business — and don't you be so cheeky. You're not old enough for that.

FLORENCE: If she's coming for her tea this afternoon she wants to tell her. If she doesn't I will. 55

BILLY: I suppose that she who's coming for her tea is Barbara and she who wants to tell her is Mother and . . .

ALICE: I've told you — shut up. I'm going to tell her, don't you fret yourself. You've never played fair with that girl. Carrying on. I'm surprised she, bothers with you. You shouldn't mess her about like that. One and then the other. That's no way to carry on. I know where you'll finish up — you'll finish up with none of them — that's where you'll finish up. 60

GEOFFREY: He'll finish up on his bloody ear-hole. I'm not having him staying out half the night. Not at his age. He's not old enough. He'll wait till he's twenty-one before he starts them bloody tricks. I've told him before, he can start coming in of a night or else go and live somewhere else. 65

BILLY: Perhaps I will do. 70

ALICE (*ignoring him*): I can't understand that Barbara — why she does bother with you. Are you supposed to be getting engaged to her or aren't you?

GEOFFREY: He doesn't know who he's bloody getting engaged to.
FLORENCE: He wants to make his mind up. 75
ALICE (*ignoring* GEOFFREY *and* FLORENCE): Because she's not like these others, you know. That time I saw you in the arcade with her she looked respectable to me. Not like that Liz or whatever her name is. That scruffy one you reckoned to be going about with. Her in that mucky skirt. Do you ever see anything of her still? 80
GEOFFREY: He sees so many bloody lasses he doesn't know who he does see.
FLORENCE: He wants to make his mind up—once and for all. He wants to make his mind up who he is going with.
BILLY: I haven't seen Liz for three months. 85
ALICE: Well, who were you with then? Down at Foley Bottoms? Last night?
BILLY: Rita.
GEOFFREY: Who the bloody hell's Rita?
FLORENCE: She wants to see that he makes his mind up. 90
ALICE: I shall tell Barbara this afternoon—I shall tell her, make no mistake about that.
GEOFFREY: He's never satisfied with what he has got—that's his bloody trouble. He never has been. It's ever since he left school. It's ever since he took that job—clerking. Clerking for that undertaker—what kind of a 95 bloody job's that?
BILLY: Perhaps I might not be doing it much longer.
GEOFFREY: You what?
ALICE: What do you mean?
BILLY: I've been offered a job in London. 100

(i) One central difference between a novel and a play is that in the drama subjective experiences—thoughts and feelings—must be represented in the form of speech and action; there is no other way in which they can be communicated unambiguously on stage. A character in a novel may be totally silent, but the author can give us privileged access to every thought that passes through his mind; in the drama thoughts and feelings have to be externalised by being spoken in dialogue—or perhaps in an aside (see page 21) or in a soliloquy (see page 184)—characters must be forced into encounters.

In passage A from the novel, particularly as it is written in the first person (Billy is telling his own story), we feel as if we are looking out on the world through Billy's eyes. In passage B, when we see much of the same material in the form of a scene from a play, there must be a strong feeling that we are looking at Billy in a more detached and objective way. Even though he is still at the centre of things, he is now a character moving among other characters.

(ii) Two points should be borne in mind here. First, you are reading the extracts in book form, and whereas this is the 'natural element' of passage A, in the case of passage B a little imagination is necessary in order to perceive the potential dramatic impact the scene might make on stage. We have to imagine the stage set—what would the Fisher's kitchen look like? We have to consider the possibilities of movement and gesture—for instance, exactly how should Billy move as he comes down the stairs? In what tone of voice does he speak? And so on.

Secondly, we think that it *is* important to remember that the extracts occur at the beginning of the works from which they are taken. To understand the contrast between them will also involve us in some generalisation about the drama and the novel. We are, of course, being introduced to the members of Billy's family and to such matters as his somewhat tangled relationships with various girlfriends. In the form of drama this kind of 'exposition' is notoriously difficult—a problem we first encountered with Episode 1 of our plot outline of a day in the life of a student (see page 2). The heart of the problem is that the information has to be conveyed through dialogue. It could be said that not much is really 'happening' until the climax of Billy's announcement at the end of the scene that he has been offered a job in London. It is easier in the novel form to convey this kind of 'introductory information' and the novelist can, perhaps, at this stage hold our interest more readily by presenting directly through his prose style the quirky immediacy of Billy's mind.

To understand how passage B would work on stage, the reader has to recognize the fundamental patterning of the dialogue; we have Billy at the centre trying to fend off the inquiries and accusations of the other three members of his family. This medley of voices has considerable dramatic potential—Billy's father is abrasively aggressive, his mother naggingly persistent and his grandmother eccentrically (but annoyingly from Billy's point of view) engaged in her own obsessive line of attack. Each member of the family, moreover, is given a distinctive speaking voice which is a register of his/her character: for instance, Geoffrey's ranting tone with 'bloody' intruding like some nervous tic or Florence's grandmotherly pronouncements in which she constantly refers to Billy (and even his mother) in the third person.

3

An actor prepares

To compare a passage from a novel with an extract of dialogue from a play will invariably produce a feeling that such a comparison is grossly unfair, because it cannot fully take into account all that may be achieved when a script is realized through its presentation on stage. This forces us to face a question that we have been pushing to one side for some time. Can we really discuss the drama as though it were a branch of literature, like the novel or lyric poetry? Like a musical score, a play exists in one sense in book form, but its fullest expression can only be realised in performance. In this book we have constantly asked you to consider the drama we have encountered so far in terms, at least, of an imagined performance. Questions such as 'What is the effect of this scene likely to be on stage?' or 'How can this material best be presented to an audience?' have never been very far from our minds. Yet it could be argued that we have taken as our starting-point a predominantly literary study of the text itself—witness our rejection of Douglas Jerrold's *Black-Ey'd Susan* as literature, linked with a grudging acceptance that some great actor might still make the play work on stage.

Great plays can legitimately be studied as works of literature, but we do not wish to suggest that this study should ever be a purely academic activity. However, when a play comes into the hands of a group of actors and a director who wish to produce it on stage, its first existence is in the form of a text which has to be understood and explored. Some plays it is true, particularly in recent years, have been written by a kind of creative collaboration between a dramatist and a company of actors, or even, in some cases, produced 'in the workshop' by means of improvisation. Yet the majority of plays come into being as the conception of a single mind—the playwright's—and the dramatic potential in the text can only be realised in performance after some initial exploration of its language, the conventions and theatrical techniques it draws on, the methods of characterisation it uses, and so on. You do not have to be a brilliant literary critic to produce a play on stage, but the best directors—and actors—certainly must know how to 'read' a dramatic text; and this activity, while not perhaps demanding the specialized technical knowledge a musician requires to bring a musical score to life in his imagination, nevertheless demands a certain training. This is where we hope this book will help—in providing the basic elements of a training in the art of recognizing the potential for dramatic life embodied in a text.

We will see later that the greatest plays offer a wide variety of potential interpretations and approaches. This is what makes the study and performance of drama so fascinating: there can never be one definitive version of *Hamlet* or *The Cherry Orchard.* Indeed, when a rich dramatic text is read closely in the study or rehearsed over a period of time, a number of complex, and often conflicting ways of presenting a scene—or of even speaking a line or a single word—will emerge, thus leading us to something of a paradox. While drama *does* exist in its fullest expressive form only in the theatre, nevertheless in performance *one* reading, one single interpretation, has to be finally adopted; whereas in rehearsal, or in an imagined performance that takes place in a reader's head, that rich, fluid complication of meaning can be retained.

The production of a play to some extent begins as a mental conception and then grows, through trial and error in rehearsal, into what the director and actors hope will be one version, one final achieved vision (which will nevertheless be slightly different each time they perform it), of what the play means to them. One of the best methods of approaching many of the longer extracts in this book is to experience drama on its home ground—that is, to involve yourself in thinking about and preparing performances of the text in front of you. Just how far you get towards a full-scale production is up to you! But do not imagine that it is only from a perfectly polished, final dramatic performance that any benefits are to be reaped. At each stage of the approach we will outline in a moment—whether it be a simple read through or a very basic workshop rehearsal with actors nervously clutching their texts—you will be discovering more about the text (and about drama), even though you may stop short of anything approaching a real performance. So the following method of approach is offered simply as a series of guidelines which may be modified as you wish. (It does take for granted, however, that you are working with a group which is keen to be involved in some practical drama.)

1. The first stage is to read through the scene you are preparing on your own. Repeat several times and try both to visualise the action and—by a process of internal ventriloquism—to hear in your inner ear the rhythms of the dialogue and the changing tones of voice you think the various speakers would adopt.

2. Now split up into groups. The size of the group will be determined by the number of parts available in the scene to be rehearsed. We suggest you begin by working on the passages from *The Corn is Green* (pages 5–7) and *Billy Liar* (pages 28–30). Decide who is going to take each part; add one extra member to your group and appoint him/her to be 'director' (more of his role in a moment). Begin with a straightforward read-through and at this stage do not expect too much in the way of incisive interpretation or vivid characterisation. The 'director' may usefully read any necessary stage directions.

3. Your read-through should lead to a number of comments and questions, and you should try to create an atmosphere in which each member of the group feels able to contribute constructively to discussion—though perhaps your director can act as a kind of chairman who will hold a balance between opposing views and supply (possibly) more objective criticism. In working towards getting the scene to sound 'right', you are likely to come up with questions of this kind:

(a) Is each reader showing due attention to the rhythms and pace of the dialogue? For instance, are readers 'picking up their cues' quickly enough? Or giving necessary pauses the right duration? Is the impetus leading up to moments of climax being maintained effectively?
(b) Is each reader adopting the voice and tone which seem right for the character he or she is portraying? Are changes of feeling being reflected in appropriate changes of tone?

4. Some readers are likely to begin to identify with the characters they are portraying; some may decide that they are not 'comfortable' with their part at all or feel no sympathy towards the role they have been asked to play. Talk about this. Try to pin down your feelings about the characters and their situation, even if such discussion means that reading is suspended for some time. Sometimes it may be useful to swop the parts around—temporarily or permanently. Sometimes you will need to focus on quite short sections of the dialogue which seem to pose particular problems. Try different ways of reading the lines in question—sometimes overplay or underplay them. If there is disagreement, always ask these two questions:

(a) What exactly do you think this character is thinking or feeling at this point?
(b) What precise dramatic effect do you think these lines should have on an audience?

Always remember you are working on a joint effort—trying to get it right!

5. At some point—early or late—you may have felt like beginning to try some 'real acting' by combining your reading of the parts with movement (those which *you* feel are appropriate, as well as those indicated by stage directions) and by matching gesture and facial expression with what you are saying. Some actors like to do this from a very early stage; some prefer to wait until they have begun 'to get the words right'. There is no correct method here: it is simply a question of how you and the other members of the group feel. Once rehearsal becomes more sophisticated, the director now has to consider how the scene looks and sounds from the perspective of a potential audience. Is each member of the cast projecting his voice properly? Is each character clearly visible or is some clumsy masking occurring? If you can now move to rehearse in a theatre or drama studio, you are lucky! But the two scenes we have suggested you work on do not

require elaborate staging—a table and chairs are all that are necessary—and an open space in a classroom can make a perfectly acceptable acting area. Do not worry too much about props. If, for instance, you want members of the Fisher family to be seen eating breakfast, this can quite effectively be mimed. In fact, avoid any tendency to become over-concerned with the demands of 'realism' in your set or props. What really matters is the honeing of the essential dramatic elements of words and action. While you should aim at excellence, the *process* of rehearsing a play can be an end in itself, a means by which we explore the text and open it up to discover its full dramatic potential. The following exchange, recorded by Stanislavsky in *An Actor Prepares*, may be instructive. An actor in rehearsal had asked for matches to light a 'real fire':

> 'What in the world do you want matches for?' asked he.
> 'To light the fire.'
> 'The fireplace is made of paper. Did you intend to burn down the theatre?'
> 'I was just going to pretend,' I explained.
> He held out an empty hand.
> 'To pretend to light a fire, pretended matches are sufficient. As if the point were to strike a match!'
> 'When you reach the point of playing Hamlet, threading a way through his intricate psychology to the moment when he kills the King, will it be important to you to have a life-size sword in your hand? If you lack one, will you be unable to finish the performance? You can kill the King without a sword, and you can light the fire without a match. What needs to burn is your imagination.'

6. Finally each group should perform its version of the scene it has prepared for the whole class. Here somebody may insist on providing the members of one group with real eggs and bacon, but just how 'professional' your production is, will depend on the circumstances under which you are operating and the time at your disposal. Whether you require actors to be word perfect in their parts again must be up to you.

Watching several productions of the same scene from *The Corn is Green* or *Billy Liar* may not at first appear to be the most exciting prospect. But you will be pleasantly surprised. You will begin to see in practice the rich variety dramatic material can take on as each group offers a slightly (or considerably) different interpretation of the text. And because by now you will be very familiar with this material, you can usually be certain that, following each performance, some excellent discussion will be generated by the basic question: 'Why did you do it that way?'.

Perhaps you do not wish to go all the way towards trying to mount something like a full performance of a scene; some of the same useful results may be achieved if each group makes a recording on tape of a 'radio drama' production of the script in question. We will shortly be giving you an extract from a play written for radio which you might like to prepare in this way (see page 00).

Any course on drama which includes the practical method of approach outlined above will avoid a narrowing down of drama to a purely literary activity—as though a dramatic text were something which, in a highly artificial way, is *only* to be experienced in the study. At the same time this approach will throw up many questions which are essentially 'literary', in that they will involve matters such as the close scrutiny of the way in which a scene is constructed or the way the language operates to achieve a particular dramatic effect. As well as being an enjoyable activity in its own right, practical experience of drama will assist you in the art of gauging the special qualities of a dramatic text, and as we have suggested before, for anybody interested in the theatre, the art of translating the notation of a script into the imagined possibilities of performance on stage must be acquired through both personal involvement and knowledge of the traditions and conventions of drama.

There is another way in which some actors and directors work. While we have started with an emphasis on an exploration of the dramatic potential of a script as the actor practises the technical means of communicating the messages encoded in a text, another approach would involve a greater stress on the psychological aspects of building a character. In its most extreme form this method requires an actor to 'find' the character he is portraying within his own experience by completely submerging himself in the role he is playing. This kind of almost total identification is achieved through self-analysis and improvisation; so the actor would be asked to take as a starting point: 'If *you* were in the position of Morgan or Billy Liar how would you feel?; what would *you* do?' The actor would be called upon to locate within his own experience memories which would arouse similar emotions to those experienced by the character in the play; with other members of the cast he would improvise scenes which involve the stage character in all manner of different situations. Thus, as an exercise the actor might improvise a scene in which Morgan talks to his friends at the pub; the character's life before the curtain rises would be investigated—perhaps through an improvisation based on how Billy Liar might have behaved in a school classroom.

This method, quite often called the 'Method', originated largely in the United States and for a time enjoyed great prominence, influencing the way actors were trained and having an effect on acting in the cinema as well as on stage. Its chief advocates were directors such as Lee Strasberg, Elia Kazan and others connected with the New York Actors' Studio, and they based their approach on a rather narrow interpretation of the practice and theory of the famous Russian director, Stanislavsky (1863–1938). The dangers of any slavish following of the Method are that first, it tends to presuppose that to have empathy with a character and to feel what he feels with sufficient intensity will in itself equip an actor to communicate on stage; second, there is the possibility that an actor will simply make the part he is playing the vehicle for a display of his own personality.

GENERAL DISCUSSION TOPIC

There may be dangers in the 'Method', but are not at least some elements of its approach compatible with a more traditional approach to acting? Could not improvisation, for instance, be very helpful in preventing an actor from becoming too sterilely preoccupied with matters of mere technique? We would like you to base a general discussion on the question of how an actor should prepare for building up a character. We hope your discussion will be stimulated by the following extracts from the Method actor's Bible, Stanislavsky's *An Actor Prepares* (1926), and by a passage from an essay critical of the Method, written by the famous British theatre director, Sir Tyrone Guthrie.

A. *A director, Tortsov—who is to be identified with Stanislavsky himself—is talking to some actors who are learning their craft.*

'To play truly means to be right, logical, coherent, to think, strive, feel and act in unison with your role.
'If you take all these internal processes, and adapt them to the spiritual and physical life of the person you are representing, we call that living the part. This is of supreme significance in creative work. Aside from the fact 5
that it opens up avenues for inspiration, living the part helps the artist to carry out one of his main objectives. His job is not to present merely the external life of his character. He must fit his own human qualities to the life of this other person, and pour into it all of his own soul. The fundamental aim of our art is the creation of this inner life of a human spirit, and its 10
expression in an artistic form.
'That is why we begin by thinking about the inner side of a role, and how to create its spiritual life through the help of the internal process of living the part. You must live it by actually experiencing feelings that are analogous to it, each and every time you repeat the process of creating it.' 15
'From what you have said I gather that to study our art we must assimilate a psychological technique of living a part, and that this will help us to accomplish our main object, which is to create the life of a human spirit,' Paul Shustov said.
'That is correct but not complete,' said Tortsov. 'Our aim is not only to 20
create the life of a human spirit, but also to "express it in a beautiful, artistic form." An actor is under the obligation to live his part inwardly, and then to give to his experience an external embodiment. I ask you to note especially that the dependence of the body on the soul is particularly important in our school of art. *In order to express a most delicate and largely* 25
subconscious life it is necessary to have control of an unusually responsive, excellently prepared vocal and physical apparatus. This apparatus must be ready instantly and exactly to reproduce most delicate and all but intangible feelings with great sensitiveness and directness. *That is why an actor of our type is obliged to work so much more than others*, both on his 30

inner equipment, which creates the life of the part, and also on his outer physical apparatus, which should reproduce the results of the creative work of his emotions with precision . . . *In our art you must live the part every moment that you are playing it, and every time.* Each time it is recreated it must be lived afresh and incarnated afresh. 35

The director discusses actors who use a 'mechanical technique':

'At first they feel the part, but when once they have done so they do not go on feeling it anew, they merely remember and repeat the external movements, intonations, and expressions they worked on at first, making this repetition without emotion. Often they are extremely skilful in technique, and are able to get through a part with technique only, and no 5 expenditure of nervous force. In fact, they often think it unwise to feel, after they have once decided on the pattern to follow. They think they are surer to give the right performance if they merely recall how they did it when they first got it right. . . To reproduce feelings you must be able to identify them out of your own experience. But as mechanical actors do not experience 10 feelings they cannot reproduce their external results. . .

The very worst fact is that *clichés will fill up every empty spot in a role, which is not already solid with living feeling.* . . A role which is built of truth will grow, whereas one built on stereotype will shrivel. . . . The false acting of passions, or of types, or the mere use of conventional gestures,—these 15 are all frequent faults in our profession. But you must keep away from these unrealities. You must not copy passions or copy types. You must live in the passions and in the types. Your acting of them must grow out of your living in them.'

An example of how to approach a part:

'Suppose you were to play a dramatisation of Chekhov's tale about an innocent farmer who unscrewed a nut off a railroad track to use as a sinker for his fishing line. For this he was tried and severely punished. This imaginary happening will sink into the consciousness of some, but for most people it will remain a "funny story". They will never even glimpse the 5 tragedy of the legal and social conditions hidden behind the laughter. But the artist who is to act one of the parts in this scene cannot laugh. He must think through for himself and, most important, he must live through whatever it was that caused the author to write the story. How would you go about it?' The Director paused. 10

The students were silent and thoughtful for a time.

'In moments of doubt, when your thoughts, feelings, and imagination are silent, remember *if*. The author also began his work that way. He said to himself:

' "What would happen *if* a simple farmer, off on a fishing expedition, 15 were to take a nut from a rail?" Now give yourselves the same problem and add: "What would I do *if* the case came up to me to judge?" '

'I would convict the criminal,' I answered, without hesitation.

'What of? On account of the sinker for his fishing line?'

'For the theft of a nut.' 20

'Of course, one shouldn't steal,' agreed Tortsov. 'But can you punish a man severely for a crime of which he is entirely unconscious?'

'He must be made to realise that he might be the cause of wrecking a whole train, killing hundreds of people,' I retorted.

'On account of one small nut? You will never get him to believe that,' argued the Director. 25

'The man is only making believe. He understands the nature of his act,' said I.

'If the man who plays the farmer has talent, he will prove to you by his acting that he is unconscious of any guilt,' said the Director. 30

As the discussion went on he used every possible argument to justify the defendant, and in the end he succeeded in making me weaken a little. As soon as he noticed that, he said:

'You felt that very same inner push which the judge himself probably experienced. If you played that part, analogous feelings would draw you close to the character. 35

To achieve this kinship between the actor and the person he is portraying add some concrete detail which will fill out the play, giving it point and absorbing action. The circumstances which are predicted on *if* are taken from sources near to your own feelings, and they have a powerful influence on the inner life of an actor. Once you have established this contact between your life and your part, you will find that inner push or stimulus. Add a whole series of contingencies based on your own experience in life, and you will see how easy it will be for you sincerely to believe in the possibility of what you are called upon to do on the stage. 40 45

'Work out an entire role in this fashion, and you will create a whole new life.

'The feelings aroused will express themselves in the acts of this imaginary person had he been placed in the circumstances made by the play.'

Stanislavsky: *An Actor Prepares* (trans. E. R. Hopgood)

B. In 1930, however, the Group* believed that good acting consisted in Being Yourself and, consistently enough, aimed to make its members better actors by making them more Aware of Themselves. Remember that this epoch coincided with the first great popular impact of psycho-analysis. At the confluence of two rivers—popular psychology and 'behaviourist' acting—like Pittsburgh, stood the Group. At the same confluence stands the Method. But twenty-seven years have passed and the waters of both streams are now less turbulent, but also far less clear and fresh. 5

In my opinion, the Method now means Behaviourist acting, which is cliché, and which is inadequate to express any wide range either of character, environment or style. It is suited only to express the very limited field of the actor's own, and his friends' experience, and in a naturalistic style. It is stylish acting (by which I do not, of course, mean merely elegant) which now needs cultivation. 10

The search by actors for the Truth Within Themselves has now gone too far. They are in grave danger of forgetting two more objective elements of truth which no artiste should dare to ignore: first, each of us is not only 15

* The Group Theater, founded by Lee Strasberg and Harold Clurman, and modelled to some extent on Stanislavsky's Moscow Art Threatre.

himself, but a member of the Human Race; second, it is the duty of an artiste to develop the Means of Communication of the truth within himself, so as to share it with fellow members of the race. 20

The Method-ists overprize the Search For Truth as opposed to the Revelation Of Truth. They have neglected the means of communication. Now the actor's principal means of expression is the voice. The expression of eyes, of the whole body, is important, too; but it is on the breathstream and by means of sounds and, more particularly, the organisation of sounds 25 into, first, syllables, then words, then sentences, that the most subtle and the most articulate communication occurs between human creatures.

Until recently the Actors' Studio has tended to pay but little attention to matters of technique. But now Mr Strasberg has said that this has been a mistake. Lessons in Voice Production and Diction are now part of the 30 curriculum. No reasonable person but will applaud when error is admitted and amendment begun. But amendment has only just begun, so it is rather too early to look for the fruits of this Revised Method. Also it is a radically new idea that anything so self-conscious and artificial as Vocal Technique, so unspontaneous, so remote from the animal life of the individual, or the 35 social life of the group, should be admissible as part of the Method. And so influential has the Method become in the contemporary theatre that it is going to be very hard to eradicate the notion that any cultivation of this Craft can only be to the detriment, not only of an actor's Art, but of his Psyche. 40

This notion has led the Method-ists into one very awkward dilemma: none of the great classics of the theatre—the Greek tragedies, French tragedy, Shakespeare, Molière, Schiller or Goethe—can be adequately performed without a real battery of technical accomplishment. An untrained beginner, however gifted, just cannot do justice to great 45 rhetorical poetry any more than an untrained beginner in music can sit right down and play a Bach fugue. So far the Method has not suggested that it aims beyond a very highly developed Behaviourism. I am not denying that in this field remarkable results have been achieved. But mere Behaviourism will not take an actor far on the way to King Lear, 50 Andromache or Faust.

Tyrone Guthrie: 'Is There Madness in the Method' (1957)

Some of the following questions should provide some starting-points for your discussion.

(i) What does Stanislavsky mean by 'truth' in the portrayal of a role on stage?
(ii) Why, in Stanislavsky's view, does a purely mechanical approach to acting miss this 'truth'?
(iii) Is it fair to say that a study of acting technique plays no part in Stanislavsky's approach?
(iv) What is the essential criticism Tyrone Guthrie makes of the 'Method' approach to acting, derived from some elements of Stanislavsky's theory and practice?

(v) Define your own views on this general question. Do you favour Stanislavsky's or Tyrone Guthrie's approach?
(vi) In connection with plays that you know well, invent suitable exercises which Stanislavsky himself might have adopted in order to prepare actors for playing certain parts.

AN IDEA FOR REHEARSAL

If possible, work in pairs. Having established the tone of voice in which the following few lines are to be spoken, decide how you would perform this short scene. Pay particular attention to the movement and positioning of the two characters relative to one another. Does one stand and the other sit? How far are they apart? Is any movement or gesture required while they speak? At what point(s) in the dialogue is eye-contact established? What are the *reasons* for the choices you make concerning the 'blocking' of this scene?

Damian and Wayne are in the same class. Damian has been 'going out' with Jane for over a year.
Set: a table and one chair (which may, or may not, be used).

WAYNE: I met Jane last night at a disco in town.
DAMIAN: Oh yes? 5
WAYNE: Had quite a nice little chat.
DAMIAN: Glad you got on so well. Jane's always friendly to everyone.
WAYNE: In fact, she's coming out with me tonight. We're going to a Bonky Squirrel concert at Droylsden.

When you have decided how you are going to perform this dialogue, invent a line or two for Damian which you think would suitably continue/close this short scene. Now arrange for a number of different versions of this scene to be performed. What do you observe? What conclusions do you come to?

4

The interdependence of situation and dialogue

We have already discovered that in drama, if we are to learn anything about characters and the situation in which they are placed, those characters must be made to 'encounter each other' and speak dialogue which appears quite naturally and spontaneously to rise out of the immediate situation. References may be made to the past and the future, but in an inescapable way drama belongs to a world in which a series of moments exist in the perpetual present as each word is uttered. In a later chapter we shall discuss the importance of observing the 'patterning' of the dialogue as a clue to understanding the underlying relationships of the characters who are speaking the lines. In order to begin our study of these important matters in a little greater detail, we would like you to consider the following simple piece of dialogue. Jot down your answers to these three questions before reading on:

(i) In what situation do you imagine these lines are spoken?
(ii) What does the dialogue tell us about each character, and in what ways are these two characters different?
(iii) What is the fundamental pattern of these lines, and what is the significance of this pattern?

ALAN: What a cold July we are having. If you weren't in England, where would you like to be at this time of the year?
ARTHUR: Haven't really thought about it.
ALAN: What beautiful flowers our hostess, Ann, always has—do you like gardening?
ARTHUR: Good Lord—No! 5
ALAN: If you were the Queen, what opera would you choose to have performed for your Gala?
ARTHUR: Opera? Don't know anything about that.
ALAN: Are you a Wimbledon fan? Have you been watching it on television? 10
ARTHUR: No. It bores the pants off me.
ALAN: Well . . . Have you had time to see the Tutankhamen exhibition?
ARTHUR: Tutankhamen?
ALAN: What delicious claret—are you a connoisseur of wine?
ARTHUR: I just drink the stuff. 15
ALAN: Do you live in London?
ARTHUR: Ealing.

ALAN: What do you do?
ARTHUR: Do? My job? I'm an accountant.
ALAN: Have you any children? 20
ARTHUR: I'm not married.
ALAN: Have you been abroad this year?
ARTHUR: Can't afford it.

(i) The situation is clearly something like a dinner-party at which two strangers, Alan and Arthur, find themselves sitting next to one other. Alan is trying to strike up a conversation, but Arthur is unhelpfully unresponsive.

(ii) Alan's unrelenting eagerness to engage Arthur in conversation probably marks him out as a sociable, garrulous kind of individual. There are certain social implications about what Alan regards as good conversational opening gambits—an interest in wine, opera, Wimbledon and so on—while Arthur's obvious lack of interest in these topics and his stolid uncommunicativeness suggest that (for reasons of his own) he is either unwilling or unable to engage in the game of making social chit-chat.

(iii) We are presented with a number of rather contrived conversation openers by Alan. If Arthur had recognized the same 'rules' of upper middle-class behaviour, he would have made some attempt to return the ball—for instance 'Well, no, he wasn't watching much Wimbledon this year because all his time was taken up with . . . . ' and so on—and the conversation might have blossomed. At this point perhaps the feelings of Alan and Arthur might have become more directly involved, and disclosures of character might have been made more frankly as they moved to greater intimacy. Instead we have the pattern of a stilted series of paired exchanges; and after each of Alan's opening questions—to which the response leaves him little room for development—we are back to square one. There would be a pause after each of Arthur's responses, and Alan's tone would perhaps increasingly register a feeling of 'Try again'. The conversation remains at the level of an arid exercise—though, incidentally, this dialogue might suggest some ways in which the skilful dramatist could use this kind of non-communication—set against the background of genteel expectations—to produce the material of social satire or comedy.

In this dialogue, in the first six questions, Alan is adopting the conversational 'openers' recommended in Debrett's *Etiquette and Modern Manners*; Debrett tells us they are designed 'to make convers-ation fluent and agreeable' and to find topics on which an interlocutor 'will speak with interest and enjoyment'. In desperation Alan finishes up with the four questions which Debrett positively advises *against* using (you might ask yourself *why* they are not to be considered wise opening questions). Somewhat mischievously we have made up Arthur's 'dead-bat' responses; the point we wish to underline, with reference to this contrived dialogue, is that even when we are considering more dramatic and sophisticated exchanges from real plays, we are going to discover the same overlapping of (a) characters in a given situation with (b) the language which is seen to grow naturally out of that situation.

To make this point more fully we want you to read this scene from Giles Cooper's radio play *Unman, Wittering and Zigo* (1958). We have divided the questions which follow into two groups: the first take the starting point of the situation and the characters involved in the scene; the second are concerned with the language and patterning of the dialogue. We think you will find that as you go more deeply into each question, you will discover that inevitably discussion of character and situation leads directly to a consideration of the language employed in dialogue—and *vice versa*.

John Ebony, a new teacher at Chantrey School, meets his class, Lower Five B, for the first time.

JOHN: (*Fading in*) Aggeridge, Ankerton, Borby, Bungabine. . . .
(*As he says each name a boy says 'here'*)
Cloistermouth, Cuthbun, Hogg, Liptstrob, Mudd,
Muffet, Munn Ma., Orris, Root. . .
CUTHBUN: Please, sir. 5
JOHN: Yes. . . er . . .
OMNES: Cuthbun, sir.
JOHN: Yes, Cuthbun?
CUTHBUN: Mr Pelham used to make a joke there sir; he used to call them out together, Orris root, you know, sir. 10
CLOISTERMOUTH: They use it for scenting soap.
ORRIS: And we used to answer together, Root and me, sir.
CUTHBUN: Root and I.
BUNGABINE: And we all laughed . . . haw haw haw!
JOHN: All right . . . er . . . 15
OMNES: Bungabine, sir.
JOHN: Bungabine. That will do. Terhew, Trindle, Unman, Wittering and Zigo.
OMNES: Absent!
JOHN: Yes, so I understand. 20
CLOISTERMOUTH: He was ill, sir.
UNMAN: With an unknown disease, sir.
LIPSTROB: And his father took him to Jamaica, sir.
CUTHBUN: To recover, sir.
ORRIS: And when he has, he'll come back, sir. 25
AGGERIDGE: That's why his name's still on the list, sir.
JOHN: Yes, thank you.
CUTHBUN: Jamaica's in the Caribbean, sir.
JOHN: Yes, Cuthbun. I know that.
TERHEW: Have you ever been there, sir? 30
JOHN: No.

AGGERIDGE: Mr Pelham went there once.
TERHEW: Twice.
AGGERIDGE: Once, the other time was Trinidad.
CUTHBUN: He went to Jamaica the time he went to Trinidad as well. 35
JOHN: Quiet! (*Dead silence*) This is all very interesting, but not to the point. (*There is the scream of a boy in pain*) Who was that? (*Wittering moans*) You? What's your name?
WITTERING: Wittering, sir.
CLOISTERMOUTH: Wet Wittering, sir. 40
JOHN: Quiet. Come out here, Wittering.
(*Movement as Wittering comes out*)
CLOISTERMOUTH: Mr Pelham called him Wet Wittering, sir.
JOHN: Quiet! Now, Wittering, why did you make that noise?
WITTERING: Sir, I was jabbed, sir. 45
JOHN: Jabbed?
WITTERING: With a compass, sir.
JOHN: Who jabbed you?
WITTERING: I don't know, sir.
JOHN: Well, go back to your place and wipe the ink off your chin. 50
WITTERING: Sir.
JOHN: And I don't want any more fooling about, or there'll be trouble.
CUTHBUN: Sir?
JOHN: Cuthbun?
CUTHBUN: I don't understand, sir. 55
JOHN: What do you not understand, Cuthbun?
CUTHBUN: 'I don't want any more fooling about or there'll be trouble.' It doesn't make sense, sir. Do you mean there'll be trouble if you do want fooling about?
JOHN: I mean that if there is any more fooling about, verbal or practical, 60 there will be trouble.
CUTHBUN: Oh, I see, sir, yes, sir.
CLOISTERMOUTH: Mr Pelham always told us we had to be frightfully careful with our English, sir.
JOHN: And he was quite right, Cloistermouth. Now then: McMorrow and 65 Purdie's history of England, chapter nine. (*A great slamming of books*) All right, all right. (*Silence*) Has anyone read chapter nine?
TERHEW: Yes, sir.
JOHN: Good . . . er, Terhew. Perhaps you'd give us an outline of its contents. 70
TERHEW: Me, sir, oh no, sir.
JOHN: And why not?
TERHEW: I haven't read it, sir.
JOHN: You said you had.
TERHEW: No, sir, you asked if anyone had read it and I said yes, sir. 75 Cuthbun has.
BUNGABINE: He's read the lot, sir.
TRINDLE: The whole book.
CUTHBUN: It ends with the General Strike.
JOHN: Does it? Well, tell us about chapter nine. 80
CUTHBUN: Actually, sir, I left that chapter out. Terhew was wrong.

TERHEW: I'm most terribly sorry, sir.
JOHN: Shut up, Terhew.
TERHEW: But I am, sir, really.
JOHN: Why did you leave that chapter out, Cuthbun? 85
CUTHBUN: Because Mr Pelham said the Wars of the Roses were not worth bothering about.
CLOISTERMOUTH: Yes, he did, sir, really.
JOHN: Oh, in that case we will read it together.
CLOISTERMOUTH: But, sir. 90
JOHN: Yes, Cloistermouth?
CLOISTERMOUTH: Mr Pelham did say, sir.
CUTHBUN: And if it's not worth bothering about surely it's a waste of time reading it.
JOHN: I consider that they are worth bothering about. 95
UNMAN: Mr Pelham was quite definite, sir.
JOHN: Nevertheless we will read it.
AGGERIDGE: Sir, please, sir . . .
JOHN: Yes, Aggeridge?
AGGERIDGE: May we have a window open? 100
JOHN: No.
AGGERIDGE: Mr Pelham said it was bad for our lungs to work in a stuffy atmosphere.
CUTHBUN: And Aggeridge has to have good lungs, sir, he's in the second eleven. 105
JOHN: Well I think it's bad for us to work in a draught. Begin reading, Wittering.
WITTERING: Me, sir?
JOHN: Yes, go on.
WITTERING: (*Slowly*) 'The Wars of the Roses. In fourteen fifty-three at the colse . . .' 110
JOHN: What?
WITTERING: Colse.
JOHN: Spell it.
WITTERING: C-L-O-S-E. 115
JOHN: Which is what?
WITTERING: *Close.* (*With a soft 's'*)
JOHN: No, close.
WITTERING: '. . . close of the Hundred Years' War, England was in a . . . '
JOHN: Well? 120
WITTERING: (*Rushing at it*) Condescension . . .
JOHN: No, Wittering! A *condition* bordering upon anarchy. Can't you read?
TERHEW: Not aloud, sir.
JOHN: I asked Wittering. 125
CUTHBUN: Mr Pelham never put him on to read. He said life was too short.
JOHN: I asked Wittering.
BUNGABINE: Mr Pelham's life was too short. Haw haw haw.
JOHN: Quiet! (*Silence*) Now I don't wish to crack the whip on our first morning together, but I will if you make me. I want no further interruptions. 130

CLOISTERMOUTH: But, sir . . .
JOHN: Did you hear me?
CLOISTERMOUTH: Sir, Mr Pelham said we were always to ask if we didn't know anything. 135
JOHN: I do not care what Mr Pelham said.
OMNES: Ooh, Sir!
JOHN: Now look here. I know his death must have been a great shock to you, but life goes on and there is work to be done. We will get through this chapter this morning, or if not we will do it this afternoon. 140
TERHEW: But, sir, it's a half-holiday.
JOHN: Yes, Terhew.
AGGERIDGE: And there's a second eleven match.
JOHN: Yes, Aggeridge. Continue reading.
AGGERIDGE: 'Many of the nobles were virtually little kings, raising their own armies and levying their own taxes.' 145
(During this, Unman begins muttering)
UNMAN: Hypotenuse, hypotenuse, hypotenuse . . .
AGGERIDGE: 'The authority of the Crown . . .'
JOHN: Stop. Who is muttering? 150
UNMAN: Me, sir.
JOHN: Unman, did you hear what I said?
UNMAN: Yes, sir.
CLOISTERMOUTH: He can't help it, sir.
CUTHBUN: He says hypotenuse, sir, all the time. 155
TERHEW: He likes the word.
AGGERIDGE: Mr Pelham said he was hypotenused by it.
(General laughter)
JOHN: Stop! *(Silence)* Very well. You have had your warning. The form will stay in this afternoon from half-past two until I am satisfied with your behaviour. 160
(Pause)
CLOISTERMOUTH: It's not a good idea, sir.
JOHN: No, Cloistermouth? Tell me why not.
CLOISTERMOUTH: Well, sir, Mr Pelham did it once. 165
CUTHBUN: The week before last, sir.
CLOISTERMOUTH: And that was why we killed him.
(Dead silence)
JOHN: Cloistermouth, take this note to the headmaster.
CLOISTERMOUTH: Now, sir? 170
JOHN: At once.
CLOISTERMOUTH: What does it say, sir?
JOHN: That you have been insolent.
CLOISTERMOUTH: But, sir, I haven't. Only truthful.
OMNES: That's right, sir. 175
JOHN: Go on, Cloistermouth.
CLOISTERMOUTH: No, sir.
JOHN: Very well. Then I shall fetch the headmaster here.
CLOISTERMOUTH: You'll look an awful fool, sir.
JOHN: *(Shouting)* Get out! 180
CLOISTERMOUTH: If you hit me, sir, there'll be a terrific row.

TERHEW: Form-masters aren't allowed to hit us.
CUTHBUN: You'll be sacked.
AGGERIDGE: And after all, he was telling the truth, sir.
CLOISTERMOUTH: I always do. 185
JOHN: Oh yes? And how did you kill Mr Pelham?
LIPSTROB: We murdered him.
CLOISTERMOUTH: On Signal Cliff, sir.
CUTHBUN: That's the big one on this side of the town.
CLOISTERMOUTH: He always went there for a walk in the afternoon, sir. 190
The day after he'd kept us in we waited for him.
TERHEW: Six of us.
CUTHBUN: In the bushes.
CLOISTERMOUTH: He came up quite slowly, panting a bit.
TERHEW: And he paused at the top and took out his handkerchief. 195
CUTHBUN: The fog was coming in from the sea.
CLOISTERMOUTH: Then we came out from the bushes all round him. He started to say something . . .
LIPSTROB: But we rushed him and got him on the ground.
AGGERIDGE: Rugger tackle. 200
CLOISTERMOUTH: His specs fell off and he started lashing out.
BUNGABINE: So we hit him on the head with a stone.
ORRIS: K.O.
LIPSTROB: Gedoing!
TERHEW: Then we carried him to the edge and chucked him over. 205
BUNGABINE: A'one, a'two, a'three . . . and away!
CLOISTERMOUTH: And there was blood on the stone, so we threw that over too.
ORRIS: Dead easy.
CUTHBUN: Nobody saw us because of the fog. 210
BUNGABINE: The perfect crime. Haw haw haw.
JOHN: Hardly.
CUTHBUN: Why not, sir?
JOHN: If you had done it . . .
OMNES: We did. 215
JOHN: You would have spoilt it all by telling me. Your vanity would have given you away.
CLOISTERMOUTH: But we have told you, sir.
JOHN: And if I believed you I'd tell the police . . . through the headmaster of course. 220
CUTHBUN: But that wouldn't do any good, sir. You don't know which of us did it.
JOHN: The police would find out. They'd get you one by one and question you.
TERHEW: We've all got alibis, sir. 225
CLOISTERMOUTH: Yes, sir, really we have. I was in Chapel with Unman and Muffet, polishing the candlesticks.
CUTHBUN: Terhew, Hogg and me were having tea in Orris's study.
LIPSTROB: Aggeridge, Root and Trindle were playing fives with me.
BUNGABINE: I was in the armoury with Borby and Ankerton. We were cleaning our equipment web for the C.C.F. parade. 230

WITTERING: And Mudd and Munn and me were doing detention.
CUTHBUN: I mean to say, sir, we can prove it. There are at least two witnesses for every member of the form.
(*Door opens*) 235
JOHN: Oh, Headmaster.
HEAD: Carry on, Mr Ebony. Take no notice of me.
JOHN: Er . . . yes . . . er.
CUTHBUN: The battle of St Albans, 1455, The Battle of Wakefield, 1461.
JOHN: Fourteen sixty, Cuthbun. 240
CUTHBUN: Sorry, sir. Hedgely Moor and Hexham, 1464. (*Door shuts*) He's gone. There you are, sir, we're good at alibis.

Giles Cooper: *Unman, Wittering and Zigo* (1958)

Situation and Character

1. What type of school is Chantrey? On what evidence do you base your answer?
2. Write brief notes on the essential characteristics of *five* boys in the class. By what means is the type of character of each boy conveyed to us?
3. How effective is John Ebony in keeping control of his class? Locate specific points in the lesson where he says or does (a) the right or (b) the wrong thing from the point of view of maintaining his own authority as a teacher.
4. What is the general attitude of the boys to Wittering, and how is this suggested?
5. What is John Ebony's initial reaction to the boys' claim that they murdered Mr. Pelham? In what way should the actor playing John's part speak the line: 'Oh yes? And how did you kill Mr Pelham?'?

Language

6. Explain briefly in what way(s) the basic pattern of the dialogue here is determined by the situation—a new teacher in a classroom with a group of pupils.
7. The class uses a number of different 'tactics' to deflect Ebony from his pedagogic purpose. What are these tactics, and what do they reveal of the boys in this class?
8. Apart from the references to Mr Pelham, how do the exchanges suggest that these boys have been together in the same class for some time?
9. Locate specific examples of the following from this scene and comment on their dramatic effect:
   (a) Increase in the pace—and perhaps the volume—of the dialogue;
   (b) Moments of tension or climax—where perhaps there is a turning point, or a dramatic pause.

General Questions

10. What features of this scene produce material which is suitable for good radio drama?

In your answers to the questions above, we hope you discovered the impossibility of discussing the situation in which characters are placed and the language in which they express themselves as though these two elements existed in separate compartments. They do not! Let us take up just one or two specific points which may have come up in your discussion of the Giles Cooper extract. The whole shape of the dialogue of the scene (Question 6) and the kind of language at work within it are determined by the classroom situation—its rapid short exchanges, its interrogatory drills and rituals and the inevitable sense (certainly on first meeting) of a conflict, a battle of wills, which is to be fought between teacher and pupils. And how do we learn about the main characteristics of the boys (Question 2)? It is, of course, through the distinctive tone of the words that are put into their mouths by the dramatist. Cuthbun, for instance, is the form 'know-all': he understands that a punctilious, ostensibly polite manner, which only partly disguises a subversive intent, is particularly difficult for the teacher who is a tyro to deal with. (Imagine the tone of his 'Oh, I see, sir, yes, sir.') The less garrulous Bungabine, on the other hand, is incapable of Cuthbun's clever thrusts and confines his contributions to simple interjections, obviously sarcastic comments and raucous laughter. This is a gauge of his character: the dramatist is portraying a number of basic types of pupil.

You probably noticed in answer to Question 3, that John Ebony shows his essential lack of experience and weakness as a teacher through a number of inept actions and comments. For instance, shortly after the opening of the scene he makes a point of calling poor Wittering to the front of the class. This is, of course, just the diversion the form wants: Wittering is their comic butt and they have rather cruelly set him up for this reprimand. Yet once John Ebony has Wittering in front of him, his words reveal that he does not really know what to do in this situation, and he ends up lamely and indecisively sending the boy back to his seat. He has not identified the pupil responsible for this piece of horseplay—first round to the class!—and when he falls back on a hackneyed piece of schoolmasterly admonition—'And I don't want any more fooling about, or there'll be trouble'—this simply gives the ever-alert Cuthbun the opportunity to have some more fun at the teacher's expense. By putting John Ebony through an obviously rehearsed series of distracting routines—Lower Five B has clearly practised these techniques for some time—the pupils in the class first test John's powers of authority, prove him to be ineffectual and then demonstrate their own corporate power; John's confidence is gradually being chipped away; the weight of the dialogue shows that quite quickly the pupils have reversed the normal balance of power. It is they who are beginning to dictate terms to the teacher.

The scene makes ideal material for radio drama for a number of reasons, perhaps most importantly the skilful variation of pace and rhythm it exhibits: there is, for instance, the tense silence which follows Cloistermouth's announcement 'And that was why we killed him' set against the contrasting and increasing rapidity of the speeches in which the members of the class, almost like voices in a single chorus, excitedly recall the details of the alleged murder of Mr Pelham. In a radio drama, aural response is everything: it is the listener who creates the scene in his own imagination by reacting to a carefully orchestrated patterning of words, rhythms and sound effects. Note, for example, the simple but totally effective shorthand that is used instantly to create in the listener's mind the scene of a classroom—the calling of the register as each boy answers to the roll-call of that amusingly evocative roster of names.

Radio drama makes us concentrate single-mindedly on words and sound—and the emotions they can trigger. That is why we feel it is worth spending some time examining the resources of language used by Giles Cooper in this extract. The frequent visits to the theatre which we have suggested it is desirable to combine with any study of the drama may not be possible for everybody, and here the radio may come to our assistance. It is well worth looking out for the plays the Drama Department of the BBC produces on Radio 3 and Radio 4. You will find that contemporary plays—some experimental, some pure entertainment—are regularly put out on the air, together with productions of drama from the classic repertory. Your radio can be a very simple (and cheap) way of familiarising yourself with a wide range of drama. Unfortunately, the genre of the play especially written for radio is often underestimated and neglected, but if you want to judge what is possible in this medium, simply sample these three very different but masterly examples:

Louis MacNeice: *The Dark Tower* (1947)
Dylan Thomas: *Under Milk Wood* (1954)
Samuel Beckett: *All That Fall* (1957)

5

Taking shape

The dialogue from the classroom scene by Giles Cooper possesses a clearly defined shape which produces the kind of momentum likely to hold an audience's attention—in contrast to the desultory conversation based on Debrett's counsel (see page 42) which, short as it is, is obviously 'not going anywhere'. If the dialogue of a play is to come to life when spoken on stage, it must possess cohesion and expressive force. (We will examine later in greater detail some of the ways in which this is achieved—see pages 81–107). Any tape-recording of our everyday speech will reveal its hesitancies and imprecisions—the way in which we stumble around what we really mean or sometimes may be totally 'lost for words'. While, of course, drawing on the rich variety of daily discourse, dramatic dialogue must—to a greater or lesser extent—offer a specially edited, more concentrated version of our normal speech habits, although there are a number of qualifications to be made here.

A dramatist may wish to show the emptiness of social chit-chat and the way in which the elaborate artifice of etiquette and convention in speech is used to blur rather than to clarify meaning; he may even wish to present characters who mangle language, like Dogberry in Shakespeare's *Much Ado About Nothing*. Many modern dramatists have been concerned to show the difficulty, the deceptions of what we take to be the communicative medium of language—with silence constantly threatening to encroach on characters' attempts to articulate. In the contemporary theatre there has been something of a reaction against eloquence and rhetoric. Buchner's *Woyzek* (1836–37), which has as its 'hero' a character of only partial articulacy, has foreshadowed a whole later modern tradition. And yet, paradoxically, even when the dramatist wishes to make it appear that we are eavesdropping on exactly the kind of rambling conversation we hear at the bus stop, close inspection of successful dramatic dialogue of this kind will reveal a patterning and editing of speech which is quite different from most everyday practice. We will give you a specific example of this contrast later (see page 77), and a study of the plays of, for instance, Pinter or Beckett would amply bear out the point we are making.

There is no getting away from the fact that in a play utterance must be a tauter, more formally arranged version of everyday language. For example, characters will tend to express feeling more nakedly or in a more heightened and striking manner than we would expect in 'real life'. With this assertion in mind, read through the following extract—the opening of Chekhov's *The Cherry Orchard* (1903).

(i) While making all due allowance for what must be something of an unknown quantity—the social behaviour of a different time and place (Russia at the end of the nineteenth century), locate examples from the dialogue which reveal characters speaking in a way you would not expect in 'real life'—for instance, with greater frankness or eloquence.

(ii) Comment on the reasons why Chekhov makes his characters speak in this way.

A room which is still known as the nursery. Half-light, shortly before sunrise. It is May already, and the cherry trees are in blossom, but outside in the orchard it is cold, with a morning frost. The windows are closed.

Enter DUNYASHA, *a parlour maid, with a candle, and* LOPAKHIN, *a business man, with a book in his hand.* 5

LOPAKHIN: God be praised, the train's arrived. What time is it?

DUNYASHA: Nearly two o'clock. (*Extinguishes the candle.*) It's light already.

LOPAKHIN: So the train's how late? Two hours, at least. (*Yawns and stretches.*) Fine one I am. Complete fool. Came all the way here to go and 10 meet them at the station, and then just dropped off while I was sitting there. It's a shame. You might have woken me.

DUNYASHA: I thought you'd gone. (*Listens.*) That sounds like them now.

LOPAKHIN (*listens*): No . . . Luggage to pick up, one thing and another . . . 15

Pause.

She's lived abroad for five years—I don't know what she'll be like now . . . She's a wonderful woman. Easy, straightforward. I remember, when I was a boy of fifteen or so, my father—he kept a shop then in the village here—dead now, of course—he hit me in the face with his fist, and 20 the blood started to pour out of my nose . . . For some reason we'd come into the yard here together, and he was drunk, he was well away. She brought me in—and I can remember it so well, she was still a girl, a slim young girl—she brought me in and she took me to the washstand in this room, in the nursery. 'Don't cry,' she says. 'Brave little peasant, now. 25 You'll live to dance at your wedding . . . '

Pause.

Brave little peasant . . . it's true, my father was a peasant—and here am I in a white waistcoat and yellow shoes. Like a pig in a pastry-cook's . . . I'm a rich man now, plenty of money, but look twice and I'm a peasant, a real 30 peasant . . . (*Leafs through the book.*) I was reading this book. Couldn't understand a word. Fell asleep over it.

Pause.

DUNYASHA: And the dogs, they haven't slept all night. They can sense that the mistress is coming. 35

LOPAKHIN: What's the matter with you, Dunyasha?

DUNYASHA: My hands are all of a tremble. I'm going to faint.

LOPAKHIN: Very tender plant, aren't you, Dunyasha? Dress like a lady, do your hair like one, too. Not the way, is it? You want to remember who you are. 40

Enter YEPIKHODOV, *a clerk on the estate, with a bouquet. He is wearing a jacket and highly polished boots that squeak loudly. As he comes in he drops the bouquet.*

YEPIKHODOV (*picks up the bouquet*): The gardener sent them. He says to put them in the dining-room. (*Gives the bouquet to* DUNYASHA.) 45

LOPAKHIN: And bring me some kvass.

DUNYASHA: Right you are. (*Goes out.*)

YEPIKHODOV: Three degrees of frost this morning, and the cherry all in blossom. I can't give our climate my seal of approval. (*Sighs.*) Indeed I can't. It never knows how to lend a helping hand at the right moment. 50 And I mean look at me—I bought myself these boots the day before yesterday, and they squeak so much, I mean it's quite impossible. I mean, put it like this—what should I grease them with?

LOPAKHIN: Leave off, will you? Pester, pester.

YEPIKHODOV: I don't know. Every day some disaster happens to me. Not 55 that I complain. I'm used to it. I even smile.

Enter DUNYASHA. *She gives* LOPAKHIN *his kvass.*

YEPIKHODOV: I'll go, then. (*Stumbles against the table, which falls over.*) There you are . . . (*As if exulting in it.*) You see what I'm up against! I mean, it's simply amazing! (*Goes out.*) 60

DUNYASHA: To tell you the truth, he's proposed to me.

LOPAKHIN: Ah!

DUNYASHA: I don't know *what* to say . . . He's all right, he doesn't give any trouble, it's just sometimes when he starts to talk—you can't understand a word of it. It's very nice, and he puts a lot of feeling into it, 65 only you can't understand it. I quite like him in a way, even. He's madly in love with me. He's the kind of person who never has any luck. Every day something happens. They tease him in our part of the house—they call him Disasters by the Dozen . . .

LOPAKHIN (*listens*): I think they're coming. 70

DUNYASHA: They're coming! What's the matter with me? I've gone all cold.

LOPAKHIN: They are indeed coming. Let's go and meet them. Will she recognize me? Five years we haven't seen each other.

DUNYASHA (*in agitation*): I'll faint this very minute . . . I will, I'll faint 75 clean away!

Two carriages can be heard coming up to the house. LOPAKHIN *and* DUNYASHA *hurry out.*

The stage is empty. Then there is noise in the adjoining rooms.

Anton Chekhov: *The Cherry Orchard* (trans. Michael Frayn)

What we have said about the construction of dramatic dialogue also applies to the way plot is developed—that is, the manner in which the narrative content of a play unfolds. In the opening passage of *The Cherry Orchard*, for instance, there may appear to be an air of inconsequentiality, but notice how skilfully we are made to anticipate the imminent arrival of Liubov Andryeevna; in the light of the whole play there is in fact nothing superfluous here—every reference, albeit sometimes in an oblique way, is preparing us for the development of future events and themes.

Before they can achieve anything in the theatre, all dramatists must have the skill of being able to organize the material that goes to make up a play: this includes, among many important structural considerations, the pacing of the narrative to create variation and balance, the manoeuvring of characters into the right combinations at the appropriate moments and the dovetailing of the individual scene into the whole structure of the drama. For a dramatist to think long and hard about these matters must not be regarded as any straitjacketing of sincerity or spontaneity, for the emotions to be expressed in a drama can only achieve the appearance of 'naturalness' if they are ordered and made to flow through carefully directed channels. Art is used to disguise art: in a drama it is only sloppy technique that draws attention to itself.

The main reason for the need to streamline a play's structure is to produce drama that will grip an audience's attention. Scenes which meander and lose their way or material which is haphazardly thrown together will not achieve this effect. While even the greatest novel may have its dull passages and while the reader may always turn back the pages if he has failed to assimilate a point, a drama which causes its audience's attention to wander is a doomed enterprise. Here again, in the way the dramatist must keep the action of the play moving in a purposeful, unified manner towards a definite end, there is a clear contrast with most of our everyday experience in which so often events occur arbitrarily with intervening periods of routine and boredom.

Of course, it is only when we study a play in its entirety that we can appreciate its formal construction—the way in which a series of moments grow organically into scenes and acts which unfold like the petals of a flower. And here we have a problem in a book of this nature, for by necessity we are considering drama in relation to a series of extracts which must mean less taken in isolation than when experienced in relation to the plays as whole. So until you have read all of *The Cherry Orchard* or seen the play performed, Chekhov's brilliance of organization in the opening scene cannot really be appreciated. Nevertheless, by means of studying the way a particular scene is put together, it is possible—in the small-scale—to gain some insight into what is demanded from a playwright in terms of construction.

The mainspring of the plot of a play is suspense, and the method by which suspense is created—and the audience's interest held—is by the arrangement of the events in the play's action in a carefully planned sequence. Suspense essentially involves the setting up of certain questions in an audience's mind. Some of these questions will be major issues: for instance, in the Chekhov extract we are clearly being made to anticipate the arrival of Liubov Andryeevna and to wonder what kind of woman she is and exactly what will be involved in her relations with Lopakhin. Again, in the scene from the Giles Cooper radio play, a most fascinating question hangs over the end of the scene and whets our appetite for the sequel: did the boys *really* murder Mr Pelham, their previous teacher?

In some plays we may be fairly certain what will happen next. For instance, in many comedies—we give you the shape of the plot outline of a 'typical' comedy on page 192—we will know the general direction in which the play is moving. Here the question will be, not what will happen, but rather, *how* will it occur? What variations on a fairly predictable pattern is the dramatist going to produce?

But suspense also works in smaller matters too; in fact, it should operate from one moment of the play to the next: how will Character A respond to what Character B has just said to him? And isn't Character C likely to arrive on the scene soon? And then what will happen? And so on. The skilful dramatist sets up wave patterns of such questions: he will certainly make us laugh and cry, but he will also make us *wait*. As we watch a play our interest is held because some of the expectations we form in response to the play's action are confirmed—while, to our surprise, others are totally reversed.

To see how this pattern can operate in a fairly basic way, read the following extract from Rattigan's *The Winslow Boy* (1946).

Make notes on (i) the general shape of the scene and (ii) the setting up of an expectation in our minds which will either be confirmed or reversed at the climax. (We will provide you with some jottings of our own later.)

Ronnie Winslow has been expelled from naval college after the authorities there have accused him of stealing a five shilling postal order from a fellow pupil. His father, Arthur, is determined to restore his son's good name and he wants the distinguished barrister, Sir Robert Morton, to take up the boy's case. The scene is set in the Winslows' drawing-room. Ronnie has just told Sir Robert that on the day the postal order was stolen he visited the locker room after lunch.

Also present are Ronnie's mother (Grace), his sister (Catherine) and the family solicitor (Desmond Curry).

SIR ROBERT: The money was perfectly safe in your pocket. Why did you suddenly feel yourself impelled to put it away in your locker?

RONNIE (*almost shouting*): I don't know.

SIR ROBERT: Was it because you knew you would be alone in the locker room at that time? 5

RONNIE: No.

SIR ROBERT: Where was Elliot's locker in relation to yours?

RONNIE: Next to it, but one.

SIR ROBERT: Next but one. What time did Elliot put his postal order in his locker? 10
RONNIE: I don't know. I didn't even know he had a postal order in his locker. I didn't know he had a postal order at all.
SIR ROBERT: Yet you say he was a great friend of yours—
RONNIE: He didn't tell me he had one.
SIR ROBERT: How very secretive of him. (*He makes a note on the document*) 15 What time did you go to the locker room?
RONNIE: I don't remember.
SIR ROBERT: Was it directly after dinner?
RONNIE: Yes, I think so.
SIR ROBERT: What did you do after leaving the locker room? 20
RONNIE: I've told you. I went for permission to go to the post office.
SIR ROBERT: What time was that?
RONNIE: About a quarter past two.
SIR ROBERT: Dinner is over at a quarter to two. Which means that you were alone in the locker room for half an hour? 25
RONNIE: I wasn't there all that time—
SIR ROBERT: How long were you there?
RONNIE: About five minutes.
SIR ROBERT: What were you doing for other twenty-five?
RONNIE: I don't remember. 30
SIR ROBERT: It's odd that your memory is so good about some things and so bad about others—
RONNIE: Perhaps I waited outside the C.O.'s office.
SIR ROBERT (*with searing sarcasm*): Perhaps you waited outside the C.O.'s office. And perhaps no one saw you there, either? 35
RONNIE: No. I don't think they did.
SIR ROBERT: What were you thinking about outside the C.O.'s office for twenty-five minutes?
RONNIE (*wildly*): I don't even know if I was there. I can't remember. Perhaps I wasn't there at all. 40
SIR ROBERT: No. Perhaps you were still in the locker room rifling Elliot's locker—
ARTHUR (*indignantly*): Sir Robert, I must ask you—
SIR ROBERT: Quiet!
RONNIE: I remember now, I remember. Someone did see me outside the 45 C.O.'s office. A chap called Casey. I remember I spoke to him.
SIR ROBERT: What did you say?
RONNIE: I said 'Come down to the post office with me. I'm going to cash a postal order.'
SIR ROBERT (*triumphantly*): *Cash* a postal order. 50
RONNIE: I mean get.
SIR ROBERT: You said cash. Why did you say cash if you meant get?
RONNIE: I don't know.
SIR ROBERT: I suggest cash was the truth.
RONNIE: No, no. It wasn't. It wasn't really. You're muddling me. 55
SIR ROBERT: You seem easily muddled. How many other lies have you told?
RONNIE: None. Really I haven't.

SIR ROBERT (*bending forward malevolently*): I suggest your whole testimony is a lie. 60

RONNIE: No! It's the truth.

SIR ROBERT: I suggest there is barely one single word of truth in anything you have said either to me, or to the Judge Advocate or to the Commander. I suggest that you broke into Elliot's locker, that you stole the postal order for five shillings belonging to Elliot, and you cashed it by 65 means of forging his name.

RONNIE (*wailing*): I didn't. I didn't.

SIR ROBERT: I suggest you did it for a joke, meaning to give Elliot the five shillings back, but that when you met him and he said he had reported the matter that you got frightened and decided to keep quiet. 70

RONNIE: No, no, no. It isn't true.

SIR ROBERT: I suggest that by continuing to deny your guilt you are causing great hardship to your own family, and considerable annoyance to high and important persons in this country—

CATHERINE (*on her feet*): That's a disgraceful thing to say! 75

ARTHUR (*rising*): I agree.

SIR ROBERT (*leaning forward and glaring at* RONNIE *with utmost venom*): I suggest that the time has at last come for you to undo some of the misery you have caused by confessing to us all now that you are a forger, a liar and a thief. 80

(GRACE *rises, crosses swiftly to* RONNIE *and envelops him.*)

RONNIE (*in tears*): I'm not! I'm not! I'm not! I didn't do it.

ARTHUR: This is outrageous, sir.

(DESMOND *crosses above* SIR ROBERT *to the table and collects the documents . . .* RONNIE *is sobbing hysterically on his mother's breast.* 85 ARTHUR *and* CATHERINE *are glaring indignantly at* SIR ROBERT, *who is putting his papers together.*)

SIR ROBERT (*to* DESMOND): Can I drop you anywhere? My car is at the door.

DESMOND: Er—no—I thank you. 90

SIR ROBERT (*carelessly*): Well, send all this stuff round to my chambers tomorrow morning, will you?

DESMOND: But—but will you need it now?

SIR ROBERT: Oh, yes. The boy is plainly innocent. I accept the brief.

(SIR ROBERT *bows to* ARTHUR *and* CATHERINE *and walks languidly to the* 95 *door . . .* RONNIE *continues to sob hysterically.*)

QUICK CURTAIN

Terence Rattigan: *The Winslow Boy* (1946)

Notes

(i) *General shape of the scene*

Winslows' drawing-room virtually becomes a courtroom—the cross-examination imposes on the dialogue a question/answer format—a naturally dramatic shape? Sir Robert presses questions with great forensic skill—moving from sarcasm, through brow-beating tactics to forthright assertion. Towards the climax Sir R's speeches lengthen—note the insistent force of his repeated 'I suggest'—while Ronnie, in contrast, becomes almost incoherent (understandably so!). Occasional interventions by other members of the family—further heighten the (unsympathetic?) hostility and harshness of Sir R.—culminates in Mr Winslow's 'This is outrageous, sir'. Effective pause follows this—tableau of the hysterically sobbing Ronnie, set against the contrasting icy coolness of Sir R. Mr Winslow and Catherine's glare direct the audience's attention. Everything focusses on Sir R. at the end of the scene. He drops his courtroom manner. Tone almost casual—relaxed—lowering the temperature for a few seconds before the final surprise which is followed by a dramatically quick curtain—gasps from the audience!—curtailing the scene at a high moment of drama.

(ii) *Audience expectations*
Sir R's cross-examination seems to have tied R. in knots—his vagueness about what he was actually doing at certain key moments, the slip over *cashing* the postal-order. We imagine Sir R. must be totally against the boy—seems to believe he is telling a pack of lies. Then the shock—after he has apparently 'demolished' R, Sir R. casually accepts the case after all. Complete reversal of our expectations. As the curtain falls we are left pondering a number of questions. What has apparently persuaded Sir R. that the boy is innocent? Why was he so hostile earlier? We realise in retrospect that Sir R. has intentionally tested R. to breaking point—adopting all the adversarial skills of the practised barrister—and R. has somehow passed the test. How? What exactly persuaded Sir R?

This leads to a couple of final questions. When Sir Robert is asked later in the play what convinced him of the boy's innocence, he replies:

> 'Three things. First of all, he made far too many damaging admissions. A guilty person would have been much more careful—much more on his guard. Secondly, I laid him a trap; and thirdly left him a loophole. Anyone who was guilty would have fallen into the one and darted through the other. He did neither.'

What is (i) the 'trap' and (ii) the 'loophole'?

The following extract from Bernard Shaw's *St Joan* (1924) presents another kind of 'courtroom drama' and the questions which follow are designed to prompt you to think about the shape of the scene and the pattern of responses it would set up in an audience.

Joan, a peasant girl who believes she has been inspired by divine voices, has led the forces of France to a number of victories against the English, but now, after being captured, she is to be tried for heresy. The scene is set in a great stone hall in the castle at Rouen. A bishop and an Inquisitor are Joan's judges, and they sit on two raised chairs, side by side. Rows of chairs radiating from them are occupied by canons, the doctors of law and theology and the Dominican monks who act as assessors. There is a stool for the prisoner. The year is 1431.

LADVENU: Joan: we are all trying to save you. His lordship is trying to save you. The Inquisitor could not be more just to you if you were his own daughter. But you are blinded by a terrible pride and self-sufficiency.
JOAN: Why do you say that? I have said nothing wrong. I cannot understand. 5
THE INQUISITOR: The blessed St Athanasius has laid it down in his creed that those who cannot understand are damned. It is not enough to be simple. It is not enough even to be what simple people call good. The simplicity of a darkened mind is no better than the simplicity of a beast.
JOAN: There is great wisdom in the simplicity of a beast, let me tell you; and 10 sometimes great foolishness in the wisdom of scholars.
LADVENU: We know that, Joan: we are not so foolish as you think us. Try to resist the temptation to make pert replies to us. Do you see that man who stands behind you? [*he indicates the Executioner*]
JOAN [*turning and looking at the man*]: Your torturer? But the Bishop said I 15 was not to be tortured.
LADVENU: You are not to be tortured because you have confessed everything that is necessary to your condemnation. That man is not only the torturer: he is also the Executioner. Executioner: let The Maid hear your answers to my questions. Are you prepared for the burning of a 20 heretic this day?
THE EXECUTIONER: Yes, Master.
LADVENU: Is the stake ready?
THE EXECUTIONER: It is. In the market-place. The English have built it too high for me to get near her and make the death easier. It will be a 25 cruel death.
JOAN [*horrified*]: But you are not going to burn me now?
THE INQUISITOR: You realize it at last.
LADVENU: There are eight hundred English soldiers waiting to take you to the market-place the moment the sentence of excommunication has 30 passed the lips of your judges. You are within a few short moments of that doom.
JOAN [*looking round desperately for rescue*]: Oh God!
LADVENU: Do not despair, Joan. The Church is merciful. You can save yourself. 35
JOAN [*hopefully*]: Yes, my voices promised me I should not be burnt. St Catherine bade me be bold.
CAUCHON: Woman: are you quite mad? Do you not yet see that your voices have deceived you?
JOAN: Oh no: that is impossible. 40
CAUCHON: Impossible! They have led you straight to your excommunication, and to the stake which is there waiting for you.
LADVENU [*pressing the point hard*]: Have they kept a single promise to you since you were taken at Compiègne? The devil has betrayed you. The Church holds out its arms to you. 45

JOAN [*despairing*]: Oh, it is true: it is true: my voices have deceived me. I have been mocked by devils: my faith is broken. I have dared and dared; but only a fool will walk into a fire: God, who gave me my commonsense, cannot will me to do that.

LADVENU: Now God be praised that He has saved you at the eleventh hour! [*He hurries to the vacant seat at the scribes' table, and snatches a sheet of paper, on which he sets to work writing eagerly*]. 50

CAUCHON: Amen!

JOAN: What must I do?

CAUCHON: You must sign a solemn recantation of your heresy. 55

JOAN: Sign? That means to write my name. I cannot write.

CAUCHON: You have signed many letters before.

JOAN: Yes; but someone held my hand and guided the pen. I can make my mark. . . .

LADVENU [*rising with the paper in his hand*]: My lord: here is the form of recantation for The Maid to sign. 60

CAUCHON: Read it to her.

JOAN: Do not trouble. I will sign it.

THE INQUISITOR: Woman: you must know what you are putting your hand to. Read it to her, Brother Martin. And let all be silent. 65

LADVENU [*reading quietly*]: 'I, Joan, commonly called The Maid, a miserable sinner, do confess that I have most grievously sinned in the following articles. I have pretended to have revelations from God and the angels and the blessed saints, and perversely rejected the Church's warnings that these were temptations by demons. I have blasphemed abominably by wearing an immodest dress, contrary to the Holy Scripture and the canons of the Church. Also I have clipped my hair in the style of man, and, against all the duties which have made my sex specially acceptable in heaven, have taken up the sword, even to the shedding of human blood, inciting men to slay each other, invoking evil spirits to delude them, and stubbornly and most blasphemously imputing these sins to Almighty God. I confess to the sin of sedition, to the sin of idolatry, to the sin of disobedience, to the sin of pride, and to the sin of heresy. All of which sins I now renounce and abjure and depart from, humbly thanking you Doctors and Masters who have brought me back to the truth and into the grace of our Lord. And I will never return to my errors, but will remain in communion with our Holy Church and in obedience to our Holy Father the Pope of Rome. All this I swear by God Almighty and the Holy Gospels, in witness whereto I sign my name to this recantation.' 70 75 80 85

THE INQUISITOR: You understand this, Joan?

JOAN [*listless*]: It is plain enough, sir.

THE INQUISITOR: And is it true?

JOAN: It may be true. If it were not true, the fire would not be ready for me in the market-place. 90

LADVENU [*taking up his pen and a book, and going to her quickly lest she should compromise herself again*]: Come, child: let me guide your hand. Take the pen. [*She does so; and they begin to write, using the book as a desk*] J.E.H.A.N.E. So. Now make your mark by yourself.

JOAN [*makes her mark, and gives him back the pen, tormented by the rebellion of her soul against her mind and body*]: There! 95

LADVENU [*replacing the pen on the table, and handing the recantation to Cauchon with a reverence*]: Praise be to God, my brothers, the lamb has returned to the flock; and the shepherd rejoices in her more than in ninety and nine just persons. [*He returns to his seat*]. 100

THE INQUISITOR [*taking the paper from Cauchon*]: We declare thee by this act set free from the danger of excommunication in which thou stoodest. [*He throws the paper down to the table*].

JOAN: I thank you.

THE INQUISITOR: But because thou has sinned most presumptuously 105 against God and the Holy Church, and that thou mayst repent thy errors in solitary contemplation, and be shielded from all temptation to return to them, we, for the good of thy soul, and for a penance that may wipe out thy sins and bring thee finally unspotted to the throne of grace, do condemn thee to eat the bread of sorrow and drink the water of affliction 110 to the end of thy earthly days in perpetual imprisonment.

JOAN [*rising in consternation and terrible anger*]: Perpetual imprisonment! Am I not then to be set free?

LADVENU [*mildly shocked*]: Set free, child, after such wickedness as yours! What are you dreaming of? 115

JOAN: Give me that writing. [*She rushes to the table; snatches up the paper; and tears it into fragments*] Light your fire: do you think I dread it as much as the life of a rat in a hole? My voices were right.

LADVENU: Joan! Joan!

JOAN: Yes: they told me you were fools [*the word gives great offence*], and 120 that I was not to listen to your fine words nor trust to your charity. You promised me my life; but you lied [*indignant exclamations*]. You think that life is nothing but not being stone dead. It is not the bread and water I fear: I can live on bread: when have I asked for more? It is no hardship to drink water if the water be clean. Bread has no sorrow for me, and 125 water no affliction. But to shut me from the light of the sky and the sight of the fields and flowers; to chain my feet so that I can never again ride with the soldiers nor climb the hills; to make me breathe foul damp darkness, and keep from me everything that brings me back to the love of God when your wickedness and foolishness tempt me to hate Him: all this is 130 worse than the furnace in the Bible that was heated seven times. I could do without my warhorse; I could drag about in a skirt; I could let the banners and the trumpets and the knights and soldiers pass me and leave me behind as they leave the other women, if only I could still hear the wind in the trees, the larks in the sunshine, the young lambs crying 135 through the healthy frost, and the blessed blessed church bells that send my angel voices floating to me on the wind. But without these things I cannot live; and by your wanting to take them away from me, or from any human creature, I know that your counsel is of the devil, and that mine is of God. 140

THE ASSESSORS [*in great commotion*]: Blasphemy! blasphemy! She is possessed. She said our counsel was of the devil. And hers of God. Monstrous! The devil is in our midst, etc., etc.

D'ESTIVET [*shouting about the din*]: She is a relapsed heretic, obstinate, incorrigible, and altogether unworthy of the mercy we have shewn her. I 145 call for her excommunication.

THE CHAPLAIN [*to the Executioner*]: Light your fire, man. To the stake with her.

The Executioner and his assistants hurry out through the courtyard.

LADVENU: You wicked girl: if your counsel were of God would He not deliver you? 150

JOAN: His ways are not your ways. He wills that I go through the fire to His bosom: for I am His child, and you are not fit that I should live among you. That is my last word to you.

The soldiers seize her. 155

Bernard Shaw: *St Joan* (1924)

(i) If we follow the different phases of Joan's response, this scene seems to fall into *three* broad 'movements'.
   (a) Explain where you would place the dividing lines of these three general movements in the scene.
   (b) Suggest what produces the transition from one phase to the next.
   (c) At each of the different stages of Joan's response, what do you think would be the audience's reaction to her? Would the audience's changing reaction be fairly straightforward, or would it sometimes/often contain an element of 'mixed feelings'?

(ii) Besides the changing pattern of Joan's feelings, what other elements in this scene create the kind of mounting tension and suspense (with variations of light and shade) which would be likely to hold an audience's attention in the theatre? (You should consider, for instance, the staging of the scene, its construction, use of language and presentation of character).

6

Dramatic irony

Dramatic irony is a characteristic device of the drama and it issues in a whole range of often complex effects which are produced by the playwright's careful structuring of the unfolding action of a play. Whereas the creation of suspense derives from our ignorance or doubt about what will happen, dramatic irony depends on the audience's privileged position of knowing more about a situation than at least one of the characters who are involved in it.

Remember the plot outline at the beginning of this book (see page 2). Let us imagine that you have dramatised this material; you begin Scene 6 with Jake throwing open the door—perhaps Spike is hovering in the background—fixing Jane and our hero with a seraphic smile and declaring: 'Great to see you! This is going to be a marvellous party!' Here we have an example of dramatic irony because the full implications of the situation make Jake's words take on a significance of which he (and Spike) can hardly be aware. Unlike us— we have observed the earlier scene—the 'victims' of the dramatic irony are not 'in the know'. In the light of what Jane has said previously, if she is to be believed (possible source of further irony?), the party, rather than being 'marvellous', is likely to prove a potential battleground for young love.

Normally in drama, as we have suggested, to create this effect of dramatic irony the audience must first be put in possession of certain vital information. For this reason the possibilities for dramatic irony will generally become richer as the action develops. However, in Greek tragedy the material from which dramatists drew their plots—a treasury of myth, legend and history—would already be familiar to audiences that assembled in Athens for the sacred festivals of drama dedicated to Dionysus. For instance, as Sophocles' *Oedipus Rex* opened, the original audience would know the following: Oedipus' father, Laius, former King of Thebes, had been informed by an oracle that he would die at the hands of his son; Oedipus survived Laius' attempts to circumvent the prophesy by destroying his son and was brought up away from the court; as a young man, ignorant of his parentage, Oedipus did in fact slay his father before he went on to Thebes, which was at that time plagued by the Sphinx; he solved the Sphinx's riddle and as a result gained the throne of Thebes and married its queen—who was no other than his own mother, Jocasta.

In the light of this knowledge, read the following extract from the play which opens as a plague is once again blighting life in Thebes. Locate and comment on the effect of dramatic irony, of which you should find numerous examples. Remember that dramatic irony begins with a situational incongruity which will then give rise to language which takes on an ironic meaning for the audience.

PRIEST: My lord and king: we are gathered here, as you see,
Young and old, from the tenderest chicks to the age-bent seniors;
Priests—I of Zeus—and the pick of our young manhood.
More sit in the market-place, carrying boughs like these,
And around the twin altars of Pallas and the sacred embers 5
Of divination, beside the river of Ismenus.
You too have seen our city's affliction, caught
In a tide of death from which there is no escaping—
Death in the fruitful flowering of her soil;
Death in the pastures; death in the womb of woman; 10
And pestilence, a fiery demon gripping the city,
Stripping the house of Cadmus, to fatten hell
With profusion of lamentation.
If we come to you now, sir, as your suppliants,
I and these children, it is not as holding you 15
The equal of gods, but as the first of men,
Whether in the ordinary business of mortal life,
Or in the encounters of man with more than man.
It was you, we remember, a newcomer to Cadmus' town, 20
That broke our bondage to the vile Enchantress.
With no foreknowledge or hint that we could give,
But, as we truly believe, with the help of God,
You gave us back our life.
Now, Oedipus great and glorious, we seek
Your help again. Find some deliverance for us 25
By any way that god or man can show.
We know that experience of trials past gives strength
To present counsel. Therefore, O greatest of men,
Restore our city to life. Have a care for your fame.
Your diligence saved us once; let it not be said 30
That under your rule we were raised up only to fall.
Save, save our city, and keep her safe for ever.
Under the same bright star that gave us then
Good fortune, guide us into good to-day.
If you are to be our King, as now you are, 35
Be king of living men, not emptiness.
Surely there is no strength in wall or ship,
Where men are lacking and no life breathes within them.
OEDIPUS: I grieve for you, my children. Believe me, I know
All that you desire of me, all that you suffer; 40
And while you suffer, none suffers more than I.
You have your several griefs, each for himself;
But my heart bears the weight of my own, and yours
And all my people's sorrows. I am not asleep.
I weep; and walk through endless ways of thought. 45

But I have not been idle; one thing I have already done—
The only thing that promised hope. My kinsman
Creon, the son of Menoeceus, has been sent
To the Pythian house of Apollo, to learn what act
Or word of mine could help you. This is the day 50
I reckoned he should return. It troubles me
That he is not already here. But when he comes,
Whatever the god requires, upon my honour
It shall be done.

PRIEST: Well said. 55
(*He descries someone approaching from a distance.*)
And look! They are making signs
That Creon is on his way. Yes. He is here!

OEDIPUS (*looking also*): And with smiling face! O Apollo!
If his news is good! 60

PRIEST: It must be good; his head is crowned with bay
Full-berried; that is a sign.

OEDIPUS: We shall soon know . . .
He can hear us now . . . Royal brother! What news?
What message for us from the mouth of God? 65

Enter CREON

CREON: Good news. That is to say that good may come
Even out of painful matters, if all goes well.

OEDIPUS: And the answer? You hold me between fear and hope.
The answer? 70

CREON:
I will tell you—if you wish me to speak in the presence of all.
If not, let us go in.

OEDIPUS: Speak before all.
Their plight concerns me now, more than my life. 75

CREON:
This, then, is the answer, and this the plain command
Of Phoebus our lord. There is an unclean thing,
Born and nursed on our soil, polluting our soil,
Which must be driven away, not kept to destroy us. 80

OEDIPUS:
What unclean thing? And what purification is required?

CREON:
The banishment of a man, or the payment of blood for blood.
For the shedding of blood is the cause of our city's peril. 85

OEDIPUS:
What blood does he mean? Did he say who it was that died?

CREON: We had a king, sir, before you came to lead us.
His name was Laius.

OEDIPUS: I know. I never saw him. 90

CREON: He was killed. And clearly the meaning of the god's command
Is that we bring the unknown killer to justice.

OEDIPUS:
And where might *he* be? Where shall we hope to uncover

The faded traces of that far-distant crime? 95
CREON: Here—the god said. Seek, and ye shall find.
Unsought goes undetected.
OEDIPUS: Was it at home,
Or in the field, or abroad on foreign soil,
That Laius met his death, this violent death? 100
CREON: He left the country, as he said, on a pilgrimage;
And from that day forth we never saw him again.
OEDIPUS: Was there no word, no fellow-traveller
Who saw what happened, whose evidence could have been used?
CREON: All died; save one, who fled from the scene in terror, 105
And had nothing to tell for certain—except one thing.
OEDIPUS:
What was it? One thing might point the way to others,
If once we could lay our hands on the smallest clue.
CREON: His story was that robbers—not one but many— 110
Fell in with the King's party and put them to death.
OEDIPUS:
Robbers would hardly commit such a daring outrage—
Unless they were paid to do it by someone here.
CREON: 115
That too was suggested. But in the troubles that followed
No avenger came forward to punish the murderers.
OEDIPUS: What troubles? Surely none great enough to hinder
A full inquiry into a royal death?
CREON: 120
The Sphinx with her riddles forced us to turn our attention
From insoluble mysteries to more immediate matters.
OEDIPUS:
I will start afresh; and bring everything into the light.
All praise to Phoebus—and thanks, for your part, to you— 125
For thus pointing out our duty to the dead.
You will find me as willing an ally as you could wish
In the cause of God and our country. My own cause too—
Not merely from a fellow-creature will I clear this taint,
But from myself. The killer of Laius, 130
Whoever he was, might think to turn his hand
Against *me*; thus, serving Laius, I serve myself.
Now, up from your seats, my children! Away with these boughs!
Bring all the people of Cadmus here, and tell them
There is nothing I will not do. Certain it is 135
That by the help of God we stand—or fall.

Sophocles: *Oedipus Rex* (trans. E. F. Watling)

So, dramatic irony derives from an audience sharing in a kind of complicity with a dramatist who presents us with knowledge of which one or more of his characters is ignorant. This will often mean that there is a striking contrast or discrepancy between what a character himself believes his words and actions mean and what the action of the play reveals about them. Dramatic irony can also be produced when a character responds in a fashion which is contrary to what an audience knows is appropriate or judicious (in terms, for instance of that character's future happiness). These types of dramatic irony can easily be located in the above passage. Oedipus is doing the 'right thing' in terms of the way a king should normally act, but by doing so he will unleash forces which will bring about his own tragic fall.

There is, too, the kind of dramatic irony which results from parallels and contrasts being developed between the responses of different characters, ironies which are implicit in the structure of a play and are part of its whole span rather than being revealed in one situation or single speech. In *Oedipus Rex*, for instance, we will be shown in a following scene that it is the literally blind Tiresias who can 'see' the truth that Oedipus himself is the source of infection in Thebes; Oedipus is 'blind' to this, though when he acquires clear vision and learns the truth of his position, in his anguish he puts out his eyes. Shakespeare, too, will use dramatic irony to explore similarly rich areas of meaning: by placing several characters in similar situations the dramatist can create a kind of parallax. So in *Hamlet*, for instance, Laertes' response to the demand to revenge a murdered father produces an ironic reflection of Hamlet's own dilemma; and in *Macbeth* dramatic irony is focussed on the contrasting reactions of Macbeth and Banquo to the witches' prophecies.

The following extract is taken from *Macbeth* and it continues the action directly from the last passage we looked at from the play on page 00. Refresh your memory of the earlier episode and then read this new material. Comment in detail on the effects of the different kinds of dramatic irony that you find here.

[*Forres. A room in the palace.*]

Flourish. Enter DUNCAN, MALCOLM, DONALBAIN *(the King's Sons), and Attendants.*

DUNCAN: Is execution done on Cawdor? Are not
  Those in commission yet return'd? 5
MALCOLM: My Liege,
  They are not yet come back; but I have spoke
  With one that saw him die: who did report,
  That very frankly he confess'd his treasons,
  Implor'd your Highness' pardon, and set forth 10
  A deep repentance. Nothing in his life
  Became him like the leaving it: he died
  As one that had been studied in his death,
  To throw away the dearest thing he ow'd,
  As 'twere a careless trifle. 15
DUNCAN: There's no art
  To find the mind's construction in the face:
  He was a gentleman on whom I built
  An absolute trust—

Enter MACBETH, BANQUO, ROSSE, *and* ANGUS. 20

O worthiest cousin!
The sin of my ingratitude even now
Was heavy on me. Thou art so far before,
That swiftest wing of recompense is slow
To overtake thee: would thou hadst less deserv'd, 25
That the proportion both of thanks and payment
Might have been mine! only I have left to say,
More is thy due than more than all can pay.

MACBETH: The service and the loyalty I owe,
In doing it, pays itself. Your Highness' part 30
Is to receive our duties: and our duties
Are to your throne and state, children and servants;
Which do but what they should, by doing everything
Safe toward your love and honour.

DUNCAN: Welcome hither: 35
I have begun to plant thee, and will labour
To make thee full of growing.—Noble Banquo,
That hast no less deserv'd, nor must be known
No less to have done so, let me infold thee,
And hold thee to my heart. 40

BANQUO: There if I grow,
The harvest is your own.

DUNCAN: My plenteous joys,
Wanton in fulness, seek to hide themselves
In drops of sorrow.—Sons, kinsmen, Thanes, 45
And you whose places are the nearest, know,
We will establish our estate upon
Our eldest, Malcolm; whom we name hereafter
The Prince of Cumberland: which honour must
Not unaccompanied invest him only, 50
But signs of nobleness, like stars, shall shine
On all deservers.—From hence to Inverness,
And bind us further to you.

MACBETH: The rest is labour, which is not us'd for you:
I'll be myself the harbinger, and make joyful 55
The hearing of my wife with your approach;
So, humbly take my leave.

DUNCAN: My worthy Cawdor!

MACBETH [*Aside.*]: The Prince of Cumberland!—That is a step
On which I must fall down, or else o'erleap, 60
For in my way it lies. Stars, hide your fires!
Let not light see my black and deep desires;
The eye wink at the hand; yet let that be,
Which the eye fears, when it is done, to see. [*Exit.*]

DUNCAN: True, worthy Banquo: he is full so valiant, 65
And in his commendations I am fed;
It is a banquet to me. Let's after him,
Whose care is gone before to bid us welcome:
It is a peerless kinsman. [*Flourish. Exeunt.*]

Lady Macbeth has received her husband's news in a letter. She accepts the necessity of killing the King, Duncan, but feels that Macbeth is likely to draw back from the act of murder. The scene is set in a room at Macbeth's castle at Inverness.

LADY MACBETH: Great Glamis! worthy Cawdor!
Greater than both, by the all-hail hereafter!
Thy letters have transported me beyond
This ignorant present, and I feel now
The future in the instant. 5
MACBETH: My dearest love,
Duncan comes here to-night.
LADY MACBETH: And when goes hence?
MACBETH: To-morrow, as he purposes.
LADY MACBETH: O! never 10
Shall sun that morrow see!
Your face, my Thane, is as a book, where men
May read strange matters. To beguile the time,
Look like the time; bear welcome in your eye,
Your hand, your tongue: look like th'innocent flower, 15
But be the serpent under't. He that's coming
Must be provided for; and you shall put
This night's great business into my dispatch;
Which shall to all our nights and days to come
Give solely sovereign sway and masterdom. 20
MACBETH: We will speak further.
LADY MACBETH: Only look up clear;
To alter favour ever is to fear.
Leave all the rest to me. [*Exeunt.*]

The royal party arrives before Macbeth's castle.

Hautboys and torches. Enter DUNCAN, MALCOLM, DONALBAIN, BANQUO, ROSSE, ANGUS, *and Attendants.*

DUNCAN: This castle hath a pleasant seat; the air
Nimbly and sweetly recommends itself
Unto our gentle senses. 5
BANQUO: This guest of summer,
The temple-haunting martlet, does approve,
By his loved mansionry, that the heaven's breath
Smells wooingly here: no jutty, frieze,
Buttress, nor coign of vantage, but this bird 10
Hath made his pendent bed, and procreant cradle:
Where they most breed and haunt, I have observ'd
The air is delicate.

Enter LADY MACBETH.

DUNCAN: See, see! our honour'd hostess.— 15
The love that follows us sometime is our trouble,

Which still we thank as love. Herein I teach you,
How you shall bid God'ild us for your pains,
And thank us for your trouble.

LADY MACBETH: All our service, 20
In every point twice done, and then done double,
Were poor and single business, to contend
Against those honours deep and broad, wherewith
Your Majesty loads our house: for those of old,
And the late dignities heap'd up to them, 25
We rest your hermits.

DUNCAN: Where's the Thane of Cawdor?
We cours'd him at the heels, and had a purpose
To be his purveyor: but he rides well;
And his great love, sharp as his spur, hath holp him 30
To his home before us. Fair and noble hostess,
We are your guest to-night.

LADY MACBETH: Your servants ever
Have theirs, themselves, and what is theirs, in compt,
To make their audit at your Highness' pleasure, 35
Still to return your own.

DUNCAN: Give me your hand;
Conduct me to mine host: we love him highly,
And shall continue our graces towards him.
By your leave, hostess. [*Exeunt.*] 40

Dramatic irony is also to be found in comedy, as the following passage from Sheridan's *School for Scandal* (1777) will amply demonstrate.

(i) Again locate particular examples of dramatic irony.
(ii) Bearing in mind what you have learnt about dramatic irony at work in tragic contexts, define the different kinds of function this device has in the world of comedy.
(iii) What future possibilities for dramatic irony are suggested at the point at which this extract ends?

Though Joseph Surface cultivates the reputation of being a virtuous man, he is, in fact, a scheming hypocrite. He has persuaded Lady Teazle, a young wife who is somewhat discontented with her older husband, Sir Peter, to visit him. In the first part of this scene Surface has been trying to persuade Lady Teazle to embark on an affair with him.

JOSEPH SURFACE: Ah, the ill effects of your country education, I see, still remain with you.

LADY TEAZLE: I doubt they do indeed; and I will fairly own to you, that if I could be persuaded to do wrong, it would be by Sir Peter's ill usage sooner than your *honourable logic*, after all. 5

JOSEPH SURFACE: Then, by this hand, which he is unworthy of—
[*Taking her hand.*]

Enter SERVANT

'Sdeath, you blockhead—what do you want?

SERVANT: I beg pardon, sir, but I thought you would not choose Sir Peter to come up without announcing him. 10

JOSEPH SURFACE: Sir Peter!—Oons and the devil!

LADY TEAZLE: Sir Peter! O Lud—I'm ruined—I'm ruined!

SERVANT: Sir, 'twasn't I let him in.

LADY TEAZLE: Oh! I'm quite undone! What will become of me now, Mr Logic? Oh! he's on the stairs—I'll get behind here—and if ever I'm so imprudent again— 15

[*Goes behind the screen.*]

JOSEPH SURFACE: Give me that book.

[*Sits down, servant pretends to adjust his hair.*] 20

Enter SIR PETER TEAZLE

SIR PETER: Aye, ever improving himself. Mr Surface, Mr Surface—

JOSEPH SURFACE: Oh, my dear Sir Peter, I beg your pardon. [*Gaping, throws away the book.*] I have been dozing over a stupid book.—Well, I am much obliged to you for this call. You haven't been here, I believe, since I fitted up this room.—Books, you know, are the only things I am a coxcomb in. 25

SIR PETER: 'Tis very neat indeed.—Well, well, that's proper; and you can make even your screen a source of knowledge—hung, I perceive, with maps. 30

JOSEPH SURFACE: Oh, yes, I find great use in that screen.

SIR PETER: I dare say you must, certainly, when you want to find anything in a hurry.

JOSEPH SURFACE: Aye, or to hide anything in a hurry either.

[*Aside.*] 35

SIR PETER: Well, I have a little private business—

JOSEPH SURFACE: You need not stay. [*To Servant*]

SERVANT: No, sir. [*Exit.*]

JOSEPH SURFACE: Here's a chair, Sir Peter—I beg—

SIR PETER: Well, now we are alone, there is a subject, my dear friend, on which I wish to unburthen my mind to you—a point of the greatest moment to my peace; in short, my good friend, Lady Teazle's conduct of late has made me very unhappy. 40

JOSEPH SURFACE: Indeed! I am very sorry to hear it.

SIR PETER: Aye, 'tis but too plain she has not the least regard for me; but, what's worse, I have pretty good authority to suspect she has formed an attachment to another. 45

JOSEPH SURFACE: You astonish me!

SIR PETER: Yes; and, between ourselves, I think I've discovered the person.

JOSEPH SURFACE: How! you alarm me exceedingly. 50

SIR PETER: Ah, my dear friend, I knew you would sympathize with me!

JOSEPH SURFACE: Yes—believe me, Sir Peter, such a discovery would hurt me just as much as it would you.

SIR PETER: I am convinced of it.—Ah! it is a happiness to have a friend whom we can trust even with one's family secrets. But have you no guess who I mean? 55

JOSEPH SURFACE: I haven't the most distant idea. It can't be Sir Benjamin Backbite!

SIR PETER: Oh no! What say you to Charles?

JOSEPH SURFACE: My brother! impossible! O no, Sir Peter, you must not credit the scandalous insinuations you may hear. No, no, Charles to be sure has been charged with many things of this kind, but I can never think he would meditate so gross an injury. 60

SIR PETER: Ah, my dear friend, the goodness of your own heart misleads you. You judge of others by yourself. 65

JOSEPH SURFACE: Certainly, Sir Peter, the heart that is conscious of its own integrity is ever slow to credit another's treachery.

SIR PETER: True; but your brother has no sentiment—you never hear him talk so.

JOSEPH SURFACE: Yet I can't but think Lady Teazle herself has too much principle. 70

SIR PETER: Aye, but what is principle against the flattery of a handsome, lively young fellow?

JOSEPH SURFACE: That's very true.

SIR PETER: And then, you know, the difference of our ages makes it very improbable that she should have any great affection for me; and if she were to be frail, and I were to make it public, why the town would only laugh at me—the foolish old bachelor, who had married a girl. 75

JOSEPH SURFACE: That's true, to be sure—they *would* laugh.

SIR PETER: Laugh—aye, and make ballads, and paragraphs, and the devil knows what of me. 80

JOSEPH SURFACE: No—you must never make it public.

SIR PETER: But then again—that the nephew of my old friend, Sir Oliver, should be the person to attempt such a wrong, hurts me more nearly.

JOSEPH SURFACE: Aye, there's the point.—When ingratitude barbs the dart of injury, the wound has double danger in it. 85

SIR PETER: Aye—I, that was, in a manner, left his guardian: in whose house he had been so often entertained; who never in my life denied him—my advice!

JOSEPH SURFACE: Oh, 'tis not to be credited! There may be a man capable of such baseness, to be sure; but, for my part, till you can give me positive proofs, I cannot but doubt it. However, if it should be proved on him, he is no longer a brother of mine—I disclaim kindred with him: for the man who can break the laws of hospitality, and attempt the wife of his friend, deserves to be branded as the pest of society. 90 95

SIR PETER: What a difference there is between you! What noble sentiments!

JOSEPH SURFACE: Yet, I cannot suspect Lady Teazle's honour.

SIR PETER: I am sure I wish to think well of her, and to remove all ground of quarrel between us. She has lately reproached me more than once with having made no settlement on her; and, in our last quarrel, she almost hinted that she should not break her heart if I was dead. Now, as we seem to differ in our ideas of expense, I have resolved she shall have her own way, and be her own mistress in that respect for the future; and, if I were to die, she will find I have not been inattentive to her interest while living. Here, my friend, are the drafts of two deeds, which I wish to have your opinion on.—By one, she will enjoy eight hundred a year independent 100 105 while I live; and, by the other, the bulk of my fortune at my death.

JOSEPH SURFACE: This conduct, Sir Peter, is indeed truly generous.—I wish it may not corrupt my pupil. [*Aside.*] 110

SIR PETER: Yes, I am determined she shall have no cause to complain, though I would not have her acquainted with the latter instance of my affection yet awhile.

JOSEPH SURFACE: Nor I, if I could help it. [*Aside.*]

SIR PETER: And now, my dear friend, if you please, we will talk over the situation of your hopes with Maria. 115

JOSEPH SURFACE: Oh, no, Sir Peter; another time, if you please.

SIR PETER: I am sensibly chagrined at the little progress you seem to make in her affections.

JOSEPH SURFACE: I beg you will not mention it. What are my disappointments when your happiness is in debate!—[*Softly*] 'Sdeath, I shall be ruined every way! [*Aside*] 120

SIR PETER: And though you are averse to my acquainting Lady Teazle with *your* passion, I'm sure she's not your enemy in the affair.

JOSEPH SURFACE: Pray, Sir Peter, now, oblige me. I am really too much affected by the subject we have been speaking of, to bestow a thought on my own concerns. The man who is entrusted with his friend's distresses can never— 125

Enter SERVANT

Well, sir? 130

SERVANT: Your brother, sir, is speaking to a gentleman in the street, and says he knows you are within.

JOSEPH SURFACE: 'Sdeath, blockhead, I'm not within—I'm out for the day.

SIR PETER: Stay—hold—a thought has struck me:—you shall be at home. 135

JOSEPH SURFACE: Well, well, let him up.—[*Exit* SERVANT.] He'll interrupt Sir Peter, however. [*Aside.*]

SIR PETER: Now, my good friend, oblige me, I entreat you. Before Charles comes, let me conceal myself somewhere—then do you tax him on the point we have been talking on, and his answer may satisfy me at once. 140

JOSEPH SURFACE: Oh, fie, Sir Peter! would you have me join in so mean a trick?—to trepan my brother too?

R. B. Sheridan: *School for Scandal* (1777)

Besides *dramatic* irony, there is a whole range of manoeuvres connected with the kind of irony which essentially derives from the tone of the language, but it is beyond the scope of this book to enter into this vast area of discussion. Let us sum up some of the general effects dramatic irony can achieve.

In the realm of tragedy this device, pointing as it does to the ignorance or half-knowledge in which characters move, can be a means of heightening a sense of foreboding: dramatic irony demonstrates how human beings tend to be unaware of, or prefer not to think about, the incongruities and complexities of their (true) situation. Dramatic irony may even be part of the expression of a whole world view, suggesting that the control characters believe they have over their own destiny is limited or perhaps totally illusory, especially since either the pressures of a given situation or characters' individual genetic, social and psychological make-up restrict them more than they imagine. In the kind of 'cosmic irony' which we find, for instance, in some Greek tragedy, it may be that Fate or the gods really determine everything and characters' blind struggle against the inescapable workings of cause and effect or the gods' will arouses our pity and fear.

Dramatic irony may involve, somewhat paradoxically, both a sympathy with and a distancing from its subject. We watch a character's actions to some extent with a detached (even critical) wisdom—largely the gift of the playwright and his medium!—which makes us recognise the inadequacies of that character's response to a certain situation; yet dramatic irony can also involve us sympathetically—in the contradictions of the character's experience. In other words, to simplify greatly, our reaction may follow something of this line: 'If he (or she) really knew the truth! . . . How blind!. . . . I'm glad I'm not in that position. . . . But I can see what it must feel like, all the same!'

In comedy, dramatic irony may be used to expose the hypocrite, to show the emptiness or deceit which underlies so much of our social intercourse or to unmask the workings of affectation and egotism. Dramatic irony, of course, feeds off the discrepancy between appearance and reality—the gap for instance, between what a character would like others to think of him and the inner reality of his nature and motives which are laid bare. Such revelations may be both entertaining and didactic; but in a comedy, while dramatic irony will have its moral functions, its harsher implications—so apparent in a tragic context—are generally softened by the warmth of laughter and the pleasure an audience will feel in seeing its own failings and foibles exposed. The contradictions of human experience revealed in a comedy are not likely in the long run to be whipped up into catastrophe.

7

Dialogue

If you go to watch a performance of *Forty Years On* by Alan Bennett, you will enter a theatre with a set designed to look like 'the Assembly Hall of Albion House, a public school on the South Downs, ... a gloomy Victorian Gothic building . . . dingy, dark and somewhat oppressive'. On stage there will be, amongst other things, a lectern, a hymn board and a War Memorial with lists and lists of names. 'When the curtain rises, the stage is dark. We hear the sounds of school, a chapel bell, the sound of a cricket match and boys repeating by rote in class. An organ plays softly. A boy enters and switches on the lights . . . the boys enter singing a processional hymn' followed by members of staff. The stage is set and the play can begin. Even before a word has been uttered, what has been called 'the language of theatre' has spoken to the audience. This 'language' of set design, sound effects, music, lighting, costume and the grouping of the actors on stage has contributed to the creation of a particular setting and a particular atmosphere—that of a minor, run-down boys' public school. Important as this 'language of theatre' is in creating these effects, one essential element for drama, however, has not yet been used—words. No actor has spoken and until someone does speak, this play, and indeed any other play, cannot begin, develop and progress to a satisfying conclusion.

Words are the *sine qua non* of drama— without them a play cannot exist. This is not to deny, of course, that set design, lighting, sound, costume and staging are unimportant, but they are the adjuncts to the words the author has written. The Italian dramatist, Pirandello, was firmly of this belief, for he claimed that 'all descriptive and narrative props should be banished from the stage' and that a dramatist should concentrate on the dialogue, as dramatic dialogue was 'spoken action, living words that move, immediate expressions inseparable from action . . . (which) belong to a definite character in a definite situation'. The example of *Our Town* by Thornton Wilder in a somewhat extreme way demonstrates this fact, for in this play, the author with a minimal use of the 'language of theatre', depicts a small New England town, Grover's Corner, and its inhabitants, relying almost totally on the power of words spoken by actors in an empty space to create the illusion of the town in the minds of the audience.

The Irishman, Samuel Beckett, is another playwright who uses the 'language of theatre' very sparingly in plays like *Waiting for Godot* and *Endgame*. At the other extreme, the over-elaborate stagings of

Shakespeare's plays in the nineteenth century when, for example, real live rabbits were used in the forest scenes in *A Midsummer Night's Dream*, served only to demonstrate theatrical ingenuity and succeeded only in getting in the way of the words.

So we can see for a play to be fully realized, there are only four elements that are absolutely necessary:

(i) a writer to pen the words;
(ii) an actor to speak them;
(iii) an open space in which to perform; and
(iv) an audience to listen to the words.

In the theatre, the word is king and in this chapter we shall be considering the nature of this monarch.

THE LANGUAGE OF EVERYDAY SPEECH AND THE LANGUAGE OF DRAMA

Many writers strive very hard to create the illusion that characters in their plays are speaking ordinary, everyday language. They want to convince an audience that what they are hearing of the dialogue, say between two people on a park bench or in a restaurant, is what they would *actually* hear if they were on the same bench or at the adjoining table in the restaurant. But this cannot be so, for if these conversations were reproduced verbatim by the playwright, he would very soon find himself without an audience, who have come to see drama, not listen to something they can hear everyday. The language of drama may appear to be the language of everyday speech, but in reality, they are very different. If this were not the case, the playwright could easily be replaced by the tape-recorder.

To illustrate that the two languages are very different, consider these two passages. The participants in both are two housewives—but one extract is from a play and the other is part of a transcript of a recorded conversation. Decide which is dramatic dialogue and which genuine conversation. You might like to discuss and make notes on the passages before comparing them with ours.

A. ANN: You got a cold?
BARBARA: No. Just a bit sniffy, 'cos I'm—I am cold and I'll be all right once I've warmed up. Do I look as though I've got a cold?
ANN: No, I thought you sounded as if you were—
BARBARA: Mm. 5
ANN: Pull your chair up if you want—Is it . . . ?
BARBARA: Yes, I'll be all right in a minute. It's just that I'm—
ANN: What have you got?
BARBARA: Stupid. I had about five thousand books to take back to Senate house yesterday—and I got all the way through the college to where the 10 car was at the parking meter at the other end and realised I'd left my coat in my locker and I just couldn't . . .

ANN: Mm.
BARBARA: . . . face going all the way back again with this great . . you know my arms were aching. . . 15
ANN: Mm.
BARBARA: and thought, well I'll get it on Tuesday—it's a bit silly 'cos I need it.
ANN: Mm. It's gone very cold, hasn't it?
BARBARA: Mm. It's freezing. 20
ANN: Mm. I'm—
BARBARA: You're knitting (*Laughs*)—what are you knitting? That's not a tiny garment.
ANN: No.
BARBARA: (*Laughs*) 25
ANN: No, it's for me, but it's very plain.
BARBARA: It's a lovely colour.
ANN: It is nice.
BARBARA: Yeah. I never did—I could never take to knitting except on those double 0 needles with string. You know that's my sort of knitting. 30

B. BEVERLY: Actually, Ang, it's going to be really nice, because I've invited Sue from Number 9.
ANGELA: Oh, lovely.
BEVERLY: Yeah, so I thought it'd be nice for you to meet her as well. Yeah, 'cos her daughter's having a party. Well, she's only a teenager, so, I 5 said, well pop down and spend the evening with us.
ANGELA: That'd be really nice, 'cos I want to meet all the neighbours.
BEVERLY: Yeah, just say hello, Ang, and break the ice.
ANGELA: 'Cos that was what was so nice when you came over, 'cos it really made me feel at home. 10
BEVERLY: Well, Ang, I know what I felt like when I moved in—I was lonely. So I thought, well, that's not going to happen to you.
ANGELA: Well, you're the friendly type, aren't you?
BEVERLY: Yeah, yeah. It's funny, 'cos as soon as we met, I knew we were gonna get on. 15
ANGELA: Well, we're alike, aren't we?
BEVERLY: Yeah, yeah.

Notes

Passage A: many speeches left incomplete (ll. 4, 6, 7); random jumps from subject to subject (colds to knitting); speeches generally short; lots of questions (ll. 1, 3, 8, 19, 22); many 'sentences' loosely constructed (e.g. Barbara's speech about taking books back, and final speech); language vague and informal (nice, my sort of, yeah, lovely, 'cos, all right); many signals that speakers are listening to each other (Mm).

Passage B: speeches show progression, no randomness (invitation → meet neighbours → made to feel at home → not lonely → friendly type); speeches are complete; longer speeches than in A; no interruptions; though language is casual/informal (yeah, 'cos, really nice, well, funny, gonna) nothing left in the air as in (A) (e.g. ll.15, 21 of passage A).

We hope that your discussion helped you to identify passage A as being the transcript of conversation (quoted in *Investigating English Style* by David Crystal and Derek Davy) and passage B as a piece of dramatic dialogue (taken from *Abigail's Party* by Mike Leigh). You will probably have observed that the dialogue from *Abigail's Party*, whilst exhibiting many of the characteristics of genuine conversation was none the less distinct from it, and that this was particularly noticeable in the way that Angela and Beverley's speeches developed. The dialogue had a shape and a progression that Ann and Barbara's lacked, and indeed, the characters from the play were prepared to listen to each other without interruption, thus allowing the speeches to be completed. So, whilst both conversations are 'informal', the scripted dialogue conveys only the illusion of informality. It is perhaps worth mentioning here that *Abigail's Party* was, in its early stages, built up by actors improvising 'ordinary conversations' around a given situation and that it was only later that the author 'shaped' the dialogue by selecting, pruning and adding narrative momentum and climaxes to what the improvisation had already suggested.

We can say then, at this early stage, that the language of drama is not the exact language of ordinary speech, though it may appear to be so, but is speech that has been selected and shaped for dramatic purposes. The language of drama *is based on*, but *is not* 'real' speech. It is very easy for us to forget this important distinction between the language of drama and the language of 'real speech' because many of the modern plays with which we are familiar have been written in the tradition of 'naturalism' where dramatists *do* try to create the illusion that what we hear on stage is what we would have heard these characters actually speaking. But, of course, as we shall see, this *is* an illusion. Naturalism, as a dramatic style, has its roots in European plays of the late nineteenth century, when writers like Ibsen, Strindberg and Chekhov strove to create plays not only whose language was seemingly as realistic as possible, but also whose setting, staging, props and costumes were similarly realistic. These three dramatists were enormously influential and, even now, both playwrights and theatre-goers are very much the inheritors of this naturalistic legacy. Many traditional theatre-goers, the legendary 'Aunt Ednas', view with suspicion any play (or theatre!) that does not seek to appear 'realistic' and similarly many writers produce plays that aim at naturalism. Those British playwrights directly influenced by European naturalism, Shaw, Galsworthy and Granville-Barker, still have their late twentieth-century followers. However, happily, this is but one stream of contemporary drama.

Before the onset of naturalism, dramatists did not seek to bring the language of common everyday speech onto the stage. Traditionally they worked with language that was distinct from the language of the street, with language that had its roots not in life, but in literature. All stage language has been, and in many cases still is, highly rhetorical and has been 'raised above the colloquial by deliberate artifice' as the critic, Eric Bentley, has noted. It is this deliberate artifice, this patterning, that we shall be examining much more closely in the section on verse and prose in drama on pp. 108–15, but you will have noticed in many of the extracts we have already cited in the book that dramatists do make use of that form of language most clearly differentiated from everyday discourse—verse. We, and the playwrights, must always remember however that dramatic language, whether verse or prose, is language intended to be spoken aloud by an actor embodying a character and must thus do two things: firstly it must be able to be spoken with ease and secondly it must convince an audience that what it is hearing is actual and 'true', at least for the duration of the play.

To give you some further practice in distinguishing between dramatic language and everyday language, here are two short extracts from twentieth-century plays, both of which are intended to be realistic. How does the language of each extract demonstrate (i) links with everyday speech, and (ii) differences from it?

A. ASTON (*attending to the toaster*): Would . . . would you like to sleep here?
DAVIES: Here?
ASTON: You can sleep here if you like.
DAVIES: Here? Oh, I don't know about that.
Pause. 5
How long for?
ASTON: Till you . . . get yourself fixed up.
DAVIES (*sitting*): Ay well, that. . . .
ASTON: Get yourself sorted out. . . .
DAVIES: Oh, I'll be fixed up . . . pretty soon now. . . . 10
Pause.
Where would I sleep?
ASTON: Here. The other rooms would . . . would be no good to you.
DAVIES (*rising, looking about*): Here? Where?
ASTON (*rising, pointing upstage right*): There's a bed behind all that. 15
DAVIES: Oh, I see. Well, that's handy. Well, that's . . . I tell you what, I might do that . . . just till I get myself sorted out. You got enough furniture here.
ASTON: I picked it up. Just keeping it here for the time being. Thought it might come in handy. 20

Harold Pinter: *The Caretaker* (1960)

B. ALICE: Oh, it's you. I hoped it was father going out.
MAGGIE: It isn't. (*She crosses and takes her place at desk.*)
ALICE: He *is* late this morning.
MAGGIE: He got up late (*She busies herself with an account book.*)
VICKEY (*Reading*): Has he had breakfast yet, Maggie? 5
MAGGIE: Breakast! With a Masons' meeting last night?

VICKEY: He'll need reviving.
ALICE: Then I wish he'd go and do it.
VICKEY: Are you expecting anyone, Alice?
ALICE: Yes, I am, and you know I am, and I'll thank you both to go when he comes. 10
VICKEY: Well, I'll oblige you, Alice, if father's gone out first, only you know I can't leave the counter till he goes.

Harold Brighouse: *Hobson's Choice* (1916)

DIALOGUE LINKS AND SEQUENCES

You will have observed from our last three extracts that the speeches in a play do not occur randomly and without structure, but that a playwright must ensure that there is a progression to his characters' utterances. Whatever a character says must, obviously, in part depend on what has just been said to (or about) him and so a dramatist must ensure that this progression seems to occur naturally. An audience must be convinced that a character is speaking without obvious premeditation and that his words are governed by the pressure of the situation of which he is part. You can see this in operation in the following passage from *The Way of the World* by William Congreve (1700), in which Mirabell is attempting to propose marriage to the independently minded Millamant.

MIRABELL:—*Like* Daphne *she, as Lovely and as Coy.* Do you lock your self up from me, to make my Search more curious? Or is this pretty Artifice contriv'd, to signifie that here the Chace must end, and my Pursuit be crown'd, for you can fly no further?—
MILLAMANT: Vanity! No—I'll fly and be follow'd to the last Moment, tho' 5 I am upon the very Verge of Matrimony, I expect you should sollicit me as much as if I were wavering at the Grate of a Monastery, with one Foot over the Threshold. I'll be sollicited to the very last, nay and afterwards.
MIRABELL: What, after the last?
MILLAMANT: O, I should think I was poor and had nothing to bestow, if I 10 were reduc'd to an inglorious Ease: and freed from the agreeable Fatigues of Sollicitation.
MIRABELL: But do not you know, that when Favours are conferr'd upon instant and tedious Sollicitation, that they diminish in their Value, and that both the Giver loses the Grace, and the Receiver lessens his 15 Pleasure?
MILLAMANT: It may be in Things of common Application; but never sure in Love. O, I hate a Lover, that can dare to think he draws a Moment's Air, independent of the Bounty of his Mistress. There is not so impudent a Thing in Nature, as the sawcy Look of an assured Man, confident of 20 Success. The Pedantick Arrogance of a very Husband, has not so Pragmatical an Air. Ah! I'll never marry, unless I am first made sure of my Will and Pleasure.
MIRABELL: Would you have 'em both before Marriage? Or will you be contented with the first now, and stay for the other 'till after Grace? 25

MILLAMANT: Ah don't be impertinent—My dear Liberty, shall I leave thee? My faithful Solitude, my darling Contemplation, must I bid you then Adieu? Ay-h adieu—My Morning Thoughts, agreeable Wakings, indolent Slumbers, all ye *douceurs*, ye *Sommeils du Matin*, adieu—I can't do't, 'tis more than impossible—Positively *Mirabell*, I'll lye a-bed in a Morning as long as I please. 30

MIRABELL: Then I'll get up in a Morning as early as I please.

MILLAMANT: Ah!. Idle Creature, get up when you will—And d'ye hear, I won't be call'd Names after I'm Marry'd ; positively I won't be call'd Names. 35

MIRABELL: Names!

MILLAMANT: Ay, as Wife, Spouse, my Dear, Joy, Jewel, Love, Sweet-heart, and the rest of that nauseous Cant, in which Men and their Wives are so fulsomely familiar,—I shall never bear that.

Congreve uses a number of devices to link the dialogue and to ensure that progression and form are maintained. Note, for instance, how some speeches pick up words that have been used in the previous speech: 'fly' (line 5); 'last' (line 9); 'sollicited', 'Sollicitation' (lines 8, 12 & 14); 'a Morning' (lines 31 & 32); 'get up' (lines 32 & 33); 'Names' (lines 35 & 36). Of course, Congreve, as a skilled dramatist knows that over-use of such 'speech-clips' would result in his dialogue becoming mechanical and so he avoids this danger and ensures progression by utilizing other types of linkage. He substitutes words: 'Will and Pleasure' (line 23) become in the subsequent speech ''em both' and 'will you be contented with *the first* now and stay for *the other*' (line 24). Where words, or substitutes for the original words are not used to clip the speeches together, then the dramatist ensures that one character responds to the ideas and sentiments the other articulates: where Mirabell expresses surprise that Millamant should want 'Sollicitation' even after accepting matrimony and she responds that she would feel unchallenged and slothful if no such 'sollicitation' took place; or where Mirabell claims that favours conferred in response to 'tedious' sollicitation lose their value and Millamant replies that this may be so in ordinary matters, but not 'in Love'. By these means, Congreve makes certain that his dialogue both avoids randomness and achieves structure and sequence. In addition, of course, by the use of a strongly interrogatory format in this battle of the sexes, Congreve supplies another binding factor in the dialogue, as the element of question and answer allows for few deviations from the matter in hand. In fact the scene is a battle of the sexes which tends to divide the audience into teams, cheering on their respective champions.

See if you can identify the methods used by Robert Bolt in this extract from his play, *A Man for All Seasons* (1960) to establish links between the speeches. Sir Thomas More is being cross-examined by Thomas Cromwell about the views he holds on King Henry VIII's claimed authority over the Church in England.

CROMWELL: Sir Thomas, there is a more serious charge—
MORE: Charge?
CROMWELL: For want of a better word. In the May of 1526 the King published a book, [*he permits himself a little smile*] a theological work. It was called *A Defence of the Seven Sacraments.* 5
MORE: Yes. [*Bitterly*] For which he was named 'Defender of the Faith', by His Holiness the Pope.
CROMWELL:—By the Bishop of Rome. Or do you insist on 'Pope'?
MORE: No, 'Bishop of Rome' if you like. It doesn't alter his authority.
CROMWELL: Thank you, you come to the point very readily; what *is* that 10 authority? As regards the Church in other parts of Europe; [*approaching*] for example, the Church in England. What exactly *is* the Bishop of Rome's authority?
MORE: You will find it very ably set out and defended, Master Secretary, in the King's book. 15
CROMWELL: The book published under the King's name would be more accurate. You wrote that book.
MORE:—I wrote no part of it.
CROMWELL:—I do not mean you actually held the pen.
MORE:—I merely answered to the best of my ability certain questions on 20 canon law which His Majesty put to me. As I was bound to do.
CROMWELL:—Do you deny that you *instigated* it?
MORE:—It was from first to last the King's own project. This is trivial, Master Cromwell.
CROMWELL: I should not think so if I were in your place. 25
MORE: Only two people know the truth of the matter. Myself and the King. And, whatever he may have said to you, he will not give evidence to support this accusation.
CROMWELL: Why not?
MORE: Because evidence is given on oath, and he will not perjure himself. If 30 you don't know that, you don't yet know him.

In this next extract, we have cheated somewhat! Only the first speech and the final one are in their original positions. See if you can arrange the other speeches into the 'correct' order. To do this you will obviously have to pay close attention to the way that a speech should grow naturally out of the preceding one and lead naturally into the next. Mr and Mrs Hardcastle are discussing their likes and dislikes and speak also of Mrs Hardcastle's son by her first marriage, Tony Lumpkin. To check whether your version agrees with the original, you will have to read the first scene of *She Stoops to Conquer* by Oliver Goldsmith (1773).

MRS HARDCASTLE: I vow, Mr Hardcastle, you're very particular. Is there a creature in the whole country but ourselves, that does not take a trip to town now and then, to rub off the rust a little? There's the two Miss Hoggs, and our neighbour, Mrs Grigsby, go to take a month's polishing 5 every winter.

HARDCASTLE: And I love it. I love every thing that's old: old friends, old times, old manners, old books, old wines; and, I believe, Dorothy, (*taking her hand*) you'll own I have been pretty fond of an old wife.

MRS HARDCASTLE: It's false, Mr Hardcastle: I was but twenty when I was brought to bed of Tony, that I had by Mr Lumpkin, my first husband; 10 and he's not come to years of discretion yet.

HARDCASTLE: Let me see; twenty added to twenty, makes just fifty and seven.

MRS HARDCASTLE: Ay, *your* times were fine times indeed; you have been telling us of *them* for many a long year. Here we live in an old rambling 15 mansion, that looks for all the world like an inn, but that we never see company. Our best visitors are old Mrs Oddfish, the curate's wife, and little Cripplegate, the lame dancing-master: And all our entertainment your old stories of Prince Eugene and the Duke of Marlborough. I hate such old-fashioned trumpery. 20

HARDCASTLE: Nor ever will, I dare answer for him. Ay, you have taught him finely.

MRS HARDCASTLE: Lord, Mr Hardcastle, you're for ever at your Dorothy's, and your old wife's. You may be a Darby, but I'll be no Joan, I promise you. I'm not so old as you'd make me, by more than one good 25 year. Add twenty to twenty, and make money of that.

HARDCASTLE: Learning, quotha! a mere composition of tricks and mischief.

MRS HARDCASTLE: No matter, Tony Lumpkin has a good fortune. My son is not to live by his learning. I don't think a boy wants much learning 30 to spend fifteen hundred a year.

HARDCASTLE: Ay, and bring back vanity and affectation to last them the whole year. I wonder why London cannot keep its own fools at home! In my time, the follies of the town crept slowly among us, but now they travel faster than a stage-coach. Its fopperies come down, not only as 35 inside passengers, but in the very basket.

MRS HARDCASTLE: Humour, my dear: nothing but humour. Come, Mr Hardcastle, you must allow the boy a little humour.

In trying to ensure that the speeches of Mr and Mrs Hardcastle were correctly sequenced, you probably found that your discussion focussed not only on what we have called 'dialogue-clips', but also on the linkage of ideas between the speeches when one character responds to or develops an idea put forward by the other; for instance, when the Hardcastles express their preferences for either the old-fashioned or for the modern. You will have noticed this technique used in all the extracts, whether it be Thomas More responding to Cromwell's challenges or Mirabell to Millamant's teasing. Just as the dramatist must convey the impression of the style of real speech as we have already noticed (pages 79–80), so too must he convey the impression of the characters' thought patterns and responses whilst not reproducing exactly the way they occur in real life. This would be sacrificing the dramatic on the altar of verisimilitude. We explore this point—that challenge and response are prerequisites for the momentum and progress of a dramatic text—in more depth on pages 94–107.

It is important that whilst dramatic dialogue does maintain momentum, the writer must ensure that this is not produced mechanically, whether in a mechanical presentation of the development of ideas or at a mechanical pace, for again the illusion of naturalness and spontaneity would be destroyed and the play would parade its over-artificiality.

Take, for instance, as an example of the mechanical, this extract from Edward Gordon Craig's *Second Dialogue on the Art of the Theatre* (1910). This is not a play, of course, but a conversation, but it is nevertheless a dialogue that sounds and moves in a false and stilted manner. The Playgoer and the Stage-director sound as if they are reading from a prepared manuscript, the language is artificial and no real action is taking place. The 'characters' are merely being paraded and do not seem to form part of an organic whole. What they are being asked to do is mechanically represent different positions in an artificial discussion about the nature of theatre: they have no other function.

PLAYGOER: I hate the theatre.
STAGE-DIRECTOR: Come now, you exaggerate; you used to love it. I remember you once asked me all sorts of questions about the Art of the Theatre, and we had no end of a talk.
PLAYGOER: I hate it now—I never go inside a theatre now, and the reports, paragraphs, announcements and interviews make me laugh. 5
STAGE-DIRECTOR: Why is that?
PLAYGOER: That is what I want to know.
STAGE-DIRECTOR: Oh, you want me to be your doctor. You are hungry for the Theatre and you can't swallow it as it is; you want a cure. Well, I can't cure you, for I cannot alter the Theatre in a day or during your lifetime, but if you would like to know what your old love the Theatre is going to be one day I will tell you. 10

So, unless we are in a very specialized situation, such as the above example, or a debating chamber or a court of law, (and not always even in these), we do not usually think in a logical manner. In discussion or argument, our thoughts do not always follow what we might call a mathematical progression, carefully moving from the first point to the second, to the third and so on until we reach a precise and satisfying conclusion, Q.E.D.; rather they, say, catch hold of an idea, circle round it, develop strongly a particular aspect, drop it, return to it with added force, are pushed out by new ideas crowding in, respond to what other people are saying and are influenced by where we are or the character(s) of the person(s) we are talking to. It would be too strong to say our thoughts were chaotic, but it is upon this 'semi-chaos' that the dramatist must seek to impose some order. Not the firmly defined order of the logical progression, for this, in a dramatic context, would be artificial and formulaic, but an order that seeks to give to an audience the impression of real people responding to real situations and pressures. The dramatist is obviously controlling the reactions and thought processes of his characters as they seem to circle around a particular theme before moving on as plot, situation and character demand. Though we may from time to time enjoy eavesdropping on a patternless, desultory conversation going on at the next table in a pub or on the bus, such dialogue does not usually hold our interest for long. How much more true this is in a play where an audience's attention needs to be gripped *and* held; consequently it is of paramount importance for the dramatist to shape and 'streamline' his dialogue to prevent his audience leaving the theatre at the interval.

Take, for example, this extract from *Roots* by Arnold Wesker (1960). In it, Beatie Bryant, who has returned for a short visit to her home in rural Norfolk is preparing to have a bath. She is talking to her mother about her boyfriend, Ronnie, whom she has met in London. Read it and make notes on how the subject matter (Ronnie; having a bath; a local scandal about Jimmy Skelton) is woven together by Wesker to suggest the movement of a real conversation. These questions may help to guide you: Where does the subject matter of the speech change? Who changes it? What has prompted the change? Where is the same theme picked up again? By whom? Why?

MRS BRYANT: You hear about Jimmy Skelton? They say he've bin arrested for accosting some man in the village.
BEATIE: Jimmy Skelton what own the pub?
MRS BRYANT: That's him. I know all about Jimmy Skelton though. He were a young boy when I were a young girl. I always partner him at whist drives. He's been to law before you know. Yes! An' he won the day too! Won the day he did. I don't take notice though, him and me gets on all right. What do Ronnie's mother do with her time? (5)
BEATIE: She've got a sick husband to look after.
MRS BRYANT: She an educated woman? (10)
BEATIE: Educated? No. She's a foreigner. Nor ent Ronnie educated neither. He's an intellectual, failed all his exams. They read and things.
MRS BRYANT: Oh, they don't do nothing then?
BEATIE: Do nothing? I'll tell you what Ronnie do, he work till all hours in a hot ole kitchen. An' he teach kids in a club to act and jive and such. And he don't stop at week-ends either 'cos then there's political meetings and such and I get breathless trying to keep up wi' him. OOOhh, Mother it's hot . . . (15)
MRS BRYANT: I'll get you some cold then.
BEATIE: No – ooh – it's lovely. The water's so soft, Mother. (20)
MRS BRYANT: Yearp.
BEATIE: It's so soft and smooth. I'm in.
MRS BRYANT: Don't you stay in too long gal. There go the twenty-minutes-past-one bus.
BEATIE: Oh Mother, me bath cubes. I forgot me bath cubes. In the little case by me pick-up. (25)
[MRS BRYANT *finds bath cubes and hands them to Beatie.*]
MRS BRYANT [*continuing her work*]: I shall never forget when I furse heard on it. I was in the village and I was talking to Reggie Fowler. I say to him,

there've bin a lot o'talk about Jimmy ent there? Disgustin', I say. Still, there's somebody wanna make some easy money, you'd expect that in a village wouldn't you? Yes, I say to him, a lot of talk. An' he stood there, an' he were a-lookin' at me an' a-lookin' as I were a-talkin' and then he say, missus, he say, I were one o' the victims! Well, you could've hit me over the head wi' a hammer. I was one o' the victims, he say. 30 35

BEATIE: Mother, these bath cubes smell beautiful. I could stay here all day.

MRS BRYANT: Still, Jimmy's a good fellow with it all—do anything for you. I partner him at whist drives; he bin had up scores o' times though.

BEATIE: Mother, what we gonna make Ronnie when he come?

As a further illustration, consider the methods used by Marlowe in the following extract to ensure a movement and progression that will not appear mechanical. Dr Faustus and Mephistopheles are bargaining over Faustus' soul.

Enter MEPHOSTOPHILIS.

FAU: Now tell me what saith Lucifer thy lord?
MEPH: That I shall wait on Faustus whilst he lives,
So he will buy my service with his soul.
FAU: Already Faustus hath hazarded that for thee. 5
MEPH: But now thou must bequeath it solemnly
And write a deed of gift with thine own blood,
For that security craves Lucifer.
If thou deny it, I must back to hell.
FAU: Stay, Mephostophilis, and tell me what good 10
Will my soul do thy lord?
MEPH: Enlarge his kingdom.
FAU: Is that the reason why he tempts us thus?
MEPH: *Solamen miseris socios habuisse doloris.*[1]
FAU: Why, have you any pain that torture other? 15
MEPH: As great as have the human souls of men.
But tell me, Faustus, shall I have thy soul?
And I will be thy slave and wait on thee
And give thee more than thou hast wit to ask.
FAU: Ay, Mephostophilis, I'll give it him. 20
MEPH: Then, Faustus, stab thy arm courageously,
And bind thy soul, that at some certain day
Great Lucifer may claim it as his own;
And then be thou as great as Lucifer.
FAU: Lo, Mephostophilis, for love of thee 25
Faustus hath cut his arm, and with his proper blood
Assures his soul to be great Lucifer's,
Chief lord and regent of perpetual night.
View here this blood that trickles from mine arm,
And let it be propitious for my wish. 30

[1] To the unhappy, it is a comfort to have had companions in misery.

MEPH: But, Faustus,
Write it in manner of a deed of gift.
FAU: Ay, so I do. But, Mephostophilis,
My blood congeals, and I can write no more.
MEPH: I'll fetch thee fire to dissolve it straight. *Exit.* 35
FAU: What might the staying of my blood portend?
Is it unwilling I should write this bill?
Why streams it not, that I may write afresh?
'Faustus gives to thee his soul': O, there it stay'd.
Why shouldst thou not? is not thy soul thine own? 40
Then write again: 'Faustus gives to thee his soul'.

Enter MEPHOSTOPHILIS *with the chafer of fire.*

MEPH: See, Faustus, here is fire; set it on.
FAU: So, now the blood begins to clear again:
Now will I make an end immediately. 45

Dr Faustus (1592)

Finally, in this section, look at this extract from *Rosencrantz and Guildenstern are Dead* (1967) by Tom Stoppard. Superficially, this might appear to be aimless dialogue but, of course, on closer examination it is anything but. Stoppard gives the illusion of momentum by a sparkling range of linguistic (and dramatic) gambits. The dialogue is pinned together by a number of 'language games'. What are the games? And what are the rules?

Stoppard imagines how the action of Shakespeare's play, Hamlet, *might have struck two minor characters who never really understand what role they are expected to play. At this point they seem to have come to a full stop in their attempts to make sense of the bewildering situation in which they find themselves.*

ROSENCRANTZ (*at footlights*): How very intriguing! (*Turns.*) I feel like a spectator—an appalling prospect. The only thing that makes it bearable is the irrational belief that somebody interesting will come on in a minute. . . .
GUILDENSTERN: See anyone? 5
ROSENCRANTZ: No, You?
GUILDENSTERN: No. (*At footlights.*) What a fine persecution—to be kept intrigued without ever quite being enlightened. . . . (*Pause.*) We've had no practice.
ROSENCRANTZ: We could play at questions. 10
GUILDENSTERN: What good would that do?
ROSENCRANTZ: Practice!
GUILDENSTERN: Statement! One—love.
ROSENCRANTZ: Cheating!
GUILDENSTERN: How? 15
ROSENCRANTZ: I hadn't started yet.

GUILDENSTERN: Statement. Two—love.
ROSENCRANTZ: Are you counting that?
GUILDENSTERN: What?
ROSENCRANTZ: Are you counting that? 20
GUILDENSTERN: Foul! No repetitions. Three—love. First game to. . . .
ROSENCRANTZ: I'm not going to play if you're going to be like that.
GUILDENSTERN: Whose serve?
ROSENCRANTZ: Hah?
GUILDENSTERN: Foul! No grunts. Love—one. 25
ROSENCRANTZ: Whose go?
GUILDENSTERN: Why?
ROSENCRANTZ: Why not?
GUILDENSTERN: What for?
ROSENCRANTZ: Foul! No synonyms! One—all. 30
GUILDENSTERN: What in God's name is going on?
ROSENCRANTZ: Foul! No rhetoric. Two—one.
GUILDENSTERN: What does it all add up to?
ROSENCRANTZ: Can't you guess?
GUILDENSTERN: Were you addressing me? 35
ROSENCRANTZ: Is there anyone else?
GUILDENSTERN: Who?
ROSENCRANTZ: How would I know?
GUILDENSTERN: Why do you ask?
ROSENCRANTZ: Are you serious? 40
GUILDENSTERN: Was that rhetoric?
ROSENCRANTZ: No.
GUILDENSTERN: Statement! Two—all. Game point.
ROSENCRANTZ: What's the matter with you today?
GUILDENSTERN: When? 45
ROSENCRANTZ: What?
GUILDENSTERN: Are you deaf?
ROSENCRANTZ: Am I dead?
GUILDENSTERN: Yes or no?
ROSENCRANTZ: Is there a choice? 50
GUILDENSTERN: Is there a God?
ROSENCRANTZ: Foul! No *non sequiturs*, three—two, one game all.
GUILDENSTERN (*seriously*): What's your name?
ROSENCRANTZ: What's yours?
GUILDENSTERN: I asked you first. 55
ROSENCRANTZ: Statement. One—love.
GUILDENSTERN: What's your name when you're at home?
ROSENCRANTZ: What's yours?
GUILDENSTERN: When I'm at home?
ROSENCRANTZ: Is it different at home? 60
GUILDENSTERN: What home?
ROSENCRANTZ: Haven't you got one?
GUILDENSTERN: Why do you ask?
ROSENCRANTZ: What are you driving at?
GUILDENSTERN (*with emphasis*): What's your name?! 65
ROSENCRANTZ: Repetition. Two—love. Match point to me.

GUILDENSTERN (*seizing him violently*): WHO DO YOU THINK YOU ARE?
ROSENCRANTZ: Rhetoric! Game and match! (*Pause.*) Where's it going to end? 70
GUILDENSTERN: That's the question.
ROSENCRANTZ: It's *all* questions.
GUILDENSTERN: Do you think it matters?
ROSENCRANTZ: Doesn't it matter to you?
GUILDENSTERN: Why should it matter? 75
ROSENCRANTZ: What does it matter why?
GUILDENSTERN (*teasing gently*): Doesn't it *matter* why it matters?
ROSENCRANTZ (*rounding on him*): What's the *matter* with you? (*Pause.*)
GUILDENSTERN: It doesn't matter. 80
ROSENCRANTZ: (*voice in the wilderness*): . . . What's the game?
GUILDENSTERN: What are the rules?

PACE AND TEMPO

Just as a dramatist must ensure that ideas and themes grow naturally from the interaction of situation and character, as we have seen, so too he must make it evident that the pace and tempo of his writing are immediately responsive to these same pressures. For tempo is as much a part of the whole meaning of a play as any other element. A simple illustration should confirm this. You will all presumably at some time or other have told a joke that falls flat; you may even have repeated it word for word on different occasions; one telling may have your audience falling about with laughter, whilst another may leave them staring glassily at you. One reason could be that your timing has gone awry. All comedians will tell you that part of the secret of a good joke lies in the timing—the variety of pace with which it is delivered, the length or shortness of the pauses and, of course, the careful timing of exactly when to deliver the punchline. If pace and tempo are essential to the miniature drama of a joke, so too are they in a play.

We can define tempo as the pace at which a particular speech, a particular scene or even a whole work moves and reaches the spectator. Naturally, this rate will vary throughout the play, depending on the effect the dramatist wishes to create in his audience at a particular stage in the play's development. We have considered elsewhere the way in which the different tempo of scenes and the relationship to each other affect the meaning of a play as a whole; in this section we shall be looking at the effect of tempo on individual speeches and scenes.

Read these lines from *Macbeth* which Macbeth speaks on hearing of the death of his wife:

Tomorrow, and tomorrow, and tomorrow,
Creeps in this petty pace from day to day (V.v. 19–20)

The way that Shakespeare has written those two lines makes it impossible for an actor to speak them anything but slowly, if he is to speak them at all meaningfully. Note that it is the repetition of certain words and preponderance of long vowels (all the 'o's in 'tomorrow', 'creeps', 'pace' and 'day to day') that force the actor to deliver the line slowly, and it is entirely appropriate to Macbeth's feelings and situation that he should speak in this way.

Another example from Shakespeare in which, this time, an actress is forced to speak the lines quickly. Rosalind in *As You Like It* replies to Orlando's question about the speed at which Time seems to move.

> By no means, sir, Time travels in divers paces with divers persons. I'll tell you who Time ambles withal, who Time trots withal, who Time gallops withal, and who he stands still withal. (III.ii)

She is forced to speak quickly—the short sentences and subordinate clauses, the predominance of plosive consonants (t, p, d, b), the repetition of grammatical structure are all playing their part in achieving a lightness that suits the playful teasing of the nature of her character and the occasion.

In these following examples, we would like you:

(i) to choose the word from the list in brackets that seems to you most precisely to describe the tempo of the lines and
(ii) to identify the means by which the dramatist has created the tempo.

A. DOLL: Why does the Prince love him so, then?
FALSTAFF: Because their legs are both of a bigness, and 'a plays at quoits well, and eats conger and fennel, and drinks off candles' ends for flap-dragons, and rides the wild mare with the boys, and jumps upon joint-stools, and swears with a good grace, and wears his boots very smooth like unto the sign of the leg, and breeds no bate with telling of discreet stories, and such other gambol faculties 'a has, that show a weak mind and an able body, for which the Prince admits him 5

Shakespeare: *Henry IV, Part 2* (II.iv) (1598)
(hesitant, rapid, deliberate, dilatory)

B. CANON CHASUBLE: My sermon on the meaning of the manna in the wilderness can be adapted to almost any occasion, joyful, or, as in the present case, distressing. I have preached it at harvest celebrations, christenings, confirmations, on days of humiliation and festal days. The last time I delivered it was in the Cathedral, as a charity sermon on behalf of the Society for the Prevention of Discontent among the Upper Orders. The Bishop, who was present, was much struck by some of the analogies I drew. 5

Oscar Wilde: *The Importance of Being Earnest* (1895)
(ponderous, tempestuous, dislocated, balanced)

C. SAMMY SAMUELS: A message for any nymphomaniacs in the audience . . . Hello. Sit down, lady, we'll have no rushing the stage. 1929 I were born. Year of the Great Crash. The sound of me father's jaw dropping. He took one look at me and said, I'm not that Jewish. Nobody's that Jewish. 5

Trevor Griffiths: *Comedians* (1976)
(sluggish, unpremeditated, swift, unhurried)

With these two final examples, you should find your own words to describe the tempo, before analysing the author's methods. The first is the opening of the play we have already discussed, *Forty Years On* by Alan Bennett (1968):

D. HEADMASTER: Members of Albion House, past and present. Parents and Old Boys. It doesn't seem so many years since I stood in this hall on November 11, 1918, to declare a half-holiday on the occasion of the Armistice. That was my first term at Albion House as a schoolboy, and now I am headmaster and it is my last term. A sad occasion 5

E. LEAR: Blow, winds, and crack your cheeks! rage! blow!
You cataracts and hurricanoes, spout
Till you have drench'd our steeples, drown'd the cocks!
You sulphurous and thought-executing fires,
Vaunt couriers of oak-cleaving thunderbolts, 10
Singe my white head!

Shakespeare: *King Lear* (1606)

All the examples we have chosen so far have been either individual speeches or short extracts from individual speeches, but it will be clear from these that even within the restricted compass of a few lines, a dramatist can successfully establish a particular tempo, which, as we shall see, he can counterpoint against the tempo of other speeches within a scene if he wishes. The musical term is not inappropriate, for a dramatic text has been described as 'a tune to be sung'. The methods open to a dramatist to vary his tempo are not far removed from those open to poets and to writers of imaginative prose and these methods are examined more fully in the chapters on rhythm in the companion volumes to this book, *Considering Prose* and *Considering Poetry*. As a general rule for drama, however, we can say that a slow tempo is often established by a dramatist using long syntactical units (sentences and clauses), with a predominance of drawn-out vowel sounds, whilst speed is generally established through the use of short syntactical units and predominance of consonants. We must stress that this can only remain a general rule!

So far in this section, we have asked you to look at changes in pace and tempo only by examining short extracts from plays, but, of course, such changes often occur during the course of much longer speeches and sections of dialogue. In the extract which follows, Jimmy Porter's wife,

Alison, has left him. His wife's friend, Helena, hands him the note which Alison has written. We would like you to imagine that you are the actor playing Jimmy and that you are preparing the speech in rehearsal. Where do you pause? Where do you quicken/slow the tempo of the speech? What variations in tone and emphasis are needed? When you have thoroughly prepared the speech, you might like to present it to the class and be responsive to any (*constructive*) criticism they make of your performance. Indeed the class would then be fulfilling one of the roles of the theatre director. The extract from *Rosencrantz and Guildenstern are Dead* which we quote on pp. 88–90 could also be prepared by two students, who should also pay close attention to the changes in pace and tone that would make their presentation most effective.

JIMMY: Oh, it's one of these, is it? (*He rips it open.*) *He reads a few lines, and almost snorts with disbelief.*
Did you write this for her! Well, listen to this then! (*Reading.*) "My dear—I must get away. I don't suppose you will understand, but please try. I need peace so desperately, and, at the moment, I am willing to sacrifice 5
everything just for that. I don't know what's going to happen to us. I know you will be feeling wretched and bitter, but try to be a little patient with me. I shall always have a deep, loving need of you—Alison". Oh, how could she be so bloody wet! Deep loving need! That makes me puke!
(*Crossing to R.*) She couldn't say "You rotten bastard! I hate your guts, 10
I'm clearing out, and I hope you rot!" No, she has to make a polite, emotional mess out of it! (*Seeing the dress in the wardrobe, he rips it out, and throws it in the corner up L.*) Deep, loving need! I never thought she was capable of being as phoney as that! What is that—a line from one of
those plays you've been in? What are you doing here anyway? You'd 15
better keep out of my way, if you don't want your head kicked in.

HELENA: (*calmly*). If you'll stop thinking about yourself for one moment, I'll tell you something I think you ought to know. Your wife is going to have a baby.
He just looks at her. 20
Well? Doesn't that mean anything? Even to you?
He is taken aback, but not so much by the news, as by her.

JIMMY: All right—yes. I am surprised. I give you that. But, tell me. Did you honestly expect me to go soggy at the knees, and collapse with remorse!
(*Leaning nearer.*) Listen, if you'll stop breathing your female wisdom all 25
over me, I'll tell you something: I don't care. (*Beginning quietly.*) I don't care if she's going to have a baby. I don't care if it has two heads! (*He knows her fingers are itching*). Do I disgust you? Well, go on—slap my face. But remember what I told you before, will you? For eleven hours, I
have been watching someone I love very much going through the sordid 30
process of dying. She was alone, and I was the only one with her. And when I have to walk behind that coffin on Thursday, I'll be on my own again. Because that bitch won't even send her a bunch of flowers—I know! . . . .
And you think I should be overcome with awe because that cruel, stupid 35
girl is going to have a baby!

(*Anguish in his voice.*) I can't believe it! I can't.
(*Grabbing her shoulder.*) Well, the performance is over.
Now leave me alone, and *get out*, you evil-minded little virgin.
She slaps his face savagely. 40

John Osborne: *Look Back in Anger* (1956)

We now move from examining individual speeches to examining the tempo of scenes or parts of scenes. For an author, a simple way of ensuring a speedy pace is to write a succession of very short speeches and trust that the actors will pick up on their cues promptly. In this example from *Waiting for Godot* by Samuel Beckett (1956), as you will see, the dialogue, thanks to the very short speeches, almost takes on the speed and character of a rapid-fire exchange at times reminiscent of two music-hall cross-talk comedians.

The scene is a country road. There is one tree. It is evening. Two tramps are in conversation.

VLADIMIR: Do you not recognize the place?
ESTRAGON: (*suddenly furious*). Recognize! What is there to recognize? All my lousy life I've crawled about in the mud! And you talk to me about scenery!
(*Looking wildly about him.*) Look at this muckheap! I've never stirred from it! 5
VLADIMIR: Calm yourself, calm yourself.
ESTRAGON: You and your landscapes! Tell me about the worms!
VLADIMIR: All the same, you can't tell me that this (*gesture*) bears any resemblance to . . . (*he hesitates*) . . . to the Macon country, for example. You can't deny there's a big difference. 10
ESTRAGON: The Macon country! Who's talking to you about the Macon country?
VLADIMIR: But you were there yourself, in the Macon country.
ESTRAGON: No, I was never in the Macon country. I've puked my puke of a life away here, I tell you! Here! In the Cackon country! 15
VLADIMIR: But we were there together, I could swear to it! Picking grapes for a man called . . . (*he snaps his fingers*) . . . can't think of the name of the man, at a place called . . . (*snaps his fingers*) . . . can't think of the name of the place, do you not remember? 20
ESTRAGON: (*a little calmer*). It's possible. I didn't notice anything.
VLADIMIR: But down there everything is red!
ESTRAGON: (*exasperated*). I didn't notice anything, I tell you!
Silence. Vladimir sighs deeply.
VLADIMIR: You're a hard man to get on with, Gogo. 25
ESTRAGON: It'd be better if we parted.
VLADIMIR: You always say that, and you always come crawling back.
ESTRAGON: The best thing would be to kill me, like the other.
VLADIMIR: What other? (*Pause.*) What other?
ESTRAGON: Like billions of others. 30

VLADIMIR: (*sententious*). To every man his little cross. (*He sighs.*) Till he dies. (*Afterthought.*) And is forgotten.
ESTRAGON: In the meantime let us try and converse calmly, since we are incapable of keeping silent.
VLADIMIR: You're right, we're inexhaustible. 35
ESTRAGON: It's so we won't think.
VLADIMIR: We have that excuse.
ESTRAGON: It's so we won't hear.
VLADIMIR: We have our reasons.
ESTRAGON: All the dead voices. 40
VLADIMIR: They make a noise like wings.
ESTRAGON: Like leaves.
VLADIMIR: Like sand.
ESTRAGON: Like leaves.
Silence. 45
VLADIMIR: They all speak together.
ESTRAGON: Each one to itself.
Silence.
VLADIMIR: Rather they whisper.
ESTRAGON: They rustle. 50
VLADIMIR: They murmur.
ESTRAGON: They rustle.
Silence.
VLADIMIR: What do they say?
ESTRAGON: They talk about their lives. 55
VLADIMIR: To have lived is not enough for them.
ESTRAGON: They have to talk about it.
VLADIMIR: To be dead is not enough for them.
ESTRAGON: It is not sufficient.
Silence. 60
VLADIMIR: They make a noise like feathers.
ESTRAGON: Like leaves.
VLADIMIR: Like ashes.
ESTRAGON: Like leaves.
Long silence. 65
VLADIMIR: Say something!
ESTRAGON: I'm trying.
Long silence.
VLADIMIR: (*in anguish*). Say anything at all!
ESTRAGON: What do we do now? 70
VLADIMIR: Wait for Godot.
ESTRAGON: Ah!
Silence.
VLADIMIR: This is awful!
ESTRAGON: Sing something. 75
VLADIMIR: No no! (*He reflects.*) We could start all over again perhaps.
ESTRAGON: That should be easy.
VLADIMIR: It's the start that's difficult.
ESTRAGON: You can start from anything.
VLADIMIR: Yes, but you have to decide. 80

ESTRAGON: True.
Silence.
VLADIMIR: Help me!
ESTRAGON: I'm trying.
Silence. 85
VLADIMIR: When you seek you hear.
ESTRAGON: You do.
VLADIMIR: That prevents you from finding.
ESTRAGON: It does.
VLADIMIR: That prevents you from thinking. 90
ESTRAGON: You think all the same.
VLADIMIR: No, no, impossible.
ESTRAGON: That's the idea, let's contradict each other.
VLADIMIR: Impossible.
ESTRAGON: You think so? 95
VLADIMIR: We're in no danger of ever thinking any more.
ESTRAGON: Then what are we complaining about?
VLADIMIR: Thinking is not the worst.
ESTRAGON: Perhaps not. But at least there's that.
VLADIMIR: That what? 100
ESTRAGON: That's the idea, let's ask each other questions.
VLADIMIR: What do you mean, at least there's that?
ESTRAGON: That much less misery.
VLADIMIR: True.
ESTRAGON: Well? If we gave thanks for our mercies? 105
VLADIMIR: What is terrible is to *have* thought.
ESTRAGON: But did that ever happen to us?
VLADIMIR: Where are all these corpses from?
ESTRAGON: These skeletons.
VLADIMIR: Tell me that. 110
ESTRAGON: True.
VLADIMIR: We must have thought a little.
ESTRAGON: At the very beginning.
VLADIMIR: A charnel-house! A charnel-house!
ESTRAGON: You don't have to look. 115
VLADIMIR: You can't help looking.
ESTRAGON: True.
VLADIMIR: Try as one may.
ESTRAGON: I beg your pardon?
VLADIMIR: Try as one may. 120
ESTRAGON: We should turn resolutely towards Nature.
VLADIMIR: We've tried that.
ESTRAGON: True.
VLADIMIR: Oh, it's not the worst, I know.
ESTRAGON: What? 125
VLADIMIR: To have thought.
ESTRAGON: Obviously.
VLADIMIR: But we could have done without it.
ESTRAGON: Que voulez-vous?
VLADIMIR: I beg your pardon? 130

ESTRAGON: Que voulez-vous?
VLADIMIR: Ah! que voulez-vous. Exactly.
Silence.
ESTRAGON: That wasn't such a bad little canter.
VLADIMIR: Yes, but now we'll have to find something else. 135
ESTRAGON: Let me see.
He takes off his hat, concentrates.
VLADIMIR: Let me see. (*He takes off his hat, concentrates. Long silence.*) Ah!
They put on their hats, relax. 140
ESTRAGON: Well?
VLADIMIR: What was I saying, we could go on from there.
ESTRAGON: What were you saying when?
VLADIMIR: At the very beginning.
ESTRAGON: The beginning of WHAT? 145
VLADIMIR: This evening . . . I was saying . . . I was saying . . .
ESTRAGON: I'm not a historian.
VLADIMIR: Wait . . . we embraced . . . we were happy . . . happy . . . what do we do now that we're happy . . . go on waiting . . . waiting . . . let me think . . . it's coming . . . go on waiting . . . now that we're happy . . . let me see . . . ah! The tree! 150
ESTRAGON: The tree?
VLADIMIR: Do you not remember?
ESTRAGON: I'm tired.
VLADIMIR: Look at it. 155
They look at the tree.
ESTRAGON: I see nothing.
VLADIMIR: But yesterday evening it was all black and bare. And now it's covered with leaves.
ESTRAGON: Leaves? 160
VLADIMIR: In a single night.
ESTRAGON: It must be the Spring.
VLADIMIR: But in a single night!
ESTRAGON: I tell you we weren't here yesterday. Another of your nightmares. 165
VLADIMIR: And where were we yesterday evening according to you?
ESTRAGON: How do I know? In another compartment. There's no lack of void.
VLADIMIR: (*sure of himself*). Good. We weren't here yesterday evening. Now what did we do yesterday evening? 170
ESTRAGON: Do?
VLADIMIR: Try and remember.
ESTRAGON: Do . . . I suppose we blathered.
VLADIMIR: (*controlling himself*). About what?
ESTRAGON: Oh . . . this and that, I suppose, nothing in particular. (*With assurance.*) Yes, now I remember, yesterday evening we spent blathering about nothing in particular. That's been going on now for half a century. 175
VLADIMIR: You don't remember any fact, any circumstance?
ESTRAGON: (*weary*). Don't torment me, Didi.

(i) How would you define the general mood generated by this dialogue? Quote key phrases or images to support your answer.
(ii) Both characters seem to possess an overwhelming urge to keep talking.
(a) Why is this?
(b) What are the devices they use to keep the conversation going?
(iii) Comment in detail on the *pace* of the dialogue.
(a) Where is the tempo fast? And where is it slow? What is the reason for these changes in pace?
(b) What is the effect of the many pauses that punctuate this dialogue?

Though it is easier to sense tempo during an actual performance, you can train yourself to respond to it when reading a text. It is obviously quicker to read a page of speeches such as in this example than it is to read a page which consists, in the main, of longer, denser and more metaphoric speeches, which in the theatre could result in a much slower pace. But, more often than not, the tempo of a particular scene does not remain one-paced throughout, for this would become monotonous. A dramatist will vary the pace of his dialogue within a particular scene as the comparisons and contrasts that this allows will not only reflect and express the action and make manifest the emotions of the characters, but also govern the reactions of the audience. Tempo is a vital and inextricable element in the whole structure of an action, so it is not something that can be added to a scene at the final revision. It provides for a dramatist a valuable way of interpreting his material. John Whiting, a modern dramatist, has said 'the shaping of prose dialogue determines the style. This does not mean the characteristic idiom of the dialogue, but the use of voices to achieve dramatic form . . . For example, the exact placing of unbroken passages for a single voice or dialogue in half speeches for two or more voices speaking together. By this method, it is possible to control from within the text of a play the speed and exact rhythm which are usually imposed by the director'. (*Writing for Actors*).

To illustrate how important a role tempo can play, consider this scene from *Macbeth* (II.ii).

Macbeth has returned to his waiting wife after having murdered his royal guest, Duncan, in the depth of night.

MACBETH: I have done the deed.—Didst thou not hear a noise?
LADY MACBETH: I heard the owl scream, and the crickets cry.
Did not you speak?
MACBETH. When?
LADY MACBETH: Now. 5
MACBETH: As I descended?
LADY MACBETH: Ay.
MACBETH: Hark!
Who lies i' th' second chamber?

LADY MACBETH: Donalbain. 10
MACBETH: This is a sorry sight.
LADY MACBETH: A foolish thought to say a sorry sight.
MACBETH: There's one did laugh in's sleep, and one cried, "Murther!"
That they did wake each other: I stood and heard them;
But they did say their prayers, and address'd them 15
Again to sleep.
LADY MACBETH: There are two lodg'd together.
MACBETH: One cried, "God bless us!" and, "Amen," the other,
As they had seen me with these hangman's hands.
List'ning their fear, I could not say, "Amen," 20
When they did say, "God bless us."
LADY MACBETH: Consider it not so deeply.
MACBETH: But wherefore could not I pronounce "Amen"?
I had most need of blessing, and "Amen"
Stuck in my throat. 25
LADY MACBETH: These deeds must not be thought
After these ways: so, it will make us mad.
MACBETH: Methought, I heard a voice cry, "Sleep no more!
Macbeth does murther Sleep,"—the innocent Sleep;
Sleep, that knits up the ravell'd sleave of care, 30
The death of each day's life, sore labour's bath,
Balm of hurt minds, great Nature's second course,
Chief nourisher in life's feast;—

(i) What pace is created by the short sentences at the beginning of the scene? What does this reveal about the state of mind of the characters?
(ii) Identify any change(s) you find in the pace of the dialogue. How does Shakespeare achieve such change(s)?
(iii) How do the changes in pace help to convey the reactions of Macbeth and Lady Macbeth to events?

Of course, not all changes of pace in scenes are as abrupt as these; not all characters experience the fear and guilt that come from having murdered a king, but this short scene from *Macbeth* does indicate how organic a role pace does play in realising the whole meaning of a scene. As an example of gentler variations in pace, we would like you to read more of the scene from *The Way of the World* that we have already quoted (p. 81). We begin with the next words that Millamant speaks.

—Good *Mirabell* don't let us be familiar or fond, nor kiss before Folks, like my Lady *Fadler* and Sir *Francis*: Nor go to *Hyde-Park* together the first *Sunday* in a new Chariot, to provoke Eyes and Whispers; And then never be seen there together again; as if we were proud of one another the first Week, and asham'd of one another ever after. Let us never Visit together, 5
nor go to a Play together, but let us be very strange and well bred: Let us be as strange as if we had been marry'd a great while; and as well bred as if we were not marry'd at all.

MIRABELL: Have you any more Conditions to offer? Hitherto your Demands are pretty reasonable. 10

MILLAMANT: Trifles,—As Liberty to pay and receive Visits to and from whom I please; to write and receive Letters, without Interrogatories or wry Faces on your part; to wear what I please; and chuse Conversation with regard only to my own Taste; to have no Obligation upon me to converse with Wits that I don't like, because they are your Acquaintance; 15 or to be intimate with Fools, because they may be your Relations. Come to Dinner when I please, dine in my Dressing-Room when I'm out of Humour, without giving a Reason. To have my Closet inviolate; to be sole Empress of my Tea-Table, which you must never presume to approach without first asking leave. And lastly where-ever I am, you 20 shall always knock at the Door before you come in. These Articles subscrib'd, if I continue to endure you a little longer, I may by degrees dwindle into a Wife.

MIRABELL: Your Bill of Fare is something advanc'd in this latter Account. Well, have I Liberty to offer Conditions—That when you are dwindled 25 into a Wife, I may not be beyond measure enlarg'd into a Husband?

MILLAMANT: You have free leave, propose your utmost, speak and spare not.

MIRABELL: I thank you. *Imprimis* then, I covenant that your Acquaintance be general; that you admit no sworn Confident, or Intimate of your own 30 Sex; no she Friend to screen her Affairs under your Countenance, and tempt you to make Trial of a mutual Secresie. No Decoy-Duck to wheadle you a *fop—scrambling* to the Play in a Mask—Then bring you home in a pretended Fright, when you think you shall be found out—And rail at me for missing the Play, and disappointing the Frolick which 35 you had to pick me up and prove my Constancy.

MILLAMANT: Detestable *Imprimis*! I go to the Play in a Mask!

MIRABELL: *Item*, I Article, that you continue to like your own Face, as long as I shall: And while it passes current with me, that you endeavour not to new Coin it. To which end, together with all Vizards for the Day, I 40 prohibit all Masks for the Night, made of Oil'd-skins and I know not what—Hog's Bones, Hare's Gall, Pig Water, and the Marrow of a roasted Cat. In short, I forbid all Commerce with the Gentlewoman in *what-d'ye-call-it* Court. *Item*, I shut my Doors against all Bauds with Baskets, and penny-worths of *Muslin, China, Fans, Atlasses*, &c.—*Item*, 45 when you shall be Breeding—

MILLAMANT: Ah! Name it not.

MIRABELL: Which may be presum'd, with a Blessing on our Endeavours—

MILLAMANT: Odious Endeavours!

MIRABELL: I denounce against all strait Lacing, squeezing for a Shape, 'till 50 you mould my Boy's Head like a Sugar-loaf; and instead of a Man-Child, make me Father to a Crooked-billet. Lastly, to the Dominion of the *Tea-Table* I submit.—But with *proviso*, that you exceed not in your Province; but restrain your self to native and simple *Tea-Table* Drinks, as *Tea, Chocolate*, and *Coffee*. As likewise to Genuine and Authoriz'd *Tea-Table* 55 Talk—Such as mending of Fashions, spoiling Reputations, railing at absent Friends, and so forth—But that on no Account you encroach upon the Mens Prerogative, and presume to drink Healths, or toast

Fellows; for prevention of which, I banish all *Foreign Forces*, all Auxiliaries to the *Tea-Table*, as *Orange-Brandy*, all *Anniseed, Cinamon, Citron* and *Barbado's-Waters*, together with *Ratafia* and the most noble Spirit of *Clary*. —But for *Couslip-Wine, Poppy-Water*, and all *Dormitives*, those I allow.—These *Proviso's* admitted, in other things I may prove a tractable and complying Husband. 60

MILLAMANT: O horrid *Proviso's*! filthy strong Waters! I toast Fellows, Odious Men! I hate your odious *Proviso's*. 65

MIRABELL: Then we're agreed. Shall I kiss your Hand upon the Contract? and here comes one to be a Witness to the Sealing of the Deed.

(i) What is the effect of the variation in the length of the speeches on (a) the pace of the scene, and (b) on its structure?
(ii) How is this related to the characters of Mirabell and Millamant and their immediate situation?
(iii) Show how Congreve has balanced the pace of Millamant's second speech with that of Mirabell's third. By what means has he achieved a particular pace and balance within the individual speeches?
(iv) In what way has Congreve achieved a satisfying conclusion to the scene?

Finally, the opening of Bernard Shaw's *St Joan* (1924). Captain Robert de Baudricourt, 'handsome and physically energetic', is 'storming terribly at his steward, a trodden worm, scanty of flesh'. Discuss any contrasts in tempo you perceive and show how they help to create an effective start to the play.

ROBERT: No eggs! No eggs!! Thousand thunders, man, what do you mean by no eggs?
STEWARD: Sir: it is not my fault. It is the act of God.
ROBERT: Blasphemy. You tell me there are no eggs; and you blame your Maker for it. 5
STEWARD: Sir: what can I do? I cannot lay eggs.
ROBERT [*sarcastic*]: Ha! You jest about it.
STEWARD: No, sir, God knows. We all have to go without eggs just as you have, sir. The hens will not lay.
ROBERT: Indeed! [*Rising*] Now listen to me, you. 10
STEWARD [*humbly*]: Yes, sir.
ROBERT: What am I?
STEWARD: What are you, sir?
ROBERT [*coming at him*]: Yes: what am I? Am I Robert, squire of Baudricourt and captain of this castle of Vaucouleurs; or am I a cowboy? 15
STEWARD: Oh, sir, you know you are a greater man here than the king himself.
ROBERT: Precisely. And now, do you know what you are?
STEWARD: I am nobody, sir, except that I have the honor to be your steward. 20

ROBERT [*driving him to the wall, adjective by adjective*]: You have not only the honor of being my steward, but the privilege of being the worst, most incompetent, drivelling snivelling jibbering jabbering idiot of a steward in France. [*He strides back to the table*].

STEWARD [*cowering on the chest*]: Yes, sir: to a great man like you I must seem like that. 25

Because most of our extracts are of necessity short, all our examples of variation of tempo have been dialogues, but we suggest that you examine some of the following longer scenes from Shakespeare in which more than two characters appear and consider how Shakespeare uses tempo in them:

Macbeth (II.iii)
Othello (II.iii)
Julius Caesar (III.ii)

SILENCES AND PAUSES

We have so far in this chapter been considering some of the ways that a dramatist uses words, but of course, words can only exist in conjunction with silence. To illustrate: no character on stage talks all the time; he listens to other characters; he may not reply instantly to what is said; he may pace his responses; what is said to him may, for instance, cause him to ponder, or may throw him off balance; he may threaten others by his silence. The silence on stage is not the silence of a room in which we are alone reading or writing, but is part of the general flow of the dialogue and consequently can be used by the playwright to create particular theatrical effects or to help in establishing a particular tempo. You will already have been aware of some of the effects that pauses and periods of silence can have from your work on the extract from *Waiting for Godot* on pp. 94–7. Nor are all silences or pauses as long as the one given by Chekhov to Trepilov at the end of *The Seagull* when he has to 'spend the next two minutes silently tearing up all his manuscripts and throwing them under the table' (this calls for acting of the highest order, if it is not to become tedious for the audience!), but even a second or two's pause or hesitation before an actor utters his next word can give heightened emphasis to that word or even create great tension, if the context of the action is appropriate.

Amongst modern playwrights, Harold Pinter is one of the most effective in using pauses and silences. Re-read the extract that we have already quoted from *The Caretaker* on page 80. Aston has brought Davies, a poorly dressed old man, back to his house, which is filled with useless objects. You will realise from a reading of the passage that Pinter has carefully orchestrated the pauses with which the dialogue is interspersed to achieve an atmosphere of tension and uncertainty. There is a veiled menace in Aston's remarks: 'Till you . . . get yourself fixed up' and 'Here. The other rooms would . . . would be no good to you' that is established by the hesitation in his speech; the uncertainty felt by Davies is indicated by the way that his remarks trail off into inconsequentiality—'Ay well, that . . . ' and 'Oh, I'll be fixed up . . . pretty soon now . . . (*Pause*) Where would I sleep?' or his line of thought changes tack. By his use of pauses, combined with a very bare, stripped dialogue, Pinter has succeeded in creating a frightening world inhabited by two inarticulate men.

Sir Peter Hall, the theatre director, has written about how he approaches a Pinter play as follows: 'The first thing to say to actors when we're beginning. . . is "Look, don't mislead yourselves into thinking that if there's a pause there, there shouldn't be a pause there, or if there's a silence, there shouldn't be a silence, because there should. Our job is to find out why. And don't in order to make it comfortable, turn a full-stop into a comma, or break it up in a colloquial way different to the way he's written it".' Clearly, he expects his actors to pay minute attention to all the nuances of Pinter's text. In this next extract, taken slightly earlier from *The Caretaker*, your 'job is to find out why' Pinter has orchestrated his pauses and silences in the way he has. You might find it useful to pay particular attention to the differing lengths of the pauses and the way Pinter signals them to his actors.

DAVIES: Nothing but wind then.
(*Pause.*)
ASTON: Yes, when the wind gets up it. . . .
(*Pause.*)
DAVIES: Yes. . . . 5
ASTON: Mmmmn. . . .
(*Pause.*)
DAVIES: Gets very draughty.
ASTON: Ah.
DAVIES: I'm very sensitive to it. 10
ASTON: Are you?
DAVIES: Always have been.
(*Pause.*)
You got more rooms then, have you?
ASTON: Where? 15
DAVIES: I mean, along the landing here . . . up the landing there.
ASTON: They're out of commission.
DAVIES: Get away.
ASTON: They need a lot of doing to.
(*Slight pause.*) 20
DAVIES: What about downstairs?
ASTON: That's closed up. Needs seeing to. . . . The floors. . . .
(*Pause.*)
DAVIES: I was lucky you come into that caff. I might have been done by that Scotch git. I been left for dead more than once. 25
(*Pause.*)
I noticed that there was someone was living in the house next door.

ASTON: What?
DAVIES (*gesturing*): I noticed. . . .
ASTON: Yes. There's people living all along the road. 30
DAVIES: Yes, I noticed the curtains pulled down there next door as we came along.
ASTON: They're neighbours.
(*Pause.*)
DAVIES: This your house then, is it? 35
(*Pause.*)
ASTON: I'm in charge.
DAVIES: You the landlord, are you?
(*He puts a pipe in his mouth and puffs without lighting it.*)
Yes, I noticed them heavy curtains pulled across next door as we came along. 40

Of course, Harold Pinter is not the only dramatist who takes great care with the organisation of pauses and silences in his texts and you can find plenty of other examples in the work of such playwrights as Samuel Beckett, Eugène Ionesco and Tom Stoppard, where the writers' intentions are clearly signalled. However, not all writers indicate by the use of stage directions where they want the pauses and silences to occur; often the clues to where they should be are contained within the text itself and the actor, director or reader has to be on the *qui vive* to locate them. In the following extracts from Marlowe and Shakespeare (a) identify where you would place the pause, and (b) see if you can suggest what clues the text contains to justify your choice.

A. *Dr Faustus begins the last hour of his life*

Ah Faustus,
Now hast thou but one bare hour to live,
And then thou must be damned perpetually:
Stand still you ever moving spheres of heaven,
That time may cease, and midnight never come. 5

Marlowe: *Doctor Faustus* (1592)

B. To be, or not to be, that is the question:
Whether 'tis nobler in the mind to suffer
The slings and arrows of outrageous fortune,
Or to take arms against a sea of troubles
And by opposing end them. To die – to sleep, 5
No more; and by a sleep to say we end
The heart-ache and the thousand natural shocks
That flesh is heir to.

Shakespeare: *Hamlet* (1601)

C. *Iago torments the jealous Othello about a handkerchief belonging to Othello's wife that he (Iago) has procured and given to Cassio in order to further Othello's suspicions.*

IAGO: Have you not sometimes seen a handkerchief
Spotted with strawberries in your wife's hand?
OTHELLO: I gave her such a one; 'twas my first gift.
IAGO: I know not that; but such a handkerchief—
I am sure it was your wife's—did I today 5
See Cassio wipe his beard with.
OTHELLO: If it be that—
IAGO: If it be that, or any that was hers,
It speaks against her with the other proofs

Shakespeare: *Othello* (1602–04)

D. *King Lear is dividing his kingdom between his daughters in proportion to their expressed love for him.*

LEAR: (*to Cordelia*) Now, our joy,
Although our last, and least; to whose young love
The vines of France and milk of Burgundy
Strive to be interess'd; what can you say to draw
A third more opulent than your sisters? Speak. 5
CORDELIA: Nothing, my lord.
LEAR: Nothing?
CORDELIA: Nothing.
LEAR: Nothing will come of nothing: speak again.
CORDELIA: Unhappy that I am, I cannot heave 10
My heart into my mouth: I love your Majesty
According to my bond; no more nor less.

Shakespeare: *King Lear* (1604–05)

DIALOGUE OF THE UNEXPECTED

Much of the dialogue we have looked at so far is intended at least to *appear* realistic, to demonstrate some links with the conventions of normal discourse, even though the emotions that lie behind it may be heightened, or the situation itself may be unusual. But dramatists have a licence to play some surprising tricks with language. They are not bound to be conventional and some of the wittiest and most effective moments in theatre can come when an audience's attention is caught by some unexpected turn in the dialogue. Take these two short extracts for example. In the first, which takes place in a Committee Room of the House of Commons, the comic surprise is gained by the secretary, Maddie's unexpected response which punctures the exaggerated pomposity of Cocklebury-Smythe. In the second, Connie's speech is a parody of romantic cliché, again deflated by the response it evokes.

A. COCKLEBURY-SMYTHE: May I be the first to welcome you to Room 3b. You will find the working conditions primitive, the hours antisocial, the amenities non-existent and the catering beneath contempt. On top of that the people are for the most part very very very boring, with interests either so generalised as to mimic wholesale ignorance or so particular as 5 to be lunatic obsessions. Their level of conversation would pass without comment in the lavatory of a mixed comprehensive and the lavatories, by the way, are few and far between.

MADDIE: It has always been my ambition to work in the House of Commons. 10

Tom Stoppard: *Dirty Linen* (1976)

B. CANON THROBBING: You're going to marry him and you don't even know his name?

CONNIE: Yes, I do know his name. His name is curtains billowing wide on a summer night. His name is a special secret rose pressed in an old book. His name is the name of all lovers down the ages who have cried their 5 challenge to the wild night and dared to cast themselves away on the frail bark of love. What is your name, by the way?

SIR PERCY: Sir Percy Shorter.

(*Connie screams and exits*)

It's not my fault if I send women mad. 10

Alan Bennett: *Habeas Corpus* (1973)

These extracts, then, demonstrate two of the methods through which dramatists can achieve surprise: by an unexpected phrase or speech and by a parody and puncturing of cliché. There are others: these have been characterised as the *mot juste*, the sudden illogicality, the paradox and the *non sequitur*. Do any of the following extracts illustrate any of these categories? Or do you need to come up with some different ones of your own?

A. *The detective, Truscott, believes that a corpse brought into the room by Dennis and Hal is a tailor's dummy.*

TRUSCOTT: What are you doing with that thing?

DENNIS: We were taking it outside.

TRUSCOTT: Why? Did it need the air?

HAL: We were putting it in the garage.

TRUSCOTT: This isn't the garage. What do you mean by bringing it back 5 into this room?

HAL: A police sergeant was in the garage.

TRUSCOTT: I'm sure he has no particular aversion to sharing a garage with a tailor's dummy.

HAL: He wanted to undress it. 10

TRUSCOTT: What possible objection could there be to an officer undressing a tailor's dummy?

DENNIS: It isn't decent.

HAL: It's a Catholic.

Joe Orton: *Loot* (1966)

B. *A married couple, Bro and Middie Paradock, have been entertaining Uncle Ted at home.*

BRO: When's your train, Uncle Ted?
UNCLE TED: It leaves Euston at nine. I shall have to be off soon.
MIDDIE: Not until you've had another read. I'm not letting you go out on a miserable two stanzas. It won't take me long to get down some more books. 5
UNCLE TED: Thank you, Middie—but I really oughtn't to stop for another read.
BRO: You're going to stay and get some prose inside you first. Don't get those down, Middie. I've got some others outside.
MIDDIE: He's got a special little store out there, for when anybody comes 10 unexpectedly. I expect he'll bring in one of the new books on the physical nature of the universe.
BRO: You've got time for a dip in one of these before you go.
UNCLE TED: Just a paragraph, then, Bro.

N. F. Simpson: *A Resounding Tinkle* (1958)

C. MRS ALLONBY: Horrid word 'health'.
LORD ILLINGWORTH: Silliest word in our language, and one knows so well the popular idea of health. The English country gentleman galloping after a fox—the unspeakable in full pursuit of the uneatable.

Oscar Wilde: *A Woman of No Importance* (1893)

Whatever conclusions you came to about the way surprise is achieved in these extracts, it should be clear that an alert ear for unusual and unexpected dialogue is needed in the appreciation of drama.

8

Verse and prose

We have already noted (on pp. 77–80) that dramatic dialogue, apart from that which seeks to be naturalistic, and thus, to imitate 'a selection of the language really used by men' has always exhibited some degree or other of rhetorical patterning. It was no part of the dramatist's purpose, before the rise of naturalism, to seek to present his audience with actors using everyday speech. Indeed, the language of the drama in some instances, such as in the French classical theatre of the 17th century, in which the actors spoke in eloquent alexandrine verse, was far removed from what one would hear either on the streets or at Court. As you will have already realised from some of the examples in the previous chapter (and throughout the book) of dramatists who used prose, they used prose that is non-naturalistic. Look, for instance, at the extracts from Congreve (p. 81), Goldsmith (p. 83), Stoppard (p. 88) and Beckett (p. 94); all of whom are using prose that is, to some degree or other, rhetorically patterned.

Of course, not all prose used in plays is equally heavily patterned; the amount of patterning depends both on the literary and dramatic conventions of the time and on the purposes of the dramatist in each particular scene. The following short extracts are taken from a variety of naturalistic and non-naturalistic plays. We would like you to read and discuss them and to see if you can identify the features of language that impose a pattern (if any). We have made notes on the first of the extracts for you. You may also like to rank the extracts in order from the least to the most heavily patterned language.

A. *Mr Hardcastle reacts to Marlow's treating Hardcastle's house as an inn.*

> HARDCASTLE: To come to my house, to call for what he likes, to turn me out of my own chair, to insult the family, to order his servants to get drunk, and then to tell me *This house is mine, Sir*. By all that's impudent, it makes me laugh. Ha! ha! ha! Pray, Sir, (*bantering*) as you take the house, what think you of taking the rest of the furniture? There's a pair of silver candlesticks, and there's a fire-screen, and here's a pair of brazen-nosed bellows, perhaps you may take a fancy to them? 5

(1st sentence—phrases of approximately same length and structure, rising to climax at 'This house is mine, Sir'. Similar patterning in last sentence—'There's a . . . there's a . . . here's a . . . '. Short sentence in middle as a contrast to longer, more rhetorical ones that surround it.)

Oliver Goldsmith: *She Stoops to Conquer* (1773)

B. *The women of Canterbury approach the Cathedral apprehensively.*

Here let us stand, close by the cathedral. Here let us wait. Are we drawn by danger? Is it the knowledge of safety that draws our feet towards the cathedral? What danger can be for us, the poor, the poor women of Canterbury? What tribulation with which we are not already familiar? There is no danger for us, and there is no safety in the cathedral. Some 5
presage of an act which our eyes are compelled to witness, has forced our feet towards the cathedral. We are forced to bear witness.

T. S. Eliot: *Murder in the Cathedral* (1935)

C. *Falstaff contemplates honour during the battle of Shrewsbury in Shakespeare's* Henry IV (Pt 1)

Well, 'tis no matter, honour pricks me on. Yea, but how if honour prick me off when I come on, how then? Can honour set to a leg? No. Or an arm? No. Or take away the grief of a wound? No. Honour hath no skill in surgery then? No. What is honour? A word. What is in that word honour? What is that honour? Air. A trim reckoning! Who hath it? He that died a- 5
Wednesday. Doth he feel it? No. Doth he hear it? No. 'Tis insensible, then? Yea, to the dead. But will it not live with the living? No. Why? Detraction will not suffer it. Therefore I'll none of it. Honour is a mere scutcheon—and so ends my catechism.

D. *Warrington is about to be tortured in the presence of the two sisters, Bodice and Fontanelle.*

BODICE: Fetch him out.

SOLDIER A *fetches* WARRINGTON *on stage. He is dishevelled, dirty and bound.*

SOLDIER A: Yer wan' 'im done in in a fancy way? Thass sometimes arst for. I once'ad t' cut a throat for some ladies t' see once. 5

FONTANELLE: It's difficult to choose.

BODICE [*sits on her riding stick and takes out her knitting.*]: Let him choose. [*Knits.*]

SOLDIER A: I once give a 'and t' flay a man. I couldn't manage that on me own. Yer need two at least for that. Shall I beat 'im up? 10

FONTANELLE: You're all talk! Wind and piss!

SOLDIER A: Juss for a start. Don't get me wrong, thass juss for a start. Get it goin' and see'ow it goes from there.

FONTANELLE: But I want something—

BODICE [*knitting*]: O shut up and let him get on with it. [*Nods at* SOLDIER A *to go on.*] 15

Edward Bond: *Lear* (1972)

E. *Mozart's wife, Constanze; addresses him.*

If I've been a bore—if I've nagged a bit about money, it didn't mean anything. It's only because I'm spoilt. You spoilt me, lovey. You've got to get well, Wolfi—because we need you. Karl and Baby Franz as well. There's only the three of us, lovey: we don't cost much. Just don't leave us—we wouldn't know what to do without you. And you wouldn't know 5 much either, up in Heaven, without us. You soppy thing. You can't even cut up your own meat without help! . . . I'm not clever, lovey. It can't have been easy living with a goose. But I've looked after you, you must admit that. And I've given you fun too—quite a lot really! . . . Are you listening?

Peter Shaffer: *Amadeus* (1979)

F. *Andrew Undershaft, an arms manufacturer, defends himself against the attacks of his son, Stephen.*

UNDERSHAFT [*with a touch of brutality*]: The government of your country! *I* am the government of your country: I, and Lazarus. Do you suppose that you and half a dozen amateurs like you, sitting in a row in that foolish gabble shop, can govern Undershaft and Lazarus? No, my friend: you will do what pays us. You will make war when it suits us, and 5 keep peace when it doesn't. You will find out that trade requires certain measures when we have decided on those measures. When I want anything to keep my dividends up, you will discover that my want is a national need. When other people want something to keep my dividends down, you will call out the police and military. And in return you shall 10 have the support and applause of my newspapers, and the delight of imagining that you are a great statesman. Government of your country! Be off with you, my boy, and play with your caucuses and leading articles and historic parties and great leaders and burning questions and the rest of your toys. *I* am going back to my counting-house to pay the piper and 15 call the tune.

Bernard Shaw: *Major Barbara* (1905)

We have not played entirely fair with you here, for one of the passages (B) was not prose, but verse, printed as prose. This should have served to remind you both that (i) much drama *is* written in verse, and (ii) perhaps a better distinction to make when dealing with dramatic language is not that between prose and poetry, but between the degrees of rhetorical patterning to be found in the language. *One* way of describing what verse is, is to say that it is the most formally patterned variety of language, with its use of rhythm, rhetorical devices, imagery and (sometimes) rhyme. Of course, you will have realised that many of the examples already quoted are written in verse, but we are still faced with the question: Why should a dramatist want to use verse in his plays? What advantages does it bring to him? Before reading on, you might like to discuss this question in your class.

A group of actors from the Royal Shakespeare Company also

conducted a similar discussion: here are some of their conclusions.

ALAN HOWARD: *It helps us to learn the lines. Verse is usually easier to learn than prose.*

JANE LAPOTAIRE: *It makes a pattern on the page which is easier for the mind to retain than prose.*

LISA HARROW: *Yes, it helps to give us our phrasing.*

DAVID SUCHET: *It's also full of acting hints if you know how to look for them.*

IAN MCKELLEN: *And because the verse is a more economical way than prose of saying something, it's likely to be more concise and more particular and exact. At the same time, because verse has a rhythm and a flow, it's perhaps more attractive to listen to and helps the actor to keep the audience's attention.*

You'll notice that the first four comments all focus on the help that verse can give an actor whether in his speech or his movements. First and foremost, because plays only come fully to life on stage, dramatic verse must be a means for the actor to communicate effectively through voice, gesture and movement; the best verse can do this through its form, through its imagery and through its rhythm, if an actor responds sensitively to what the author has written.

Ian McKellen's comment reminds us of the other related function of dramatic verse: because it is the most heightened form of language, then it is the most suitable form to express the heightened emotions that we find in drama. Often, in everyday life, when we are faced with a situation that demands a very strong emotional response, for example, the death of a close relative or when we wish to express our love for someone, we lapse into inarticulacy. A dramatist cannot afford such inarticulacy, so he must find a form of language that can do justice to his characters' emotions when they are at their most intense and consequently he may use verse (or a particularly heightened form of prose) for this purpose. J. L. Styan in *The Elements of Drama* suggests that the effect of poetry in the theatre is 'to secure the depth and intensity of poetic method. . . . It will extend the range and power of the author's meaning . . . the poetry is there to express and define patterns of thought and feeling otherwise inexpressible and indefinable'.

It is true to say, however, that the most successful verse drama is drama that has been written at a time when the verse used has had links with the language commonly used by the people. Much of the verse of the 20th century has not had these links and with one or two notable exceptions such as the historical drama, *Murder in the Cathedral*, by T. S. Eliot, the majority of modern verse drama has been a failure. Indeed, it can be argued that there has been no completely successful verse drama since the Age of Shakespeare.

SHAKESPEARE AND BLANK VERSE

When we think of dramatists who use verse, we automatically think of Shakespeare, but of course, most dramatists of the Elizabethan and Jacobean era wrote much of their work in verse, and it is additionally a valuable corrective to remember that Shakespeare did not use verse all the time—some 28 % of his work is in prose. But the norm for him was to write in blank verse. What is this? Unrhymed lines of ten syllables with an alternation of light and strong stresses, technically known as iambic pentameter. When you hear a regular line of blank verse, you can hear its characteristic rhythm underneath the words: de dum/de dum/de dum/de dum/de dum/, a series of five 'feet', each foot consisting of an unstressed syllable (◡) followed by a stressed one (\\). Here is a passage from *Richard II* in which we have marked the rhythmic pattern for you:

> GAUNT: This roy / al throne / of kings, / this scep / t'red isle /
> This earth / of ma / jesty /, this seat / of Mars /
> This oth / er E / den de / mi-pa / radise /
> This for / tress built / by Na / ture for / herself /

But, as you will have no doubt realised, to write or listen to a whole play in regular blank verse would be rather monotonous. It is the variation on the basic rhythm of iambic pentameter that gives Shakespeare much of his dramatic effectiveness, whether it be slight variation in the number of syllables per line or in the rhythmic stresses. The character and the situation in which the character finds himself dictate the rhythm of the line. Shakespearean blank verse is not a straitjacket in which to imprison the actor, but is an infinitely variable medium which is capable of helping the actor the more fully to communicate exactly what his 'character' is feeling at each moment in the play. Obviously we cannot illustrate here every possible effect that Shakespeare is capable of in his variations on basic iambic pentameter, but in the following examples, we would like you to (i) mark where you think the variations occur, and (ii) say why you think Shakespeare has made them. To help, you ought to consider how *you* would normally speak the lines, paying attention to their meaning, and this ought to give you a reliable indication as to where to place the stresses in the verse.

A. Henry V rallies his troops during the attack on Harfleur (*Henry V*, III. i).

> HENRY: Once more unto the breach, dear friends, once more,
> Or close the wall up with our English dead!
> In peace there's nothing so becomes a man
> As modest stillness and humility,
> But when the blast of war blows in our ears, 5
> Then imitate the action of the tiger,
> Stiffen the sinews, conjure up the blood,

Disguise fair nature with hard-favoured rage.
Then lend the eye a terrible aspect:
Let it pry through the portage of the head 10
Like the brass cannon; let the brow o'erwhelm it
As fearfully as doth a gallèd rock
O'erhang and jutty his confounded base,
Swilled with the wild and wasteful ocean.
Now set the teeth and stretch the nostril wide; 15
Hold hard the breath, and bend up every spirit
To his full height!

B. Leontes speaks of his wife's supposed adultery, whilst his son plays (*The Winter's Tale*, I.ii, 187–98).

Go play, boy, play: thy mother plays, and I
Play too—but so disgraced a part, whose issue
Will hiss me to my grave; contempt and clamour
Will be my knell. Go play, boy, play. There have been,
Or I am much deceived, cuckolds ere now, 5
And many a man there is, even at this present,
Now, while I speak this, holds his wife by th' arm,
That little thinks she has been sluiced in 's absence,
And his pond fished by his next neighbor, by
Sir Smile, his neighbour: nay, there's comfort in 't, 10
Whiles other men have gates, and those gates opened,
As mine, against their will.

C. Claudio contemplates death as he lies in prison (*Measure for Measure*, III.i, 117–31).

CLAUDIO: Ay, but to die, and go we know not where,
To lie in cold obstruction and to rot;
This sensible warm motion to become
A kneaded clod; and the delighted spirit
To bathe in fiery floods, or to reside 5
In thrilling region of thick-ribbèd ice;
To be imprisoned in the viewless winds,
And blown with restless violence round about
The pendent world; or to be worse than worst
Of those that lawless and incertain thought 10
Imagine howling—'tis too horrible!
The weariest and most loathèd worldly life
That age, ache, penury, and imprisonment
Can lay on nature is a paradise
To what we fear of death. 15

VERSE AND POETRY

Later, during the same discussion we have already referred to, Ian McKellen says that 'the verse is there to *help* the actors, and not for the audience to wallow in something vaguely poetic'. Clearly, attending a performance of a play is not like closely reading a poem, and even reading a verse play in the study or classroom is not the same as doing a piece of poetry practical criticism. But it is true, nonetheless, that many of Shakespeare's plays have been seen as 'dramatic poems' in which the full resources of poetry, not just the rhythm and stress of the iambic pentameter and its variations, are used. Shakespeare, in using iambic pentameter, uses the verse that usually lies the closest to the rhythms of everyday speech and we have seen how this can be dramatically very effective. These effects, however, are considerably enhanced by his use of those other elements that separate 'verse' from 'poetry', such as concentrated imagery and diction. Here, we must restrict our discussion to illustrating briefly how poetry can be inherently dramatic, by showing a mind at work. Even the most highly wrought poetic language which appears artificial can be dramatic. For instance, take this example from *Macbeth*; Macbeth has just heard of the death of his wife.

> Tomorrow, and tomorrow, and tomorrow,
> Creeps in this petty pace from day to day
> To the last syllable of recorded time;
> And all our yesterdays have lighted fools
> The way to dusty death. Out, out, brief candle! 5
> Life's but a walking shadow; a poor player,
> That struts and frets his hour upon the stage,
> And then is heard no more; it is a tale
> Told by an idiot, full of sound and fury,
> Signifying nothing. 10

Without, of course, a full knowledge of the play and the circumstances that have led up to Macbeth's making this speech, much of its impact will be lost, but even the briefest glance will show Shakespeare using poetry of the highest order to communicate Macbeth's feelings. The first two lines alone illustrate his variations on iambic pentameter—where in line 1 the rhythm seems to stagger, befitting Macbeth's weary despair and line 2 sees a reversed foot with the stress on 'creeps' at the very start of the line and the despairing scorn can be heard in the recurring 'Ps'. Shakespeare also makes full use of imagery, imagery connected with light and darkness (ll. 4–6), with the end of the world (ll. 3,5 & 10) and with acting (ll. 6–9), all of which serve to embody the psychological state of a world-weary man whose own self-deception during the course of the play has led him to lose the ability to distinguish between good and evil, illusion and reality. To Macbeth, in the context of time which endlessly repeats itself, all human life and ambition have come to seem meaningless.

Clearly, there is much, much more that could be said about this speech than we have space for, but even such a cursory piece of practical criticism should suffice to show Shakespeare using not verse, but poetry. If you would like to try a similar exercise, perhaps in more depth than this, we suggest you look at some of the following passages.

King Lear (II.iv, 266–89): 'O reason not the need . . . O Fool! I shall go mad'

Antony and Cleopatra (II.ii, 191–204): 'The barge she sat in . . . what they undid did'

Richard II (III.ii, 155–70): 'For God's sake . . . and farewell king!'

The Tempest (III.ii, 133–41): 'Be not afeard . . . I cried to dream again'

Hamlet (III.i, 60–8): 'To be or not to be . . . must give us pause.'

9

Character

Begin by jotting down your reaction to these two statements before you read on.

(i) A playwright's ability to create character is *the* most important single element that determines the success of a play.
(ii) What is required in a play is the portrayal not of types but of three-dimensional characters who seem to have a life of their own beyond the confines of the play.

We feel that both statements are in need of considerable qualification. Understandably, when we begin to consider a set play in class, a discussion of the characters and their inter-relationships may seem to be the most suitable starting point; perhaps when we have seen a play performed in the theatre, we are inclined first to think of how the different roles have been portrayed. Yet it is wrong to imagine that, as statement (i) suggests, character is virtually the 'be all and end all' of drama—as though a play were simply a gallery in which a number of highly detailed portraits were to be exhibited. Moreover, we need to remind ourselves that, while for the purposes of criticism we often single out elements such as 'character', 'plot', 'theme' and 'structure' as though they were clearly separable ingredients of the drama, such an approach is largely an abstract (though convenient) fiction. All these different aspects, and many others, are in fact integral to the whole design of a play and must be kept in a delicate balance. So, for instance, the development of character is constrained by the playwright's need to ensure that the length and weight of dialogue a character speaks bears on the play as a whole and does not deflect its steady, purposive advancement. It is only a novice in the craft who will totally suspend the action of a drama while one character 'reveals himself'. In so far as we can ever unscramble or quantify the part played by characterisation in the success of a play, we might risk the generalisation that any playwright who is interested solely in creating characters should probably be working in a different medium and that a play's quality is likely to depend more on the coherence of its structure than on its presentation of uniquely interesting characters. Characterisation is simply *one* item on the dramatist's agenda.

In relation to the second statement made above, it is certainly true that some great dramatists have created characters who strike us as possessing a complexity and a profundity of psychological depth—Shakespeare's Hamlet might be one such instance—which gives us the illusion that in some way they exist 'beyond the confines of the play'. But this is only an illusion, and it becomes a dangerous one if we insist on divorcing such characters from the dramatic world in which they truly have their being and treating them as though they were simply individual 'case studies' for psychological investigation. We must never forget that a character in a play grows out of a given (then changing) situation, is revealed through a whole range of interactions with other characters and exists only by means of a process of vital interdependence with the drama's plot, themes and structure.

We also need to remember that relatively few dramatic characters are ever intended to be fully 'rounded' or 'three-dimensional' creations. For instance, minor characters in a play may have a very limited function—perhaps to convey a message or to trigger the response of some other character. Moreover, particularly in comedy or in drama in which an intricate plot or a strong didactic or satirical element predominates, character will frequently be presented as a series of recognisably broad types of human behaviour in whom it would be a mistake to expect psychological depth. (Remember, for example, the boys in John Ebony's class—see page 44.) There is a long-established dramatic tradition in which a character is to be seen as the concentration or exaggeration of one single aspect or 'humour' of human nature, and to demonstrate that this approach to characterisation does not necessarily limit a playwright to a simple-minded view of his creations or rule out subtlety, we need only recommend the following short-list of reading: Ben Jonson's *Volpone* (1605–6), any English comedy of manners, such as Sheridan's *The Rivals* (1775) and Joe Orton's *Loot* (1966).

Whether the dramatist works in the assemblage of types of character in a complex pattern or is concerned to create fully rounded characters, he is in one sense to be seen as providing an actor with the blueprint for a performance. The portrayal of a character on stage depends on so much which is not actually in the text, or is only sketchily indicated in stage directions. An actor brings a character to life through the rhythms and accent of a particular voice—and a certain way of walking or a detail of costume may be central to the characterization. We have previously noted (see page 24) the way in which an actor of genius can work on what seems a relatively thin text to produce a virtuoso act of secondary creation. However, discussion of drama as an art can become very limited if we surrender to the personality cult of the great actor and never get beyond the level of 'Did you see *X*'s performance as Lear or *Y*'s Cleopatra?'. Our main task in a book of this nature must be to suggest the ways in which the dramatist encodes his conception of a character in the text, and it is to the methods of dramatic characterisation that we must now turn our attention.

METHODS OF CHARACTERISATION

At a primary level, character must be revealed in speech and in action. Character A, for instance, speaks like a brave man and acts heroically; while, in a slightly more complex fashion, Character B, says he is heroic and self-sacrificing, but his actions reveal him to be quite the opposite. For this process of character revelation to take place, characters have to be made to 'encounter each other', for as we have observed before, the playwright, unlike the novelist, cannot disclose to an audience the unspoken thoughts of a character—except through the devices of the aside or the soliloquy—nor can he add directly comments in his own person (except through stage directions which remain in practice for the actor's or reader's benefit only). What the characters say about each other will also often be a significant method of characterisation. For instance, the early scenes of Shakespeare's *Julius Caesar* emphasise the important fact that Brutus is widely regarded as 'noble'—a man of unimpeachable integrity—while in *Othello*, in a powerfully ironic way, the general (and entirely mistaken) view of Iago is that he is 'honest'. As we listen to the views that characters in a play express about each other, every comment must, of course, be evaluated in terms of an audience's appreciation of the strengths and limitations of a particular speaker's viewpoint. The reasons why judgements are at variance will usually be highly significant. In Shakespeare's *Antony and Cleopatra* a whole range of views of Antony's character is expressed. There are many contrasting moral perspectives. For example, to many Romans, Antony is a profligate who has been seduced by lust into deserting his public duty; but there is another aspect to the dialectic from which Antony may be seen as a hero of great personal magnetism who has found a transcending value in his love for Cleopatra—a view which is manifested not only through what other characters say about Antony, but also by means of the intensity of the poetic utterance that both Antony and Cleopatra can attain. For speech is a powerful indicator of character. A character is portrayed not only by what he or she says, but also by *how* it is said. And the creation of a distinctive 'voice' for a character is one of the main weapons in the dramatist's armoury.

Our own everyday experience will confirm the extent to which we relate the sound of a person's voice to our sense of what kind of person we are dealing with. We instantly recognise a friend's voice from its individual accent, mannerisms and rhythms, and the way in which a person relates just how he grew that splendid crop of tomatoes or won a recent game of tennis is an instant expression of his character. As one simple test of the power of a disembodied voice, ask yourself what is going through your mind the next time you hear somebody speak on the radio. As well as listening to the actual content, are you not also making certain assumptions, on the basis of the sound of the voice, about the speaker's background and character—and even perhaps imagining a face? As soon as we open our mouths to speak, we give away a lot of information about ourselves. The English, for instance, are often said to be peculiarly alert and sensitive when it comes to picking up the give-away signs of a speaker's social origins and educational background; but, more importantly, the tone of our voice is likely to suggest what we are feeling at a given moment and what attitude we are expressing—or perhaps trying to hide—towards the person we are addressing.

The fact that our voices are almost as strong a distinguishing feature as our fingerprints is something which the dramatist can turn to his own creative advantage. He can convey a sense of character by, quite literally, providing each individual in a play with his or her own unique voice—with its own immediately recognisable ranges of tone, its speech habits and its personal resonance. To see how this works, read the following scene from Rattigan's *The Winslow Boy* (1946). This is the first occasion in the play on which we meet these members of the Winslow family. Write down some notes on what we learn about their characters from (i) what they have to say, and (ii) the way in which they say it. In the second part of this question, concentrate particularly on the contrast between the voices of Arthur Winslow and his son, Dickie, and suggest what this contrast reveals about their respective characters.

Some notes of our own follow, together with an example of how these notes might be used to produce a brief essay on this topic.

The Winslow family returns from church on a Sunday morning. The scene is set in their drawing-room.

ARTHUR WINSLOW, RONNIE'S *father, is about sixty with a rather deliberately cultured patriarchal air. He is leaning heavily on a stick.*
GRACE, *his wife, is about ten years younger and has the faded remnants of prettiness.*
CATHERINE, *their daughter, is approaching thirty and has an air of masculinity about her which is at odd variance with her mother's intense femininity. She carries a handbag.* 5
DICKIE, *their elder son, is an Oxford undergraduate, large, noisy and cheerful.*

GRACE (*entering*): But he's so old, dear. From the back of the church you really can't hear a word he says. 10
ARTHUR: He's a good man, Grace.
GRACE: But what's the use of being good, if you're inaudible?
CATHERINE: A problem in ethics for you, Father. (*She puts her handbag on the table, takes up a book, sits and reads.*) . . . 15
DICKIE: I'm on Mother's side. The old boy's so doddery now he can hardly finish the course at all. I timed him to-day. It took him seventy-five seconds dead from a flying start to reach the pulpit, and then he needed the whip coming round the bend. I call that pretty bad going.
ARTHUR: I'm afraid I don't think that's very funny, Richard. 20
DICKIE: Oh, don't you, Father?
ARTHUR: Doddery though Mr Jackson may seem now, I very much doubt if, when he was at Oxford, he failed in his pass mods.

DICKIE (*aggrieved*): Dash it, Father—you promised not to mention that again this vac— 25

GRACE: You did, you know, Arthur.

ARTHUR: There was a condition to my promise—if you remember—that Dickie should provide me with reasonable evidence of his intentions to work.

DICKIE: Well, haven't I, Father? Didn't I stay in all last night—a Saturday night—and work? 30

ARTHUR: You stayed in, Dickie. I would be the last to deny that.

GRACE: You *were* making rather a noise, dear, with that old gramophone of yours. I really can't believe you could have been doing much work with that going on all the time. 35

DICKIE: Funnily enough, Mother, it helps me to concentrate.

ARTHUR: Concentrate on what?

DICKIE: Work, of course.

ARTHUR: That wasn't exactly what you appeared to be concentrating on when I came down to fetch a book—sleep, may I say, having been rendered out of the question, by the hideous sounds emanating from this room. 40

DICKIE: Edwina and her brother just looked in on their way to the Grahams' dance—they only stayed a minute.

GRACE: What an idiotic girl that is! Oh, sorry, Dickie—I was forgetting. You're rather keen on her, aren't you? 45

ARTHUR: You would have had ample proof of that fact, Grace, if you had seen them in the attitude in which I found them last night.

DICKIE: We were practising the Bunny Hug.

GRACE: The what, dear? 50

DICKIE: The Bunny Hug. It's the new dance.

CATHERINE (*helpfully*): It's like the Turkey Trot—only more dignified.

GRACE: Oh, I thought that was the tango.

DICKIE: No. More like a Fox Trot, really. Something between a Boston Glide and a Kangaroo Hop. 55

ARTHUR: We appear to be straying from the point. Whatever animal was responsible for the posture I found you in has little to do with the fact that to my certain knowledge that you have not yet done one single stroke of work so far this vacation.

DICKIE: Oh. Well, I do work awfully fast, you know—once I get down to it. 60

ARTHUR: Indeed? That assumption can hardly be based on experience, I take it.

DICKIE: Dash it, Father! You are laying in to me, this morning.

ARTHUR: I think it's time you found out, Dickie, that I'm not spending two hundred pounds a year keeping you at Oxford, merely that you may make a lot of useless friends and learn to dance the Bunny Hop. 65

DICKIE: Hug, Father.

ARTHUR: The exact description of the obscenity is immaterial.

(i) Typical 'respectable' upper middle-class family—of period around the beginning of this century? Conversation apparently inconsequential—but establishes each character's credentials. *Mr Winslow*: stern, dominant father—takes a dim view of Dickie's weak joke; turns his son's levity back on him. Though is he quite as forbidding as he seems? He stresses principle—in contrast to *Mrs Winslow* who seems more straightforwardly practical (see her view on the parson's audibility). Difference between husband and wife to be brought out later? *Catherine*: only given a couple of lines. Playfully punctures her father's tendency to pomposity. Then she retreats to her book. Why silent? Somewhat detached from rest of family—and their values? Obviously quite a clever young lady. *Dickie*: no books for him! Clearly life revolves around the latest dance crazes and horse-racing—while trying to keep his father's demands at bay.

(ii) *Mr Winslow*: Poised, almost pedantic manner of speech. Often bristles with formality—particularly when he wants to enforce criticism of his son—though there is an edge of irony. Habit of correcting loose language in others. Is he quite as cold as his punctilious speech suggests? *Dickie*: his light-headed chatter makes a clear contrast with his father's measured speech. Lots of slang of period. Suggests rather superficial young man—familiar type of undergraduate of period. *Mrs Winslow*: softer in tone and more placatory in manner than her husband—see her remarks to Dickie and her apology.

We have often suggested you adopt this kind of note-taking technique to record your initial impressions of a passage (or of one aspect of it) before turning them into a more polished piece of writing. As one example of this second stage, here is the way in which one writer used these notes to produce a short essay on Rattigan's introduction of the members of the Winslow family to an audience. It is worth underlining the importance of *close reference* and *quotation* when you are discussing the style and tone of language: this is necessary to give generalisation some concrete force.

Like any respectable family of the period just before the First World War, the Winslow family has just returned from Sunday morning church, and the members of the family are involved in what appears to be an inconsequential discussion of the sermon they have just heard. However, Rattigan uses this conversation to establish very economically the credentials of each character. With Mr Winslow, it is his sternest face we see first. He takes a dim view of Dickie's attempt to make a weak joke about the parson's 'doddery' performance and is inclined to stress the clergyman's inner qualities: 'He's a good man'. In contrast, his wife takes a more straightforwardly commonsensical view: 'But what's the use of being good, if you're inaudible?'. Already, in their first exchange over this very minor matter, we can see a difference in approach between husband and wife which is likely to be developed later in the play; but clearly it is Mr Winslow who is the dominant influence in the family. In the way he turns Dickie's levity back on him to remind his son of a promise to work hard after failing his exams at Oxford, he shows himself to be a demanding father who adopts a high moral tone on most matters and, where his children's future is concerned, expects them to take life seriously.

In the first part of this scene, Catherine has only one line which is probably intended to deflate what she judges to be her father's tendency to stiff high-mindedness. She is obviously not in awe of him, and on the issue of whether the parson can be both good and inaudible she says playfully, 'A problem in ethics for you, Father'. Then she retreats to her book. Catherine's relative silence and her apparent detachment from the rest of the family serve to arouse the interest of the audience in her. She is obviously quite a clever and independent young lady. Is she above all this small talk? Could it be that her outlook makes her stand slightly apart from the rest of the family? Or is she possibly preoccupied with some important event which she knows is in the offing?

Rattigan has already begun to sketch in some of his characters' essential qualities, and just as importantly he is creating a sense of the types of character we are being presented with by giving each one a recognisable 'voice' of his or her own. Consider, for instance, the contrast between the way in which father and son speak. Mr Winslow articulates in a poised, almost pedantic, manner. His sentences are carefully formulated and his speech is full of rather formal language—'Dickie should provide me with reasonable evidence of his intentions to work'. We also observe the little habit he has of seizing on what he considers to be loose or imprecise language in other speakers: he picks up Dickie's slang word 'doddery' and, in the punctilious tone of a man who holds the offending term wriggling between forceps, he witheringly reminds his son of his own limitations. Yet there are suggestions of a certain playfulness and irony behind Mr Winslow's patriarchal manner, as though he is adopting the tone he thinks appropriate for his son's best good and using the distancing formality of his language with some awareness that he is slotting into a familiar paternal role. It is likely that he is not quite such a cold, forbidding man as he may appear. Yet what a contrast his 'voice' makes with his son's light-headed chatter. Dickie's speech lacks any sense of premeditation and it is full of the upper-class slang of the period—'Dash it, Father! You are laying in to me, this morning'—which marks him out as the familiar figure of the drone-like Edwardian undergraduate. References to the latest fashionable dances and to horse-racing are never far from his lips and illustrate his rather superficial range of interests. He is a lively and likeable enough young man, but just his sister's relatively few words serve to emphasise, by comparison, his shallowness. There is also something of a contrast between Mr Winslow's rather harsh words to Dickie and his wife's softer tone and more placatory manner: 'You *were* making rather a noise, dear, with that old gramophone of yours' she says, and she is quick to apologise to Dickie after she has inadvertently criticised one of his girlfriends.

READING THE SUBTEXT

The members of an audience will constantly be asking themselves what the words and tone of the speeches they hear indicate about the characters they see moving across the stage. When we are reading a play we face the much harder task of imagining the tone which we feel would match the speaker's response to a particular situation. Very often what is not said—witness Catherine's relative taciturnity in the scene we have just been examining—or what is implied can be just as important as what is stated explicitly, because we know that people frequently suggest their deeper feelings—or try to suppress them—even as they are engaged in discussing some apparently trivial matter. For instance, a man says to his wife: 'There is no food in the fridge'. These words could simply be an objective statement of fact, or they might be spoken in the tone of someone extremely angry at this lack or resigned to what may be an habitual state of affairs. Perhaps the man is really implying something along these lines: 'I consider a wife's role is to cater for her husband's every need. You don't care about me any more—you can't even be bothered to do the shopping'. A whole range of other interpretations is possible. (Think of some of them for yourself.)

When meaning is communicated in this 'latent' way in a play, through some implicit or suggested statement, we often call this the 'subtext'. The subtext is that part of human communication which, like most of an iceberg, is hidden beneath the surface. In a poetic drama, the subtext may be present in networks of imagery; in an Ibsen play such as *The Wild Duck* (1884) it is often through symbolism that the buried realities of a character's situation and identity are uncovered. Of course, aspects of the subtext in drama can also be communicated by non-verbal means—through a gesture, a moment of silence, a detail of costume and many other theatrical devices. Reading the subtext, because it concerns the revelation of deeper realities than the merely superficial or strictly objective, may lead us into areas of ambiguity. You will remember that there was a whole range of possible ways of interpreting just what the man meant when he said to his wife 'There is no food in the fridge'. So, how are we to know which subtext is the relevant one? Obviously the key here is our understanding of the particular context and our general interpretation of the whole play which would include our appreciation of the nature of the relationship between this man and his wife. Even so, though a reading of the subtext must take place within these defined limits, there will often be a rich variety of acceptable readings of a line of dialogue, and an understanding of this is one of the pleasures of dramatic criticism to which we will return in our chapter on 'Interpretation'.

As a fairly straightforward exercise to consolidate some of the general points we have made so far, we want you to look carefully at a scene from Robert Bolt's *A Man for All Seasons* (1960). The questions which follow are designed to provide some practice in 'reading a subtext' and in distinguishing between explicit and implicit meaning.

Sir Thomas More, who was Henry VIII's Lord Chancellor, has been imprisoned in the Tower of London for refusing to swear an oath which would ratify the divorce the King wished to effect from Queen Catherine and recognise the King's position as Supreme Head of the Church of England.

In this scene Sir Thomas receives a visit from his wife (Alice), daughter (Margaret) and son-in-law (Will Roper).

JAILER: Wake up, Sir Thomas! Your family's here!
MORE (*starting up. A great cry*): Margaret! What's this? You can visit me? (*Thrusts arms through cage.*) Meg. Meg. (*She goes to him. Then horrified.*) For God's sake, Meg, they've not put *you* in here?
JAILER (*reassuring*): No-o-o, sir. Just a visit; a short one. 5
MORE (*excited*): Jailer, jailer, let me out of this.
JAILER (*stolid*): Yes, sir. I'm allowed to let you out.
MORE: Thank you. (*Goes to door of cage, gabbling while* JAILER *unlocks it.*) Thank you, thank you. (*Comes out. He and she regard each other; then she drops into a curtsey.*) 10
MARGARET: Good morning, Father.
MORE (*ecstatic, wraps her to him*): Oh, good morning—Good morning. (*Enter* ALICE, *supported by* WILL. *She, like* MORE, *has aged and is poorly dressed.*) Good morning, Alice. Good morning, Will.
ROPER *is staring at the rack in horror.* ALICE *approaches* MORE *and peers at him technically.* 15
ALICE (*almost accusatory*):Husband, how do you do?
MORE (*smiling over* MARGARET): As well as need be, Alice. Very happy now. Will?
ROPER: This is an awful place! 20
MORE: Except it's keeping me from you, my dears, it's not so bad. Remarkably like any other place.
ALICE (*looks up critically*): It drips!
MORE: Yes. Too near the river. (ALICE *goes apart and sits, her face bitter.*)
MARGARET (*disengages from him, takes basket from her mother*): We've brought you some things. (*Shows him. There is constraint between them.*) Some cheese. . . . 25
MORE: Cheese.
MARGARET: And a custard. . . .
MORE: A custard! 30
MARGARET: And, these other things. . . . (*She doesn't look at him.*)
ROPER: And a bottle of wine. (*Offering it.*)
MORE: Oh. (*Mischievous.*) Is it good, son Roper?
ROPER: I don't know, sir.
MORE (*looks at them, puzzled*): Well. 35
ROPER: Sir, come out! Swear to the Act! Take the oath and come out!
MORE: Is this why they let you come?
ROPER: Yes. . . Meg's under oath to persuade you.
MORE (*coldly*): That was silly, Meg. How did you come to do that?
MARGARET: I wanted to! 40
MORE: You want me to swear to the Act of Succession?
MARGARET: 'God more regards the thoughts of the heart than the words of the mouth' or so you've always told me.

MORE: Yes.

MARGARET: Then say the words of the oath and in your heart think otherwise. 45

MORE: What is an oath then but words we say to God?

MARGARET: That's very neat.

MORE: Do you mean it isn't true?

MARGARET: No, it's true. 50

MORE: Then it's a poor argument to call it 'neat', Meg. When a man takes an oath, Meg, he's holding his own self in his own hands. Like water (*cups hands*) and if he opens his fingers *then*—he needn't hope to find himself again. Some men aren't capable of this, but I'd be loathe to think your father one of them. 55

MARGARET: So should I. . . .

MORE: Then—

MARGARET: There's something else I've been thinking.

MORE: Oh, Meg!

MARGARET: In any state that was half good, you would be raised up high, not here, for what you've done already. 60

MORE: All right.

MARGARET: It's not your fault the State's three-quarters bad.

MORE: No.

MARGARET: Then if you elect to suffer for it, you elect yourself a hero. 65

MORE: That's very neat. But look now . . . if we lived in a State where virtue was profitable, common sense would make us good, and greed would make us saintly. And we'd live like animals or angels in the happy land that *needs* no heroes. But since in fact we see that avarice, anger, envy, pride, sloth, lust and stupidity commonly profit far beyond humility, chastity, fortitude, justice and thought, and have to choose, to be human at all . . . why then perhaps we *must* stand fast a little—even at the risk of being heroes. 70

MARGARET (*emotional*): But in reason! Haven't you done as much as God can reasonably *want*? 75

MORE: Well . . . finally . . . it isn't a matter of reason; finally it's a matter of love.

ALICE (*hostile*): You're content then, to be shut up here with mice and rats when you might be home with us!

MORE (*flinching*): Content? If they'd open a crack that wide (*between finger and thumb*) I'd be through it. (*To* MARGARET.) 80
Well, has Eve run out of apples?

MARGARET: I've not yet told you what the house is like, without you.

MORE: Don't, Meg.

MARGARET: What we do in the evenings, now that you're not there. 85

MORE: Meg, have done!

MARGARET: We sit in the dark because we've no candles. And we've no talk because we're wondering what they're doing to you here.

MORE: The King's more merciful than you. He doesn't use the rack.

Enter JAILER. 90

JAILER: Two minutes to go, sir. I thought you'd like to know.

MORE: Two minutes!

JAILER: Till seven o'clock, sir. Sorry. Two minutes.

Exit JAILER.

(i) Why is Alice's greeting to her husband 'almost accusatory' (l. 17) and what is the significance of her silence throughout much of this scene?
(ii) What is the reason why More says of the prison: 'it's not so bad. Remarkably like any other place' (l. 21)?
(iii) What is the atmosphere like while Margaret is showing her father the food the family has brought him (ll. 25–35)? Consider the following points in your answer:
(a) Why does Margaret not look at her father?
(b) What is More probably thinking at this point?
(c) Do the stage directions offer any interpretative help?
(iv) At what stage in the scene does the real reason for the visit become apparent, and how does this affect More's mood?
(v) 'The meaning of the second half the extract is nearly all presented in *explicit* terms.' Do you agree? Why (or why not) is this so?
(vi) Drawing on some of the points in your earlier answers, summarise the changing emotions that are apparent in More as the scene unfolds.

General questions

(vii) 'As in real life we generally make a spontaneous reaction to the people we meet, without any thought of conscious analysis, so it is with drama: we either find a character sympathetic and interesting—or we do not. There is, therefore, little point in painstaking analysis.' Do you agree? Why (not)?
(viii) How much help do you think a dramatist should give the reader/performer in his stage directions concerning the tone in which a line is to be spoken or the motive that lies behind some words or a piece of action? Do you welcome fairly exact and detailed directions, or do you feel the playwright should trust the reader/performer to interpret the lines? And must a dramatist's stage directions *always* be observed to the letter? (You might find it illuminating to compare the nature of the stage directions given in a play by Shakespeare with those which a playwright such as George Bernard Shaw was in the habit of including in his text. Have you come across any dramatists who present their texts in a fashion which suggests that they intend their work to be *read*, almost as the reader might approach a novel, as well as performed?)

10

Tone: levels of formality and intimacy

It should be clear, from what we have said already, that when we are thinking about the ways in which character and feeling are expressed in a play, a crucial element is the appreciation of the *tone* (or the possible range of different tones) of the lines. Once we have established some idea of the likely tone a character would adopt in a given situation, we are well on the way to producing an interpretation of what he or she is feeling—though the order in which we make these judgements is rather like the old problem of what comes first, the chicken or the egg. The extent to which a playwright should help us in this 'testing for tone' is a question we left you to decide for yourself at the end of the last chapter. What needs to be emphasised at this stage is that the tone of the dialogue spoken by a character is *the* responsive indicator of the pressure of the character's immediate feelings; tone also embodies the speaker's attitude towards and relationship with the person he or she addresses. The means by which tone is produced—by a whole variety of linguistic elements such as the level of diction (choice of words) and the rhythms of a sentence or phrase—and the methods by which it is to be analysed in detail, are questions largely beyond the scope of this book.

However, in the context of a study of dramatic literature, it will help us to pin down the crucial importance of tone if we consider the extent to which our everyday speech is influenced by two important factors—the levels of (i) intimacy, and (ii) status that we believe we share (or do not share) with the person we are speaking to. As a starting point, consider these two examples of invitations to an evening drink at a pub. In each case, what is likely to be the relationship between the speakers?

(a) Do you fancy popping down to the Arden Arms later on for a quick one?
(b) If you're free . . . I mean if you've not got any previous engagement, do you think you might possibly be able to come out with me this evening for a drink?

The language used in each request is a gauge of the kind of relationship the speaker believes he has with his interlocutor. While the first speech is obviously spoken by one friend to another—it has the ring of chatty intimacy—the second invitation, with its slightly greater formality and the hesitating rhythm at the outset, would most probably be addressed to somebody (perhaps of the opposite sex) whom the speaker does not know well—but would like to know better. Our own experience will tell us that, for instance, the way we would speak to a close friend differs greatly from the way, on the one hand, we would address somebody we regarded (in a particular situation) as our 'superior'—say, the headmaster of a school—or, on the other hand, the manner in which we would engage a young child in conversation. You could easily prove how the factors of 'perceived intimacy and relative status' affect our everyday language in different social contexts by simulating the following situations and improvising appropriate dialogue which might grow out of these encounters:

(a) You are in conversation with a close friend on the topic of the kind of career you would like to follow in the future.
(b) You are being interviewed by a potential employer for a job you really want.
(c) Having just graduated from university you return to your former school or college to address some pupils who are just about to embark on the same 'A' level course you yourself followed some years earlier.

Almost unconsciously we learn the appropriate 'registers' for speaking to a particular individual in a given situation, and it is perhaps only when we have to speak a foreign language abroad that we discover the problems of switching to usages which seem alien to us—for instance, in French, when are we to use *tu* and when *vous*?—because they are the product of another culture, the language of which embodies slightly different customs and values.

The way in which particular kinds of language are generally deemed to be appropriate to certain situations is a complex study for students of socio-linguistics, and we only have space here to define sketchily some of its basic principles. There are, of course, many other factors which influence the kind of language we use when we engage in conversation—factors such as the age, sex and number of those involved. The *setting* will also provide a frame to discourse: for example, the kind of cross-examination which belongs to the world of the courtroom (see pages 56 and 60) or a lesson in a classroom (see pages 5 and 44) will each tend to trigger certain characteristic rhythms and speech habits—as will be the case with a conversation at the bar of the Arden Arms or one which takes place over the telephone. We need to take into account, too, the *function* of any kind of discourse. Do the participants wish, for example, to communicate certain information or facts? Do they set out to express their own feelings or to change those of the people they are addressing, perhaps by persuading them to a particular point of view? Is it the aim of the speaker(s) to create a sense of sociability—to win friends and to influence people? Or is a combination of these intentions (and many others) simultaneously involved?

In the study of the language of social interaction, there can be no 'hard and fast' rules because, of course, we can never predict the extent to which a particular individual is going to correspond to the conventional expectations of behaviour in a given situation—how tedious if we could make such binding predictions!—and the way in which individuals adapt their language and conduct is inevitably connected with their own way of perceiving 'social reality': two individuals, for instance, may not agree on their relative standing—in terms, perhaps, of social class or their power to dominate the situation—or one person may presume on a level of intimacy which another fails to acknowledge. Interesting and varied linguistic encounters will result! It should also be noted that the conventions which influence the way people communicate differ greatly from one time or place to the another: it is likely, for example, that few modern fathers would address their recalcitrant sons with the formality of a Mr Winslow (see page 119). Moreover, in modern society the roles we adopt are perhaps peculiarly fluid; and, as has always been the case, the roles we play are coloured by our particular prejudices and values. So, when one motorist is stopped by a policeman for speeding, he may acknowledge with cringing servility (for genuine or for tactical reasons) the dominance of this 'authority figure', while another man in exactly the same position, who perhaps regards the police as rotten and corrupt, will go out of his way to avoid using any expression which might be interpreted as being deferential. Looking at the roles people play is a complex business, but it can be useful to bear in mind what we might define as 'norms of behaviour'—the conventional expectations of how most people would react in a given situation—which we may use as touchstones to enable us to measure the departures from and adaptations of these anticipated 'norms' that we practise. If we carry over some of these insights to our study of drama, we shall find that it is often helpful to examine the actions and speech of characters in a play as an indicator of their (often changing) perception of their relative intimacy and status. With this approach in mind, we should be equipped to analyse what characters feel about themselves and about each other; we should be in a position to interpret the tone which signals, for instance, 'I know you are in some ways in power over me, but I want to get to know you better' or the subtext which is to be read as 'Keep your distance!'.

In the case of the following extract, taken from J. M. Barrie's *The Admirable Crichton* (1902), the questions are designed to focus your attention on the language the characters use and the way in which it reflects their perception of the relationships they share with each other.

The members of an aristocratic family have been shipwrecked on a desert island. Ernest is reading to the three ladies who, as they listen, keep one apprehensive eye on the unpleasant things that are liable to fall from the trees above them. Occasionally Crichton and Treherne come momentarily into sight; they are hacking and hewing the bamboo from which they are building a hut.

ERNEST (*who has written on the fly-leaf of the only book saved from the wreck*): This is what I have written. 'Wrecked, wrecked, wrecked! on an island in the Tropics, the following: the Hon. Ernest Woolley, the Rev. John Treherne, the Ladies, Mary, Catherine, and Agatha Lasenby, with two servants. We are the sole survivors of Lord Loam's steam yacht *Bluebell*, which encountered a fearful gale in these seas, and soon became a total wreck. The crew behaved gallantly, putting us all into the first boat. What became of them I cannot tell, but we, after dreadful sufferings, and insufficiently clad, in whatever garments we could lay hold of in the dark'— 5 10

LADY MARY:Please don't describe our garments.

ERNEST:—'succeeded in reaching this island, with the loss of only one of our party, namely, Lord Loam, who flung away his life in a gallant attempt to save a servant who had fallen overboard.'

(*The ladies have wept long and sore for their father, but there is something in this last utterance that makes them look up.*) 15

AGATHA: But, Ernest, it was Crichton who jumped overboard trying to save father.

ERNEST (*with the candour that is one of his most engaging qualities*): Well, you know, it was rather silly of uncle to fling away his life by trying to get into the boat first; and as this document may be printed in the English papers, it struck me, an English peer, you know— 20

LADY MARY (*every inch an English peer's daughter*): Ernest, that is very thoughtful of you.

ERNEST (*continuing, well pleased*):—'By night the cries of wild cats and the hissing of snakes terrify us extremely'—(*This does not satisfy him so well, and he makes a corrrection*)— 'terrify the ladies extremely. Against these we have no weapons except one cutlass and a hatchet. A bucket washed ashore is at present our only comfortable seat'— 25

LADY MARY (*with some spirit*): And Ernest is sitting on it. 30

ERNEST: H'sh! Oh, do be quiet. —'To add to our horrors, night falls suddenly in these parts, and it is then that savage animals begin to prowl and roar.'

LADY MARY: Have you said that vampire bats suck the blood from our toes as we sleep? 35

ERNEST: No, that's all. I end up, 'Rescue us or we perish. Rich reward. Signed Ernest Woolley, in command of our little party.' This is written on a leaf taken out of a book of poems that Crichton found in his pocket. Fancy Crichton being a reader of poetry! Now I shall put it into the bottle and fling it into the sea. 40

(*He pushes the precious document into a soda-water bottle, and rams the cork home. At the same moment, and without effort, he gives birth to one of his most characteristic epigrams.*)

The tide is going out, we mustn't miss the post.

(*They are so unhappy that they fail to grasp it, and a little petulantly he* 45 *calls for* CRICHTON, *ever his stand-by in the hour of epigram.* CRICHTON *breaks through the undergrowth quickly, thinking the ladies are in danger.*)

CRICHTON: Anything wrong, sir?

ERNEST (*with fine confidence*): The tide, Crichton, is a postman who calls at our island twice a day for letters. 50

CRICHTON (*after a pause*): Thank you, sir.

(*He returns to his labours, however, without giving the smile which is the epigrammatist's right, and* ERNEST *is a little disappointed in him.*)

ERNEST: Poor Crichton! I sometimes think he is losing his sense of humour. Come along, Agatha. 55

(*He helps his favourite up the rocks, and they disappear gingerly from view.*)

CATHERINE: How horribly still it is.

LADY MARY (*remembering some recent sounds*): It is best when it is still.

CATHERINE (*drawing closer to her*): Mary, I have heard that they are always very still just before they jump. 60

LADY MARY: Don't. (*A distinct chopping is heard, and they are startled.*)

LADY MARY (*controlling herself*): It is only Crichton knocking down trees.

CATHERINE (*almost imploringly*): Mary, let us go and stand beside him.

LADY MARY (*coldly*): Let a servant see that I am afraid! 65

CATHERINE: Don't, then; but remember this, dear, they often drop on one from above.

(*She moves away, nearer to the friendly sound of the axe, and* LADY MARY *is left alone. She is the most courageous of them as well as the haughtiest, but when something she had thought to be a stick glides toward her, she forgets her dignity and screams.*) 70

LADY MARY (*calling*): Crichton, Crichton!

(*It must have been* TREHERNE *who was tree-felling, for* CRICHTON *comes to her from the hut, drawing his cutlass.*)

CRICHTON (*anxious*): Did you call, my lady? 75

LADY MARY (*herself again, now that he is there*): I! Why should I?

CRICHTON: I made a mistake, your ladyship. (*Hesitating*) If you are afraid of being alone, my lady—

LADY MARY: Afraid! Certainly not. (*Doggedly*) You may go.

(*But she does not complain when he remains within eyesight cutting the bamboo. It is heavy work, and she watches him silently.*) 80

LADY MARY: I wish, Crichton, you could work without getting so hot.

CRICHTON (*mopping his face*): I wish I could, my lady.

(*He continues his labours.*)

LADY MARY (*taking off her oilskins*): It makes me hot to look at you. 85

CRICHTON: It almost makes me cool to look at your ladyship.

LADY MARY (*who perhaps thinks he is presuming*): Anything I can do for you in that way, Crichton, I shall do with pleasure.

CRICHTON (*quite humbly*): Thank you, my lady.

(*By this time most of the bamboo has been cut, and the shore and sea are visible, except where they are hidden by the half completed hut. The mast rising solitary from the water adds to the desolation of the scene, and at last tears run down* LADY MARY'*s face.*) 90

CRICHTON: Don't give way, my lady, things might be worse.

LADY MARY: My poor father! 95

CRICHTON: If I could have given my life for his—

LADY MARY: You did all a man could do. Indeed I thank you, Crichton. (*With some admiration and more wonder*) You are a man.

CRICHTON: Thank you, my lady.

LADY MARY: But it is all so awful. Crichton, is there any hope of a ship coming? 100

CRICHTON (*after hesitation*): Of course there is, my lady.

LADY MARY (*facing him bravely*): Don't treat me as a child. I have got to know the worst, and to face it. Crichton, the truth.

CRICHTON (*reluctantly*): We were driven out of our course, my lady; I fear far from the track of commerce. 105

LADY MARY: Thank you; I understand.

(*For a moment, however, she breaks down. Then she clenches her hands and stands erect.*)

CRICHTON (*watching her, and forgetting perhaps for the moment that they are not just a man and woman*): You're a good plucky 'un, my lady. 110

LADY MARY (*falling into the same error*): I shall try to be. (*Extricating herself.*) Crichton, you presume!

CRICHTON: I beg your ladyship's pardon; but you are.

(*She smiles, as if it were a comfort to be told this even by* CRICHTON.) 115

And until a ship comes we are three men who are going to do our best for you ladies.

LADY MARY (*with a curl of the lip*): Mr Ernest does no work.

CRICHTON (*cheerily*): But he will, my lady.

LADY MARY: I doubt it. 120

CRICHTON (*confidently, but perhaps thoughtlessly*): No work—no dinner—will make a great change in Mr Ernest.

LADY MARY: No work—no dinner. When did you invent that rule, Crichton?

CRICHTON (*loaded with bamboo*): I didn't invent it, my lady. I seem to see it growing all over the island. 125

LADY MARY (*disquieted*): Crichton, your manner strikes me as curious.

CRICHTON (*pained*): I hope not, your ladyship.

LADY MARY (*determined to have it out with him*): You are not implying anything so unnatural, I hope, as that if I and my sisters don't work there will be no dinner for *us*? 130

CRICHTON (*brightly*): If it is unnatural, my lady, that is the end of it.

LADY MARY: If? Now I understand. The perfect servant at home holds that we are all equal now. I see.

CRICHTON (*wounded to the quick*): My lady, can you think me so inconsistent? 135

LADY MARY: That is it.

CRICHTON (*earnestly*): My lady, I disbelieved in equality at home because it was against nature, and for that same reason I as utterly disbelieve in it on an island. 140

LADY MARY (*relieved by his obvious sincerity*): I apologise.

CRICHTON (*continuing unfortunately*): There must always, my lady, be one to command and others to obey.

LADY MARY (*satisfied*): One to command, others to obey. Yes. (*Then suddenly she realises that there may be a dire meaning in his confident words.*) Crichton! 145

CRICHTON (*who has intended no dire meaning*): What is it, my lady?
(*But she only stares into his face and then hurries from him. Left alone he is puzzled, but being a practical man he busies himself gathering firewood.*)

(i) What impressions do you form of Ernest, both from the nature of the letter he writes and the way in which he speaks?

(ii) From the way in which Ernest, Lady Mary and Agatha talk to each other, what indicates that
 (a) they belong to the same class and
 (b) share both a degree of intimacy and certain social values?
 (c) What is suggested about the way in which they perceive the different roles of men and women?

(iii) In the conversation between Lady Mary and Crichton in the second half of the extract, select and comment on *three* occasions when an exchange between them is obviously conditioned by their sense of the class divisions of mistress and servant which separate them.

(iv) Select and comment on *three* examples which show that an increasing familiarity is becoming temporarily apparent in the way Lady Mary and Crichton address one another.

(v) (a) What factors are tending to produce the developments you have noted in your previous answer?
 (b) How would you account for the rather contradictory attitude of Lady Mary towards Crichton?

(vi) Crichton defines his position on 'equality' towards the end of this scene (see ll. 121–43). Basing your answer on the last part of the extract, suggest in what way you think the playwright is likely to develop this idea in the rest of the play.

General Question

(vii) 'Because the play is obviously based on a now outmoded view of the old English class system, it will seem largely irrelevant to a modern audience.' Do you agree? Why (or why not)?

The next passage also concerns the relationship between a mistress and a servant, and it provides a fascinating study of the way in which the language of dialogue signals both a constant 'power struggle'—a veritable battle of the sexes—and an oscillating movement towards greater intimacy. You will see that this dialogue contains a continuously engrossing subtext, for beneath the conversation run the driving imperatives of sexual passion.

If you are working as a member of a class, split up into pairs and prepare a reading of this extract, *paying particular attention to what the lines suggest each character is feeling from one moment to the next.* Then jot down notes which record what you have discovered. Finally, you should compare your findings and judge the extent to which you can agree on a common interpretation with the other members of the class.

To give you some idea of the kind of notes you might aim at, we provide you with our reading of the first section of the scene. You are, of course, entirely at liberty to disregard our notes. The extract is taken from Strindberg's *Miss Julie* (1888).

In the absence of her father, the Count, Miss Julie is caught up in the revelry of the celebrations for Midsummer's Eve. After she has danced with Jean, her father's valet, she tells him to change out of his servant's uniform. The other character present during the first part of this scene which takes place in a large kitchen of the Count's house is Christine, a cook with whom Jean has an 'unofficial engagement'.

JEAN *enters in black tails and a black bowler hat.*
MISS JULIE: *Très gentil, monsieur Jean! Très gentil!*
JEAN: *Vous voulez plaisanter, madame!*
MISS JULIE: *Et vous voulez parler francais!* Where did you learn that?
JEAN: In Switzerland. I was wine waiter at the biggest hotel in Lucerne. 5
MISS JULIE: You look quite the gentleman in those tails. *Charmant!* [*Sits at the table.*]
JEAN: Oh, you're flattering me.
MISS JULIE: [*haughtily*]: Flattering *you*?
JEAN: My natural modesty forbids me to suppose that you would pay so high a compliment to one as humble as myself, so I assumed you were exaggerating, for which I believe the polite word is flattering. 10
MISS JULIE: Where did you learn to talk like that? You must have spent a lot of your time at the theatre.
JEAN: Yes. And I've been around a bit, too. 15
MISS JULIE: But you were born here, weren't you?
JEAN: My father worked on the next farm to yours. I used to see you when I was a child, though you wouldn't remember me.
MISS JULIE: No, really?
JEAN: Yes. I remember one time especially—no, I oughtn't to mention that. 20
MISS JULIE: Oh, yes! Tell me. Come on! Just this once.
JEAN: No, I really couldn't now. Some other time, perhaps.
MISS JULIE: Some other time means never. Is it so dangerous to tell it now?
JEAN: It isn't dangerous, but I'd rather not. Look at her!
[*Indicates* CHRISTINE, *who has fallen asleep in a chair by the stove.*] 25
MISS JULIE: A charming wife she'll make. Does she snore too?
JEAN: She doesn't do that, but she talks in her sleep.
MISS JULIE [*cynically*]: How do you know?
JEAN [*coolly*]: I've heard her.
Pause. They look at each other. 30
MISS JULIE: Why don't you sit?
JEAN: I wouldn't permit myself to do that in your presence.
MISS JULIE: But if I order you to?
JEAN: Then I shall obey.
MISS JULIE: Sit, then. No, wait. Can you give me something to drink first? 35
JEAN: I don't know what we have in the ice-box. Only beer, I think.
MISS JULIE: What do you mean, only beer? My taste is very simple. I prefer it to wine.

JEAN *takes a bottle of beer from the ice-box, opens it, gets a glass and plate from the cupboard and serves her.* 40

MISS JULIE: Thank you. Won't you have something yourself?

JEAN: I'm not much of a drinker, but if madam orders me—

MISS JULIE: Orders? Surely you know that a gentleman should never allow a lady to drink alone.

JEAN: That's perfectly true. [*Opens another bottle and pours a glass.*] 45

MISS JULIE: Drink my health, now! [JEAN *hesitates.*] Are you shy?

JEAN [*kneels in a parody of a romantic attitude, and raises his glass*]: To my mistress's health!

MISS JULIE: Bravo! Now kiss my shoe, and ceremony is complete.

JEAN *hesitates, then boldly takes her foot in his hands and kisses it lightly.* 50

MISS JULIE: Excellent. You ought to have been an actor.

JEAN: [*gets up*]: We mustn't go on like this, Miss Julie. Someone might come in and see us.

MISS JULIE: What then?

JEAN: People would talk, that's all. And if you knew how their tongues 55 were wagging up there just now—

MISS JULIE: What kind of thing were they saying? Tell me. Sit down.

JEAN [*sits*]: I don't want to hurt you, but they were using expressions which—which hinted that—well, you can guess! You aren't a child, and when people see a lady drinking alone with a man—let alone a servant— 60 at night—then—

MISS JULIE: Then what? Anyway, we're not alone. Christine is here.

JEAN: Asleep.

MISS JULIE: Then I shall wake her. [*Gets up.*] Christine! Are you asleep?

CHRISTINE *mumbles to herself in her sleep.* 65

MISS JULIE: Christine! My God, she is asleep!

CHRISTINE [*in her sleep*]: Are his lordship's boots brushed? Put on the coffee. Quickly, quickly, quickly! [*Laughs, then grunts.*]

MISS JULIE [*takes her by the nose*]: Will you wake up?

JEAN: [*sharply*]: Leave her alone! 70

MISS JULIE [*haughtily*]: What!

JEAN: People who stand at a stove all day get tired when night comes. And sleep is something to be respected—

MISS JULIE: A gallant thought, and one that does you honour. [*Holds out her hand to* JEAN.] Come outside now, and pick some lilac for me. 75

During the following dialogue, CHRISTINE *wakes and wanders drowsily right to go to bed.*

JEAN: With you?

MISS JULIE: With me.

JEAN: Impossible. I couldn't. 80

MISS JULIE: I don't understand. Surely you don't imagine—?

JEAN: I don't, but other people might.

MISS JULIE: What? That I should have an *amour* with a servant?

JEAN: I'm not being conceited, but such things have happened—and to these people, nothing is sacred. 85

MISS JULIE: Quite the little aristocrat, aren't you?

JEAN: Yes, I am.

MISS JULIE: If choose to step down—

JEAN: Don't step down, Miss Julie, take my advice. No one will believe you did it freely. People will always say you fell— 90

MISS JULIE: I have a higher opinion of people than you. Come and see! Come!

She fixes him with her eyes.

JEAN: You know, you're strange.

MISS JULIE: Perhaps. But so are you. Everything is strange. . . . Come, now! Just into the park! 95

She offers him her arm, and they go.

JEAN: We must sleep with nine midsummer flowers under our pillow tonight, Miss Julie, and our dreams will come true!

They turn in the doorway. JEAN *puts a hand to one of his eyes.* 100

MISS JULIE: Have you something in your eye?

JEAN: It's nothing. Only a speck of dust. It'll be all right.

MISS JULIE: My sleeve must have brushed it. Sit down and I'll take it out. [*Takes him by the arm, makes him sit, takes his head and pushes it backwards, and tries to remove the dust with the corner of her handkerchief.*] Sit still now, quite still! [*Slaps his hands.*] Come, obey me! I believe you're trembling, you great, strong lout! [*Feels his biceps.*] What muscles you have! 105

JEAN [*warningly*]: Miss Julie!

MISS JULIE: Yes, monsieur Jean? 110

JEAN: *Attention! Je ne suis qu'un homme!*

MISS JULIE: Sit still, will you! There! Now it's gone. Kiss my hand and thank me.

JEAN [*gets up*]: Miss Julie, listen to me. Christine's gone to bed now—will you listen to me! 115

MISS JULIE: Kiss my hand first.

JEAN: Listen to me!

MISS JULIE: Kiss my hand first.

JEAN: All right. But you've only yourself to blame.

MISS JULIE: For what? 120

JEAN: For what? Are you a child? You're twenty-five. Don't you know it's dangerous to play with fire?

MISS JULIE: Not for me. I am insured.

JEAN [*boldly*]: No, you're not. And if you are, there's inflammable material around that isn't. 125

MISS JULIE: Meaning you?

JEAN: Yes. Not because I'm me, but because I'm a young man—

MISS JULIE: Of handsome appearance! What incredible conceit! A Don Juan, perhaps? Or a Joseph! Yes, upon my word, I do believe you're a Joseph! 130

JEAN: Do you?

MISS JULIE: I almost fear it.

JEAN *moves boldly forward and tries to take her round the waist to kiss her.*

MISS JULIE [*slaps him*]: Stop it!

JEAN: Are you joking or serious? 135

MISS JULIE: Serious.

JEAN: Then you were being serious just now too. You play games too seriously, and that's dangerous. Well, now I'm tired of this game and with your permission I'll get back to my work. His lordship's boots must be ready in time, and it's long past midnight. 140

MISS JULIE: Forget the boots.

JEAN: No. They're part of my job, which doesn't include being your playmate. And never will. I flatter myself I'm above that.

MISS JULIE: Aren't we proud!

JEAN: In some respects. In others, not. 145

MISS JULIE: Have you ever been in love?

JEAN: We don't use that word. But I've been fond of a lot of girls, and once I was sick because I couldn't get the one I wanted. Yes, sick, do you hear, like those princes in the Arabian Nights, who couldn't eat or sleep because of love. 150

MISS JULIE: Who was she? [JEAN *is silent.*] Who was she?

JEAN: You cannot order me to answer that.

MISS JULIE: If I ask you as an equal? As a friend! Who was she?

JEAN: You.

MISS JULIE [*sits*]: How absurd! 155

JEAN: Yes, if you like. It was absurd.

Strindberg: *Miss Julie* (1888) (trans. by Michael Meyer)

Miss Julie is coyly flirtatious—playing games, but the stakes are high. She toys with Jean—though his reply in French slightly surprises her. Jean takes the chance to 'show-off'—he is no mere uncultivated servant—he can speak 'genteel French'. Miss J. patronizes him—he *looks* 'quite the gentleman'—but the implication is that he is simply performing the part. When Jean says 'Oh, you're flattering me' he presumes on a degree of intimacy which Miss J. will not concede: perhaps to admit flattering him would be to accept him as a social equal—you don't flatter servants—and to suggest a desire for further intimacy. Hence her 'haughty' response—'Flattering you?'—which puts him in his place. This causes Jean to retreat into tight-lipped formality—to put distance between them. Yet even while apparently demeaning himself—'one as humble as myself'—Jean's tactics here offer a form of self-assertion: just as when he spoke French he is, in effect, suggesting 'I can master this kind of courtly utterance just as well as any of my "betters".' Miss J. recognises his expertise, but again in the form of a barbed 'put down'—i.e. Jean is simply aping the manners of his social superiors; if she congratulates him it is only in the tone of praising some performing seal which has learnt its tricks well. She wants both to maintain her power over Jean and to feel he desires her as a woman; she uses her social position to assert her power, but also to add a frisson of furtive excitement to the dangerous game she is playing. As soon as Jean assumes too much, he gets his knuckles rapped; but, perversely, even as she rejects, she 'leads him on'.

(Correct according to your own impressions—and continue.)

A footnote to the above passage. The original is written in Swedish. As it is an obvious fact that each language contains its own nuances which may be very difficult, or even impossible, to translate exactly, this raises the question of the adequacy with which we can study drama in translation. An important prerequisite, of course, is to make sure that the translation we are working with is a good one—as the example above, translated by Michael Meyer, undoubtedly is. Our justification for including in this book extracts from plays in translation is that to fail to consider at least some examples of the work of dramatists such as Chekhov, Strindberg and Brecht would be to ignore the tremendous influence many foreign playwrights have had on English drama and to limit greatly the boundaries (and enjoyment) of our study.

QUESTIONS TO BE ASKED

We should now be in a position to draw some general conclusions about the sort of questions we should ask when we are thinking about characterisation in a scene of drama. It is perfectly reasonable to assert that, as in all areas of literary criticism, the response of a sensitive reader (or of a member of an audience) to a particular piece of dramatic writing will, in itself, suggest what kind of questions are of interest. However, to start the current flowing it can sometimes be helpful in the early stages of analysis, to approach a consideration of character with a number of staple questions in mind which usually lead to productive answers. Although we would not wish to suggest that there is any kind of 'all-purpose-character-analysis kit', in fact, whether we are considering the most stumbling piece of dialogue, based on a blind following of Debrett's recommended conversational gambits (see page 42) or examining the most sophisticated dramatic study of shifting character relationships, the *basic* questions will invariably be of the same type—and we would list them as follows:

1. What is (a) the setting and (b) the situation in which the characters find themselves? (This would involve a consideration of such factors as the characters' previous relationship, their age and sex and the number of people present.)

2. Do the characters perceive the situation in the same way? (If not, what are the differences?)

3. What is the function of the dialogue? Is the intention of each participant clear? (That is, for instance, do we know what each character essentially wants from the other(s)?)

4. How do the characters rate on a scale which assesses:

   (a) the degree of intimacy they feel for each other, and
   (b) the nature of their relative status, as they perceive it?
   (c) How do these factors affect the interaction of the characters?

5. How much is communicated between the characters explicitly—and how much implicitly? Is there any significant 'subtext'?

6. What changes in feeling and mood have the characters undergone during the scene? Has the nature of their relationship or the situation in which they find themselves changed in any significant way? (eg. Are the characters moving into a closer intimacy or beginning to share the same view of 'reality'?)
7. What are the main theatrical devices—we have been concentrating in this chapter on the dynamics of language—by means of which the dramatist effects his characterisation?

It should be emphasised that Question 7 cannot be treated as a 'separate issue': it will be involved in your discussion of all the previous points. If you are studying a play in its entirety—which is, of course, how plays should really be studied!—we would add one final, vital question:

8. In what ways does the development of character in a particular scene relate to the characterization in the rest of the play—and to the unfolding of the drama's plot, themes and structure?

To see how these signposting questions will generally point us in the right direction, we would like you to answer Questions 1–7 in relation to one final extract which deals with another mistress/servant relationship. The passage is taken from *The Changeling* (1622) by Middleton (and Rowley).

Beatrice-Joanna, daughter of the Governor of Alicant, has always felt a fierce physical repugnance towards the ugly De Flores, her father's servant, who, unbeknown to Beatrice is infatuated with her. Nevertheless, when her father commands her to marry Alonzo de Piracquo–she is in love with Alsemero–she accepts De Flores' offer to murder Alonzo.
De Flores has just reported that he has carried out the murder.

BEATRICE: 'Tis resolv'd then;
Look you, sir, here's three thousand golden florins;
I have not meanly thought upon thy merit.
DE FLORES: What, salary? Now you move me.
BEATRICE: How, De Flores? 5
DE FLORES: Do you place me in the rank of verminous fellows,
To destroy things for wages? Offer gold?
The life blood of man! Is anything
Valued too precious for my recompense?
BEATRICE: I understand thee not. 10
DE FLORES: I could ha' hir'd
A journeyman in murder at this rate,
And mine own conscience might have slept at ease,
And have had the work brought home.
BEATRICE [*aside*]: I'm in a labyrinth; 15
What will content him? I would fain be rid of him.—
I'll double the sum, sir.
DE FLORES: You take a course
To double my vexation, that's the good you do.

BEATRICE [*aside*]: Bless me! I am now in worse plight than I was; 20
I know not what will please him.—For my fear's sake,
I prithee make away with all speed possible.
And if thou be'st so modest not to name
The sum that will content thee, paper blushes not[1];
Send thy demand in writing, it shall follow thee, 25
But prithee take thy flight.
DE FLORES: You must fly too then.
BEATRICE: I?
DE FLORES: I'll not stir a foot else.
BEATRICE: What's your meaning? 30
DE FLORES: Why, are you not as guilty, in, I'm sure,
As deep as I? And we should stick together.
Come, your fears counsel you but ill; my absence
Would draw suspect[2] upon you instantly;
There were no rescue for you. 35
BEATRICE [*aside*]: He speaks home[3].
DE FLORES: Nor is it fit we two engag'd so jointly,
Should part and live asunder.
BEATRICE: How now, sir
This shows not well. 40
DE FLORES: What makes your lip so strange[4]?
This must not be betwixt us.
BEATRICE [*aside*]: The man talks wildly.
DE FLORES: Come, kiss me with a zeal now.
BEATRICE [*aside*]: Heaven, I doubt[5] him! 45
DE FLORES: I will not stand so long to beg 'em shortly.
BEATRICE: Take heed, De Flores, of forgetfulness,
'T will soon betray us.
DE FLORES: Take you heed first;
Faith, y'are grown much forgetful, y'are to blame in't. 50
BEATRICE [*aside*]: He's bold, and I am blam'd for't!
DE FLORES: I have eas'd
You of your trouble, think on't, I'm in pain,
And must be eas'd of you; 'tis a charity,
Justice invites your blood[6] to understand me. 55
BEATRICE: I dare not.
DE FLORES: Quickly!
BEATRICE: Oh, I never shall!
Speak it yet further off that I may lose
What has been spoken, and no sound remain on't. 60
I would not hear so much offence again
For such another deed.

---

[1] i.e. you may express on paper without any embarrassment the sum you require.
[2] suspicion.
[3] presses his point, strikes home.
[4] unfriendly.
[5] suspect.
[6] both her passion and her nature as a woman of aristocratic class.

DE FLORES: Soft, lady, soft;
The last[7] is not yet paid for. Oh, this act
Has put me into spirit; I was as greedy on't 65
As the parch'd earth of moisture, when the clouds weep.
Did you not mark, I wrought myself into't,
Nay, sued and kneel'd for't? Why was all that pains took?
You see I have thrown contempt upon your gold,
Not that I want it not, for I do piteously; 70
In order I will come unto't, and make use on't,
But 'twas not held so precious to begin with;
For I place wealth after the heels of pleasure,
And were I not resolv'd in my belief
That thy virginity were perfect in thee, 75
I should but take my recompense with grudging,
As if I had but half my hopes I agreed for.
BEATRICE: Why, 'tis impossible thou canst be so wicked,
Or shelter such a cunning cruelty,
To make his death the murderer of my honour! 80
Thy language is bold and vicious,
I cannot see which way I can forgive it
With any modesty.
DE FLORES: Push[8]! You forget yourself!
A woman dipp'd in blood, and talk of modesty! 85
BEATRICE: Oh, misery of sin! Would I had been bound
Perpetually unto my living hate
In that Piracquo, than to hear these words.
Think but upon the distance that creation
Set 'twixt thy blood and mine[9], and keep thee there. 90
DE FLORES: Look but into your conscience, read me there,
'Tis a true book, you'll find me there your equal.
Push! Fly not to your birth, but settle you
In what the act has made you, y'are no more now.
You must forget your parentage to[10] me: 95
Y'are the deed's creature; by that name
You lost your first condition, and I challenge you,
As peace and innocency has turn'd you out,
And made you one with me.
BEATRICE: With thee, foul villain? 100
DE FLORES: Yes, my fair murd'ress; do you urge[11] me?
Though thou writ'st maid, thou whore in thy affection!
'Twas chang'd from thy first love, and that's a kind
Of whoredom in thy heart; and he's chang'd[12] now,
To bring thy second on, thy Alsemero, 105

---

[7] i.e. the act of murder.
[8] an ejaculation—compare 'tush'.
[9] i.e. the gap between our social status.
[10] in your dealings with.
[11] provoke.
[12] i.e. transformed by my murder of him—to death.

Whom (by all sweets that ever darkness tasted)
If I enjoy thee not, thou ne'er enjoy'st;
I'll blast the hopes and joys of marriage,
I'll confess all; my life I rate at nothing.
BEATRICE: De Flores! 110
DE FLORES: I shall rest from all lovers' plagues then;
I live in pain now; that shooting eye
Will burn my heart to cinders.
BEATRICE: Oh, sir, hear me.
DE FLORES: She that in life and love refuses me, 115
In death and shame my partner she shall be.
BEATRICE [*kneels*]: Stay, hear me once for all; I make thee master
Of all the wealth I have in gold and jewels;
Let me go poor unto my bed with honour,
And I am rich in all things. 120
DE FLORES: Let this silence thee:
The wealth of all Valencia shall not buy
My pleasure from me;
Can you weep Fate from its determin'd purpose?
So soon may you weep me. 125
BEATRICE: Vengeance begins;
Murder, I see, is followed by more sins.
Was my creation in the womb so curs'd,
It must engender with a viper first?
DE FLORES: Come, rise, and shroud your blushes in my bosom; 130
[*Raiser her.*]
Silence is one of pleasure's best receipts;
Thy peace is wrought for ever in this yielding.
'Las, how the turtle[13] pants! Thou'lt love anon
What thou so fear'st and faint'st to venture on. 135
Exeunt.

General Questions

1. 'For characters to interest and involve an audience, they must be brought into conflict.' How true do you find this statement to be, bearing in mind the scenes you have studied in this chapter?
2. Which are the most interesting characters you have been introduced to so far in this book? Justify your choice.

[13] dove—reference to Beatrice as a vulnerable object of love.

11

Interpretation

When it comes to interpretation, drama is probably the most concrete, yet fluid, of all art forms. Drama is 'concrete' because in the theatre it involves the embodiment by real people—actors and actresses—of the issues and human relationships which a play presents. The word is made flesh. Drama requires, too, an audience's active participation while a series of 'live moments' unfolds before its very eyes. We have also claimed that to read a dramatic text properly demands the imaginative capacity to visualise a scene—and to 'hear' it with our inner ear. Yet the interpretation of drama is 'fluid' because of the wide variety of responses that are possible to the words and images we experience in the theatre—or bring to life in our imagination as we read a text. To refer to an example we introduced earlier, we can never hear in the theatre or read in a script anything quite like this: ' "There is no food in the fridge," Brian said in a querulous tone, feeling once again in his puerile way that Lilian was simply not looking after him as a good wife should.' As spectators of a drama only the first seven words of that sentence are going to come our way—and it is up to us to work out from the actor's tone and emphasis just what we are to make of the line. To study drama, therefore, as an actor, spectator or reader, is to be constantly challenged to *interpret for ourselves*—and to become aware of the wide range of possible interpretations that a dramatic text offers.

Plays in performance can appear to possess a protean form; they undergo all kinds of sea changes. When a director approaches a classic play, he may feel that its interpretation has become straitjacketed by a conventional way of presenting it. Perhaps he has already in mind the adoption of a different style of acting—maybe a move from a naturalistic to a more stylised mode—which will force an audience to see the play with fresh eyes. It could be that the director has been influenced by a literary critic who has emphasised a reading of the play which depends on an underlining of a set of related images, or maybe in rehearsal a new slant on one central character or theme emerges. A director may choose to adopt a novel method of staging—a topic we will discuss in some detail in a later chapter—or decide that he will use modern costume for an old play or set it in some unexpected period or locale. Most directors will focus on certain moments they regard as central to their interpretation of a play, and they will make sure that in their production the full weight of the resources of the theatre comes to rest on these key moments. Each director, of course, will choose a different emphasis which subtly (or unsubtly) moves the balance of the play's structure this way or that. The pace at which a production moves is another vital interpretative matter. Here a dramatist such as Chekhov is a classic test case. To put the question at its simplest, does the director of *The Cherry Orchard* wish to make the play move along slowly, stressing its inherently tragic qualities and giving full value to the futility, the emptiness and restricted possibilities for fulfilment of most of the lives we see portrayed, or does he want the action to develop more briskly, the tone to be lighter, less portentous, so that the play's considerable comic possibilities ring out, while the more sombre elements sound a distant ground bass?

The fact is that in the richest dramatic texts there are often so many different sides to a play's themes and presentation of character that any single production will necessarily address itself to only a selected number of interpretative possibilities. This is certainly true of a play such as Shakespeare's *Hamlet*. There can be no definitive production. Hamlet's character, for instance, is so complex that any director and actor are almost bound to bring certain aspects of the hero's character into full dramatic focus, while other elements remain blurred or perhaps almost disappear from the frame. As a demonstration of this, read the following extracts which have been taken virtually at random from reviews of various productions of *Hamlet*. Even allowing for the subjective nature of the critics' response, might we not find it difficult to accept that all these comments are written in connection with the portrayal of just *one* character in a play? Might they not almost seem to apply to a number of different individuals?

> '(The playing) of the part is too light . . . it gives the impression of a man little engaged in intellectual struggle (but) dominated by emotional impulse.' (Olivier as Hamlet, Old Vic, 1937)

> 'Evidently Mr Guthrie intends that this Hamlet should suffer as plainly as possible from an Oedipus complex.' (Guinness as Hamlet, directed by Guthrie—in modern dress—at the Old Vic, 1938)

> 'A picturesque and romantic performance . . . This Hamlet wears his pessimism as lightly as he wears his madness.' (John Byron as Hamlet, Stratford-upon-Avon, 1944)

> 'Mr Scofield's frail and youthful Hamlet is haunted by phantoms of the mind so direful that in colloquy he scarcely dare utter words that give positive shape to his doubts and fears. He is a spiritual fugitive who seeks not so desperately the fulfilment of his earthly mission as some steadfast refuge for the hard-driven imagination, and only in death the refuge is found.' (Scofield as Hamlet, Stratford-upon-Avon, 1948)

> '(Hamlet) to his loss, has always been a favourite adolescent role: one in which parents and authority figures can be flouted with impunity and in which the vast unfocussed sense of dissatisfaction and injustice can be

indulged in a delicious environment of isolated self-righteousness. And it is mainly on this level that McKellen operates.' (Ian McKellen as Hamlet, Cambridge Arts, 1971)

'Behind Mr Pennington's infinitely adaptable face there is always nightmare . . . This is Hamlet with bad dreams . . . obsessed with revenge . . . Both sharp-brained and sweet-souled, he is a natural rationalist who views his own bloodthirsty impulses with a self-critical amazement.' (Michael Pennington as Hamlet, Aldwych, 1981)

'Anton Lesser plays the Prince like an exasperated wasp . . . It is a highly intelligent reading, but it somehow falls short of nobility, partly because the actor's inches fall short of everyone in the Court . . . The revenge motif is reduced to a matter of abstract speculation.' (Anton Lesser as Hamlet, Warehouse, 1982)

In the production of a play, the director and actors finally have to settle on one interpretation—one way of speaking a line, making a move or staging a scene. Yet we have seen that this choice will probably involve a selection from a whole range of possible (and perhaps equally interesting) alternatives which have emerged in rehearsal or from a close reading of the text. We would like you to experience for yourself the process by which these rich and perhaps even ambiguous or contradictory discoveries are made. We want you to study closely the following scene from *Hamlet* (1601). If you are working as a member of a class, you should split up into pairs for this exercise, the first stage of which is to absorb the bare details of the background to a complex situation from a necessarily sketchy summary. If you can read the whole play and therefore see exactly what leads up to this episode, so much the better.

Hamlet, Prince of Denmark, is beset by problems which centre around the need to avenge a murdered father, the former king. The fact that Hamlet's mother, the Queen, is now married to the usurper who murdered to gain the crown, fills Hamlet with a disillusionment which undermines his faith in all women.

In the scene you will be studying, we see Hamlet with Ophelia. Hamlet certainly was once deeply in love with this young woman, but what he feels for her now must be in question after Ophelia, acting on her father's command, has denied Hamlet her presence. Doubless one part of Hamlet regards Ophelia as someone who, like his mother, has betrayed him by apparently siding with his enemies. Ophelia's father is the present King's chief adviser, and when she meets Hamlet in this scene she is once again acting on her father's directions: her father has arranged for the King and himself to be in hiding so they can eavesdrop on the conversation—they want to know whether Hamlet's melancholia has been caused by his thwarted love for Ophelia.

Now read the scene through, and then adopt the approach we suggest at the end of the extract.

OPHELIA: Good my lord,
How does your honour for this many a day?
HAMLET: I humbly thank you, well.
OPHELIA: My lord, I have remembrances[1] of yours
That I have longed long to redeliver. 5
I pray you now receive them.
HAMLET: No, not I.
I never gave you aught.
OPHELIA: My honour'd lord, you know right well you did,
And with them words of so sweet breath compos'd 10
As made the things more rich. Their perfume lost,
Take these again; for to the noble mind
Rich gifts wax poor when givers prove unkind.
There, my lord.
HAMLET: Ha, ha! Are you honest[2]? 15
OPHELIA: My lord?
HAMLET: Are you fair?
OPHELIA: What means your lordship?
HAMLET: That if you be honest and fair, your honesty should admit no discourse to your beauty. 20
OPHELIA: Could beauty, my lord, have better commerce than with honesty?
HAMLET: Ay, truly, for the power of beauty will sooner transform honesty from what it is to a bawd[3] than the force of honesty can translate beauty into his likeness. This was sometime[4] a paradox, but now the time gives it 25 proof. I did love you once.
OPHELIA: Indeed, my lord, you made me believe so.
HAMLET: You should not have believed me; for virtue cannot so inoculate our old stock but we shall relish of it[5]. I loved you not.
OPHELIA: I was the more deceived. 30
HAMLET: Get thee to a nunnery[6]. Why, wouldst thou be a breeder of sinners? I am myself indifferent honest, but yet I could accuse me of such things that it were better my mother had not borne me. I am very proud, revengeful, ambitious, with more offences at my beck[7] than I have thoughts to put them in, imagination to give them shape, or time to act 35 them in. What should such fellows as I do crawling between earth and heaven? We are arrant[8] knaves all, believe none of us. Go thy ways to a nunnery. Where's your father?
OPHELIA: At home, my lord.
HAMLET: Let the doors be shut upon him, that he may play the fool 40 nowhere but in's own house. Farewell.

---

[1] gifts, love-tokens.
[2] virtuous, chaste.
[3] prostitute.
[4] once.
[5] i.e. grafting virtue on to our original sinful nature cannot effect a complete change.
[6] In a nunnery Ophelia's virtue will be protected; but a 'nunnery' was also a slang term for a brothel.
[7] bidding.
[8] thorough.

OPHELIA: O help him, you sweet heavens.
HAMLET: If thou dost marry, I'll give thee this plague for thy dowry: be thou as chaste as ice, as pure as snow, thou shalt not escape calumny. Get thee to a nunnery, farewell. Or if thou wilt needs marry, marry a fool; for 45 wise men know well enough what monsters you make of them. To a nunnery, go—and quickly too. Farewell.
OPHELIA: Heavenly powers, restore him.
HAMLET: I have heard of your paintings[9] well enough. God hath given you one face and you make yourselves another. You jig and amble, and you 50 lisp, you nick-name God's creatures, and make your wantonness your ignorance[10]. Go to, I'll no more on't, it hath made me mad. I say we will have no mo marriage. Those that are married already—all but one—shall live; the rest shall keep as they are. To a nunnery, go. *Exit.*
OPHELIA: O, what a noble mind is here o'erthrown! 55
The courtier's, soldier's, scholar's, eye, tongue, sword,
Th'expectancy and rose of the fair state,
The glass of fashion and the mould of form,
Th'observ'd of all observers, quite, quite down!
And I, of ladies most deject and wretched, 60
That suck'd the honey of his music vows,
Now see that noble and most sovereign reason
Like sweet bells jangled out of tune and harsh,
That unmatch'd form and feature of blown youth
Blasted with ecstasy[11]. O woe is me 65
T'have seen what I have seen, see what I see.

Working in pairs, if this is possible, first prepare a reading of Hamlet's part which is all savage anger and bitter repudiation: he feels totally betrayed by Ophelia.

Then read the part in a way which stresses that Hamlet is not so much angry as hurt, depressed, confused: he is still deeply in love with Ophelia and can show tenderness towards her.

Now consider the following questions.

1. What particular parts of the text would you draw on to support each of the two general interpretations of Hamlet's response to Ophelia which we have outlined above?
2. Are these two views of Hamlet's feelings mutually exclusive?
3. As we indicated in our introduction to this scene, the audience will be aware that Ophelia's father and the King are in hiding and eavesdropping on Hamlet and Ophelia. Some critics have suggested that during the scene Hamlet himself becomes aware of this fact.
   (a) What is the evidence in the text for this view? How convincing is it?
   (b) If Hamlet does realise that he is being spied on, at what point in the scene would he show this awareness?

---

[9] i.e. of the face, make-up.
[10] i.e. pretend that what is really seductively affected behaviour is the result of your innocence.
[11] madness.

(c) If we accept this interpretation, how would it affect the way Hamlet acts?

4. Discuss the particular passages in the scene which suggest a sense of ambiguity about what Hamlet is feeling. Do not be afraid here to offer a considerable range of speculation (grounded, of course, in the text), or even to express puzzlement at certain points.
5. Basing your answer on some of the points that have emerged in response to the previous question, what other possible approaches are there to playing the part of Hamlet in this scene? For instance, what about Ophelia's view that Hamlet is 'blasted with ecstacy' (l. 65)—i.e. suffering from madness? Hamlet's 'madness' is a vexed issue in the play. At certain moments in *Hamlet*, the Prince certainly feigns madness—largely for tactical reasons—and sometimes his imaginative, sensitive mind may be for a time genuinely unbalanced. Do you find any signs of mental instability in this scene?
6. What are the different ways in which Ophelia's part might be played? What is she feeling at various points in the scene? For example, at the beginning of the scene, is she really eager to return Hamlet's love tokens, or is she hoping Hamlet will refuse to accept them and that her action will prompt him to a new declaration of love?
7. Suggest the ways in which the use of certain gestures and the positioning and movement of one character relative to the other might register on stage the feelings of Hamlet and Ophelia.

This last question should only be attempted after you have discussed the first seven questions in some depth:

8. Write an essay in which you define in detail what you feel is the nature of the relationship between Hamlet and Ophelia at this point in the play.

Finally, prepare a reading or a performance of this scene which embodies the interpretation you offer in question 8. If you are working as the member of a class, compare your reading/performance—use the partner you were working with earlier—with that of other students. (Please note: the part of Hamlet *has* been played by a woman!)

WHERE ARE WE? WHAT IS HAPPENING?

Hamlet is a very complex play, but at least we know where the action is taking place and what is the *general* nature of the relationships between the characters. The traditional kind of play usually begins with an exposition which provides an audience with a firm framework within which the relationship between the characters and their background can readily be appreciated. (Remember how this was done in the extracts we considered from *Billy Liar*—see page 28—and from *The Winslow Boy*—see page 119). However, a number of dramatists in our own century have not worked in this orthodox manner, and they pose particularly demanding problems—as the following extract will demonstrate. The passage is taken from the opening of Jean-Paul Sartre's *Huis-clos* (1944), translated here as *In Camera* by Stuart Gilbert.

A drawing-room in Second Empire style. A massive bronze group stands on the mantelpiece.

GARCIN [*enters, accompanied by the* ROOM-VALET, *and glances round him*]: Mm! So here we are?
VALET: Yes, Mr Garcin.
GARCIN: And this is what it looks like?
VALET: Yes. 5
GARCIN: Second Empire furniture, I observe . . . Well, well, I dare say one gets used to it in time.
VALET: Some do. Some don't.
GARCIN: Are all the other rooms like this one?
VALET: How could they be? We cater for all sorts: Chinamen and Indians, 10 for instance. What use would they have for a Second Empire chair?
GARCIN: And what use do you suppose *I* have for one? Do you know who I was? . . . Oh, well, it's no great matter. And, to tell the truth, I'd quite a habit of living amongst furniture that I didn't relish, and in false positions. I'd even come to like it. A false position in a Louis-Philippe 15 dining-room—you know the style?—well, that had its points, you know. Bogus in bogus, so to speak.
VALET: And you'll find that living in a Second Empire drawing-room has its points.
GARCIN: Really? . . . Yes, yes, I dare say . . . [*He takes another look* 20 *round.*] Still, I certainly didn't expect—this! You know what they tell us down there?
VALET: What about?
GARCIN: About [*makes a sweeping gesture*] this—er—residence.
VALET: Really, sir, how could you believe such cock-and-bull stories? Told 25 by people who'd never set foot here. For, of course, if they had. . .
GARCIN: Quite so. [*Both laugh. Abruptly the laugh dies from* GARCIN'S *face.*] But, I say, where are the instruments of torture?
VALET: The what?
GARCIN: The racks and red-hot pincers and all the other paraphernalia? 30
VALET: Ah, you must have your little joke, sir!
GARCIN: My little joke? Oh, I see. No. I wasn't joking. [*A short silence. He strolls round the room.*] No mirrors, I notice. No windows. Only to be expected. And nothing breakable. [*Bursts out angrily*]. But, damn it all, they might have left me my toothbrush! 35
VALET: That's good! So you haven't yet got over your—what-do-you-call-it?—sense of human dignity? Excuse me smiling.
GARCIN [*thumping ragefully the arm of an armchair*]: I'll ask you to be more polite. I quite realise the position I'm in, but I won't tolerate . . .
VALET: Sorry, sir. No offence meant. But all our guests ask me the same 40 questions. Silly questions, if you'll pardon me saying so. Where's the torture-chamber? That's the first thing they ask, all of them. They don't

bother their heads about the bathroom requisites, that I can assure you. But, after a bit, when they've got their nerve back, they start in about their toothbrushes and what-not. Good heavens, Mr Garcin, can't you use your brains? What, I ask you, would be the point of brushing your teeth? 45

GARCIN [*more calmly*]: Yes, of course you're right. [*He looks round again.*] And why should one want to see oneself in a looking-glass? But that bronze contraption on the mantelpiece, that's another story. I suppose there will be times when I stare my eyes out at it. Stare my eyes out—see what I mean? . . . All right, let's put our cards on the table. I assure you I'm quite conscious of my position. Shall I tell you what it feels like? A man's drowning, choking, sinking by inches, till only his eyes are just above water. And what does he see? A bronze atrocity by—what's the fellow's name?—Barbedienne. A collector's piece. Like in a nightmare. That's their idea, isn't it? . . . No, I suppose you're under orders not to answer questions; and I won't insist. But don't forget, my man, I've a shrewd notion of what's coming to me, so don't you boast you've caught me off my guard. I'm facing up to the situation, facing up. [*He starts pacing the room again.*] So that's that; no toothbrush. And no bed, either. One never sleeps, I take it? 50 55 60

VALET: That's so.

GARCIN: Just as I expected. *Why* should one sleep? A sort of drowsiness steals on you, tickles you behind the ears, and you feel your eyes closing—but why sleep? You lie down on the sofa and . . . in a flash, sleep flies away. Miles and miles away. So you rub your eyes, get up, and it starts all over again. 65

VALET: Romantic, that's what you are.

GARCIN: Will you keep quiet, please! . . . I won't make a scene, I shan't be sorry for myself, I'll face up to the situation, as I said just now. Face it fairly and squarely. I won't have it springing at me from behind, before I've time to size it up. And you call that being 'romantic'! . . . So it comes to this; one doesn't need rest. Why bother about sleep if one isn't sleepy? That stands to reason, doesn't it? Wait a bit, there's a snag somewhere; something disagreeable. Why, now, should it be disagreeable? . . . Ah, I see; it's life without a break. 70 75

VALET: What do you mean by that?

GARCIN: What do I mean? [*Eyes the* VALET *suspiciously.*] I thought as much. That's why there's something so beastly, so damn' bad-mannered, in the way you stare at me. They're paralysed. 80

VALET : What are you talking about?

GARCIN: Your eyelids. We move ours up and down. Blinking, we call it. It's like a small black shutter that clicks down, and makes a break. Everything goes black; one's eyes are moistened. You can't imagine how restful, refreshing, it is. Four thousand little rests per hour. Four thousand little respites—just think! . . . So that's the idea. I'm to live without eyelids. Don't act the fool, you know what I mean. No eyelids, no sleep; it follows, doesn't it? I shall never sleep again. But then—how shall I endure my own company? Try to understand. You see, I'm fond of teasing, it's a second nature with me— and I'm used to teasing myself. Plaguing myself, if you prefer; I don't tease nicely. But I can't go on 85 90

doing that without a break. Down there I had my nights. I slept. I always had good nights. By way of compensation, I suppose. And happy little dreams. There was a green field. Just an ordinary field. I used to stroll in it . . . Is it daytime now? 95
VALET: Can't you see? The lights are on.
GARCIN: Ah yes, I've got it. It's *your* daytime. And outside?
VALET: Outside?
GARCIN: Damn it, you know what I mean. Beyond that wall. 100
VALET: There's a passage.
GARCIN: And at the end of the passage?
VALET: There's more rooms, more passages and stairs.
GARCIN: And what lies beyond them?
VALET: That's all. 105
GARCIN: But surely you have a day off sometimes. Where do you go?
VALET: To my uncle's place. He's the head valet here. He has a room on the third floor.
GARCIN: I should have guessed as much. Where's the light-switch?
VALET: There isn't any. 110
GARCIN: What? Can't one turn off the light?
VALET: Oh, the management can cut off the current, if they want to. But I can't remember their having done so on this floor. We have all the electricity we want.
GARCIN: So one has to live with one's eyes open all the time? 115
VALET: To *live*, did you say?
GARCIN: Don't let's quibble over words. With one's eyes open. For ever. Always broad daylight in my eyes . . . and in my head. [*Short silence.*] And suppose I took that contraption on the mantelpiece and dropped it on the lamp—wouldn't it go out? 120
VALET: You can't move it. It's too heavy.
GARCIN [*seizing the bronze ornament and trying to lift it*]: You're right. It's too heavy.
[*A short silence follows.*]
VALET: Very well, sir, if you don't need me any more, I'll be off. 125

(i) Where do you think this scene is taking place? On what evidence do you base your view?
(ii) What effect on an audience is Sartre trying to achieve here, and how successful is this scene as the opening of a play?

In fact, if you read on in Sartre's play, you will find that the cloudy liquid soon begins to clear and an audience will have few doubts about where the action is taking place and what significance it has. There are, however, some modern plays which remain almost continuously enigmatic. Not only may we remain uncertain about the precise location of the action; as Martin Esslin observes in *An Anatomy of Drama*, 'we may well no longer ask the question which most conventional drama poses for the spectator: what's going to happen next? but the more general question: what's happening?' In Beckett's *Waiting for Godot* (1955), a passage from which we have already examined (see p. 94), we know that the scene is set as follows: 'A country road. A tree. Evening.' Yet we have a strong impression that the real scene is as much a landscape of the mind as an actual location. And what *is* happening? Not very much, if we are expecting the momentum of a constantly onward-moving plot—one which, in a traditional play, develops through a series of contrasts and varied situations to lead us to a clear-cut resolution. The end of Act I neatly encapsulates much of the mood of *Waiting for Godot*.

VLADIMIR: . . . Come on.
He draws him after him. As before.
ESTRAGON: Wait.
VLADIMIR: I'm cold!
ESTRAGON: Wait! (*He moves away from Vladimir.*) I wonder if we wouldn't have been better off alone, each one for himself. (*He crosses the stage and sits down on the mound.*) We weren't made for the same road. 5
VLADIMIR: (*without anger*). It's not certain.
ESTRAGON: No, nothing is certain.
Vladimir slowly crosses the stage and sits down beside Estragon. 10
VLADIMIR: We can still part, if you think it would be better.
ESTRAGON: It's not worth while now.
Silence.
VLADIMIR: No, it's not worth while now.
Silence. 15
ESTRAGON: Well, shall we go?
VLADIMIR: Yes, let's go.
They do not move.

CURTAIN

Why do Beckett's two tramps not move? And who exactly is this 'Godot' that they are waiting for? His name certainly suggests he might have something to do with the Deity, but it cannot be that simple, can it? What are we to make of the fact that Godot never actually turns up, though he does send a boy who is (allegedly) his messenger? And what is the significance of the detail that when Act II begins the scene is exactly the same as before, except for 'four or five leaves' which have sprouted on the tree? We could go on listing a number of puzzling questions which the play poses, leaving an audience uncertain of its exact bearings. If the play has a meaning, it is an emergent one, and to arrive at an interpretation we have to decode cryptic suggestions and realise that Beckett is using the theatre to present an audience with an ambiguous situation which unfolds in the manner of a complex, poetic metaphor. In many plays written by dramatists such as Beckett and Ionesco—their kind of drama is often labelled 'Theatre of the Absurd'—we are presented with a dramatic world which does not correspond at all to our rational expectations, our preconceptions about what goes to produce a 'well-made play' or our sense that drama should clearly relate to an immediately recognisable social context. The plays may not appear to develop in a linear way, but rather to move in circles—or in labyrinths; we are given distortions of reality, strange dream (or nightmare) images and fantasies. These plays are not really vehicles for telling a story; they have rather become a way of exploring a state of mind, in a highly idiosyncratic and often symbolic manner.

For our final exercise in interpretation, we would like you to read this extract from Max Frisch's *Biedermann und die Brandstifter* (1953/58), translated by Michael Bullock as *The Fire Raisers*. We present some of the interpretative issues raised by the passage in the form of a summary of several different approaches which have been made to the play's meaning.

Gottlieb Biedermann (his name in German suggests a pious and conventionally respectable citizen) accepts the invasion of the attic of his house by some highly dubious characters who are clearly practising arsonists.

Eisenring is singing Lili Marlene, then there is a knock at the door.
EISENRING: Come in.
He goes on whistling, but no one comes in.
Come in.
Enter Biedermann in shirtsleeves, his cigar in his hand. 5
Morning, Herr Biedermann.
BIEDERMANN: May I?
EISENRING: How did you sleep?
BIEDERMANN: Wretchedly, thank you.
EISENRING: Me too. It's that south wind . . . 10
He continues working with the cord and the reel.
BIEDERMANN: I hope I'm not disturbing you.
EISENRING: But of course not, Herr Biedermann, you're at home here.
BIEDERMANN: I don't want to be in the way.
The cooing of pigeons is heard. 15
Where has our friend got to?
EISENRING: Joe? At work, the lazy dog. He didn't want to go without breakfast! I sent him to get some wood-wool.
BIEDERMANN: Wood-wool—?
EISENRING: Wood-wool carries the sparks furthest. 20
Biedermann laughs faintly as though at a poor joke.
BIEDERMANN: What I was going to say, Herr Eisenring—
EISENRING: Are you going to throw us out again?
BIEDERMANN: In the middle of the night (my sleeping tablets are all gone) it suddenly occurred to me that you haven't a toilet up here— 25
EISENRING: We have the gutter.
BIEDERMANN: As you like gentlemen, as you like It just crossed my mind. All night long. Perhaps you'd like to wash or take a shower. Don't hesitate to use my bathroom. I told Anna to put out towels for you.
Eisenring shakes his head. 30
Why do you shake your head?
EISENRING: Where on earth has he put it?
BIEDERMANN: What?

EISENRING: Have you seen a primer anywhere?
He looks here and there. 35
Don't worry about the bathroom, Herr Biedermann. Seriously. There was no bathroom in prison either, you know.
BIEDERMANN: Prison?
EISENRING: Didn't Joe tell you I had just come out of prison?
BIEDERMANN: No. 40
EISENRING: Not a word?
BIEDERMANN: No.
EISENRING: He talks of nothing but himself all the time. There are people like that. I mean, is it our fault that he had such a tragic youth? Did you have a tragic youth, Herr Biedermann? I didn't!—I could have gone to 45 the university, Father wanted me to be a lawyer.
He stands at the skylight conversing with the pigeons:
Grrr! Grrr! Grrr!
Biedermann re-lights his cigar.
BIEDERMANN: Herr Eisenring, I didn't sleep all night. Tell me frankly, is there really petrol in those drums? 50
EISENRING: Don't you trust us?
BIEDERMANN: I'm only asking.
EISENRING: What do you take us for, Herr Biedermann, tell me frankly, what do you take us for?
BIEDERMANN: You mustn't think I have no sense of humour, my friend, 55 but the kind of jokes you make are really a bit much.
EISENRING: That's something we've learnt.
BIEDERMANN: What is?
EISENRING: Joking is the third best method of hoodwinking people. The second best is sentimentality. The kind of stuff our Joe goes in for—a 60 childhood with charcoal burners in the forest, an orphanage, the circus and so on. But the best and safest method—in my opinion—is to tell the plain unvarnished truth. Oddly enough. No one believes it. . .
Eisenring is standing working, Biedermann is standing smoking. 65
EISENRING: What on earth is keeping Joe so long? Wood-wool is easy enough to get hold of. I hope they haven't nabbed him.
BIEDERMANN: Nabbed him?
EISENRING: Why does that amuse you?
BIEDERMANN: You know, when you talk like that, Herr Eisenring, you 70 seem to me to come from another world. Nabbed! I find it fascinating. From another world! I mean, in the circles in which we move people hardly ever get nabbed—
EISENRING: Because in such circles people don't steal wood-wool, that's obvious, Herr Biedermann, that's class distinction. 75
BIEDERMANN: Nonsense!
EISENRING: You don't mean, Herr Biedermann—
BIEDERMANN: I don't believe in class distinctions!—You must have felt that, Eisenring, I'm not old-fashioned. On the contrary. I'm genuinely sorry that among the lower classes people still blather about class 80 distinctions. Aren't we all creatures of one creator nowadays, whether we're rich or poor? The middle class too. Aren't we both flesh and blood,

you and I? . . . I don't know, Herr Eisenring, whether you also smoke cigars?

He offers one, but Eisenring shakes his head. 85

I don't say all men are equal, of course; there will always be the competent and the incompetent, thank God; but why don't we just shake hands? A little good will, damn it all, a little idealism, a little—and we could all live in peace, rich and poor, don't you agree?

EISENRING: If I may be frank, Herr Biedermann— 90

BIEDERMANN: Please do.

EISENRING: You won't take it amiss?

BIEDERMANN: The franker the better.

EISENRING: I mean, quite frankly, you ought not to smoke here.

Biedermann starts and puts out his cigar. 95

It's not for me to tell you what to do here, Herr Biedermann, after all this is your house, but you understand—

BIEDERMANN: Of course!

Eisenring bends down.

EISENRING: There it is! 100

He picks something up from the floor and blows it clean before attaching it to the cord, once more whistling Lili Marlene.

BIEDERMANN: Tell me, Herr Eisenring: What are you doing all the time? If I may ask. And what's that thing?

EISENRING: The primer. 105

BIEDERMANN: —?

EISENRING: And that's the fuse.

BIEDERMANN: —?

EISENRING: There are supposed to be even better ones now, Joe says, new models. But they're not in the arsenals yet, and it's out of the question for 110 us to buy them. Everything connected with war is terribly expensive, nothing but the top quality.

BIEDERMANN: Fuse, you say?

EISENRING: Detonating fuse.

He gives Biedermann one end of the fuse: 115

Will you be so kind as to hold this end, Herr Biedermann, so that I can measure it?

Biedermann holds the fuse.

BIEDERMANN: Joking apart, my friend—

EISENRING: Only for a moment! 120

He whistles Lili Marlene and measures the fuse.

Thanks, Herr Biedermann, thanks very much.

Biedermann bursts out laughing.

BIEDERMANN: No, Willie, you can't kid me. Not me! But I must say you put a great deal of trust in people's sense of humour. A great deal! If you 125 talk like that I can well believe you get arrested now and then. Not everyone has as much sense of humour as I have, my friend!

EISENRING: We have to find the right people.

BIEDERMANN: At the local, for instance, they fly off the handle if you so much as say you believe in the goodness in man. 130

EISENRING: Ha.

BIEDERMANN: And yet I donated a sum to our Fire Brigade so big I won't even tell you how much it was.
EISENRING: Ha.
He lays the fuse. 135
The people who have no sense of humour are just as lost when the balloon goes up; don't worry about that!
Biedermann has to sit down on a drum, sweating.
What's the matter, Herr Biedermann? You're quite pale!
He slaps him on the back. 140
I know, it's this smell, when you're not used to the smell of petrol it can upset you—I'll open a window.
Eisenring opens the door.
BIEDERMANN: Thank you . . .

The following imaginary conversation raises some views about the 'meaning' of this scene. To which of these several interpretations would you give some weight? Why (or why not)?

A: This is obviously a scene from the kind of play which is meant to puzzle an audience: the point is, there is no final solution. The playwright himself tells us as much in the play's subtitle—'A Morality without a Moral'.

B: That's just Frisch's little joke! In fact, when he wrote the play we know he had in mind the political situation in Czechoslovakia after the war when President Benes, a Social Democrat, invited the Communists to join his government, even though they were determined to take away his country's independence. Many critics have pointed out this parallel.

C: But that seems to me a far too specific interpretation. How many people know about the post-war political situation in Czechoslovakia? Even if Frisch had that in mind, audiences today will certainly not make the link. Surely Frisch is thinking about Germany and—something everyone knows about—the insidious way Hitler came to power, while both the intellectuals and bourgeoisie simply refused to see that Hitler was going to do precisely what he said he would.

D: And how much relevance do you think that can really havc for today's audience? For young people Hitler is simply someone they learn about in history lessons. The play needs to be more up to date than that—it must be set in the context of the war in Vietnam when the South Vietnamese government virtually invited the Americans into their country to burn and destroy it. But I think it's got to be even more topical. The play is obviously about neo-colonialism in the Third World—when a major power gains access to a poor country by making all sorts of promises, but ends up by undermining the country's economy. It's also a play about the way we are all stock-piling our own attics with nuclear warheads.

E: You're making the play sound like a political tract. And you're moving further and further from what we actually would see on stage. Let me remind you what the play's 'about': Biedermann's attic has been taken over by these characters who are obviously going to start a fire, but poor Biedermann will not face up to what is happening. That's it—a human situation. And then what interests Frisch as a dramatist is to make something 'happen' on stage. So we've got to look at the rhythms and patterning of the dialogue. Just accept what we are given—at face value. Look at the actual situation and the speech of these characters. And don't rush into forcing massive historical or political statements on the play. That stops you experiencing what is really involved here.

F: No. I don't want to make the play 'topical at all costs' either, but I do get the definite sense that there is some kind of parable here. It's not just a case of 'drama for drama's sake'. It's a morality play for all times and seasons. Look at it this way: the scene suggests the very ordinary, apparently innocuous way evil presents itself; it creeps into our lives, not in any obviously diabolic manner; it seems quite plausible. And we keep on, apparently powerless to stop the encroachment of evil; we're weak because we even refuse to believe 'the plain, unvarnished truth' that fire-raisers start fires. Soon evil is in residence; it's taken over our lives . . .

G: But doesn't that interpretation mean that we have to identify with Biedermann, to see him as our representative? Speak for yourself, but I know I'm not such a fool as Biedermann! He is such an ineffectual and fatuous type that nobody is going to judge this caricature as an emblem of average humanity. He's a comic butt—he simply cannot bear all the metaphysical weight you are making him carry.

H: I think you're all tending to miss the point about Biedermann. He's not a fool at all. He's tolerant, liberal and generous—a nice man. He just wants to get on with people, even though this means others may sometimes take advantage of him for a while. But Biedermann really knows the score. He sees that Eisenring is having a little joke at his expense; he plays along with it, but when the right moment comes he will show that he is a positive force for good. I think Frisch approves of him and of what he does. The playwright is saying: don't leap to conclusions about people based on mere prejudices. Try to sympathise with everyone—whether he's a criminal or not doesn't matter.

I: Really, I agree with A—if I agree with anybody. If the play can make you think of all these different things, then it seems to me it can be about anything—or nothing. And that suggests that in the first place the dramatist himself probably didn't know what he meant. Certainly he can't say it clearly. I mean if you have a message, you make sure people understand what you want to say. He was just writing a play for the commercial theatre—probably to make as much money as he could. He puts in a few hints that there might be some great hidden meaning to start all the critics off—just like you—airing their pet theories. And all the time Frisch is probably having a jolly good laugh at you all.

WRITING REVIEWS

Remember the short extracts from reviews of *Hamlet* that we quoted earlier (see page 144)? Reviews of plays in the press are, like all dramatic criticism, necessarily subjective, and often 'instant': the newspaper reviewer hardly has any time to reflect deeply on his reaction before meeting the deadline for his copy. This kind of criticism ranges from the indulgent parading of the reviewer's own ego to writing which is produced in the spirit of a real love for the theatre and a concern for the maintenance of its highest standards. If the reviewer's art also moves easily between the extremes of the bestowal of the supreme accolade and the crudest kind of hatchet job, this only reflects most people's experience of living (or dead) drama: you can leave a theatre exhilarated, but then there is nothing quite like a really bad theatrical experience, a third-rate show, for inducing the kind of depression that carries with it a strong urge for retribution.

What we would like to suggest is that the next time you go to the theatre, you try your hand at writing a review. Make your own deadline! If you are going to see a performance with a number of other people, all the better: you will be able to compare your reviews. The point of this suggestion is that often it is not until we are obliged to sit down and write a reasoned response to a production we have seen that we sort out what we really feel about it. We provide you below with a kind of check-list of obvious points to consider. It would be advisable to jot down notes as soon as possible after you have seen a play, and then to use these notes to produce a more polished piece of writing. The particular weight you give to some of the items on our check-list will depend on the nature of the production you see—and on your own response. For instance, in one production you may notice that the use of certain lighting effects plays a vital part; in connection with another production you may feel there is not all that much to say on this topic. As in all criticism, the trick is to be able to analyse the effect produced by the separate elements we list below, while recognising areas of overlapping and moving towards a statement of how these different aspects of theatre function as an entity to give a unified impression—or how they fail to achieve this end.

1. *The play*: its genre (see pages 189–95) and the nature of the story it tells (though avoid long summaries). Major themes and issues it raises; any special problems it poses the director or actor.
2. *Direction*: its quality and nature. For example, did the director impose the stamp of his own interpretation on the play? Was the pace of the production correctly gauged? Any tedious moments? How effective were the groupings of actors on stage? Was a common approach to acting style established, or was each actor apparently allowed to arrive at his/her own individual way of playing a role? How well were the items listed under points 4 and 5 integrated in the production?
3. *Individual acting performances*: e.g. How successful was the use of voice and movement in creating character? Which actors impressed you—or failed to do so? Why?
4. *Method of staging and set*: what type of staging was adopted (see pages 167–8)? What was the effect of the relation between the acting area and the audience? What kind of set was used? (Did it, to take two extremes, aim at complete realism or a 'bare stage' effect?) Any changes of set? How effective? Did the play have 'visual variety'? Any

particularly memorable images? Note clear overlap here with items listed under 5.

5. *Use of lighting, stage properties, costume and make-up, sound effects and music*: discuss in terms of both the creation of (i) specific theatrical effects and (ii) general mood and atmosphere. Avoid being purely descriptive here. Link your comments on the use of the technical resources of the theatre to the specific way in which they contributed to the effect of the production and to your enjoyment of it.
6. *Audience reaction*: what impressions did you form about the way the audience was responding to the play? Did audience response contribute to the play's success—or failure?
7. *A final judgement*: how would you sum up the production and your reaction to it? Were you moved or involved in the issues the play raises? What general impression has it left in your mind? If you saw a production of a play you already knew fairly well, did you find it challenged or added anything new to your previous conception of the play?

12

Staging

Theatre needs only three elements: actors, space to perform and audience. Whether this 'theatre' consists of a fire-eater performing in the open-air before a crowd of curious Saturday shoppers or the Royal Shakespeare Company at the Stratford Memorial Theatre playing *King Lear* to a full house, if you remove any one of these elements—though you will have something left—it won't be 'theatre'. 'Theatre' can exist in many unlikely places—a school hall, a church, a converted engine shed, a warehouse or a pub, for example, but if you mention 'theatre' to most people, they will immediately call to mind a building, generally rectangular, in which people sit in tiered rows facing an opening in a wall, in which, as in a picture, actors perform on a stage that extends away from the audience. Around this space where the actors perform, will be scenery and probably, hidden away, more scenery for different parts of the play, together with lighting equipment, both above the stage and to its sides.

Clearly, the type of theatre in which a play is performed will affect not only what an audience expects of a play, but will also impose certain constraints on the actors: for example, on their acting styles, on the way they move and on the way they relate to that audience. Of course, that traditional (or 'proscenium', as it is sometimes known) theatre that we have just described will be no exception. Here, as the audience is all sitting facing the actors, as if watching a framed painting with moving figures, the actors will have to ensure that they are always, more or less, facing the front of the stage so they may be seen and heard; the 'picture-frame' allows a director to organise actors in fairly complex groupings without there being any grave danger of some member of the audience complaining that his view was being obscured; the fact that the audience sits in darkness means that its attention can be focussed precisely on the stage action and that lighting and scenery can both play their parts in creating the atmosphere that playwright and director require. In such a theatre, it is as if the spectators are secretly spying on a world that has been carefully created before them, but yet it is a world from which in many ways they may remain detached.

It was not always so, as we have briefly mentioned on pages 16–22. You'll remember that theatrical conditions in Ancient Greece were very different from those we are used to, as was the way in which the medieval Corpus Christi plays were performed on carts that travelled round the town. Shakespeare's *Hamlet* gives us hints about another very different theatrical style and performance from those we might be tempted to view as 'traditional'. In *Hamlet*, we meet a troupe of strolling professional players who travel around the country, prepared to perform from a clearly limited repertoire of plays in noble houses and royal palaces, with a minimum of props and technical equipment. A performance from such a company of actors would markedly differ from, say, one put on by a modern repertory company or one by actors in a Restoration theatre.

To examine in more detail the way that theatrical conditions can affect the nature of plays and performances, we are going to look at theatres in two very different periods—the Elizabethan and the Victorian.

THE ELIZABETHAN THEATRE

This is the well-known drawing by Johannes de Witt of the Swan (1596)

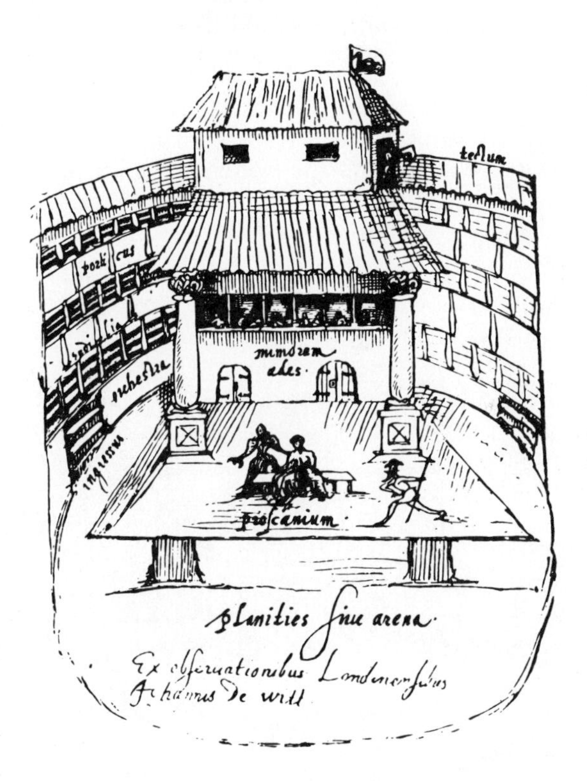

and is the type of theatre that Shakespeare and his contemporaries would have been working for. You can easily see how it differs from the 'proscenium arch' theatre that we are so familiar with:

(i) the stage is a large open platform thrusting out into the middle of the audience, raised about five feet. The acting area was estimated to be about 40 feet wide and 30 feet deep—much, much larger than most modern stages;

(ii) there is no 'set', as the rear of the acting area is a permanent feature, providing a number of acting levels;
(iii) there is an 'inner' stage at the back of the main stage that could be curtained off;
(iv) there were only two doorways at the back for entrances and exits;
(v) the spectators surrounded the acting area on three sides and it is estimated that over 2000 would be present at each performance, with some actually sitting on the stage and some standing in the 'pit' below the acting area;
(vi) the plays were acted in daylight, in the open air and thus the 'director' had to forego the benefits of complex lighting, scenic, and set effects.

We have listed a number of possible consequences that may stem from such theatrical conditions and we would like you to discuss them and decide whether:

(a) these consequences are likely to occur;
(b) they are unlikely to occur; or
(c) it is difficult to be sure from the evidence you have.

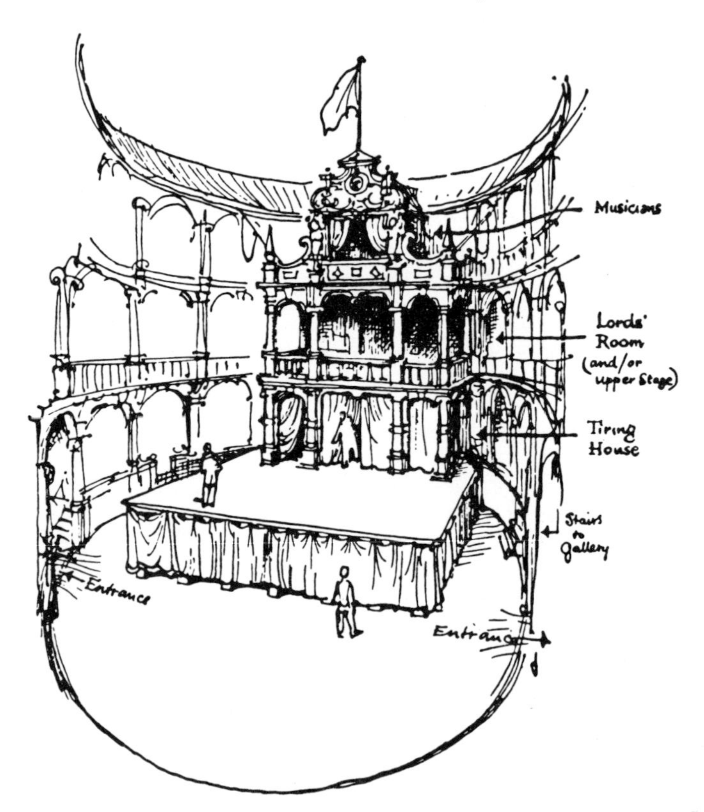

Reconstruction of the Globe Theatre

1. There can be rapid changes of scene.
2. Only one centre of interest is possible on stage at a time.
3. Much emphasis is placed on the actor, his voice and gesture to create meaning and atmosphere.
4. Location of scenes in a particular place and time is very important.
5. Actors have the possibility of being either intimate with or very detached from an audience.
6. The dramatist's language would have a crucial role in creating a sense of place and atmosphere.
7. Comic scenes are likely to be more successful than tragic ones.
8. Acting is likely to be very static and formal.
9. Audiences are required to be very involved with plays and to have to use their imaginations a great deal, as in modern radio dramas.
10. Exits and entrances will be very laboured.
11. Great opportunities for soliloquies and asides are offered.
12. The dramatists can write plays that switch rapidly from one tone and one pace to another within the same play.
13. Plays are likely to have small casts.
14. Costumes, sound effects and music will play an important role.
15. Stage sets would be of the very realistic kind which make an audience gasp as a new scene is revealed.

(To discover our conclusions, turn to page 165.)

We can see, as an example from the opening few lines of *Antony and Cleopatra*, how such conditions may have affected both the writing and staging of the play.

The scene is set in a room in Cleopatra's palace and two Romans, Philo and Demetrius, are discussing how Antony's relationship with the Egyptian queen has affected his abilities as a soldier and statesman.

PHILO: Nay, but this dotage of our general's
O'erflows the measure: those his goodly eyes,
That o'er the files and musters of the war
Have glowed like plated Mars, now bend, now turn,
The office and devotion of their view
Upon a tawny front. His captain's heart, 5
Which in the scuffles of great fights hath burst
The buckles on his breast, reneges all temper,
And is become the bellows and the fan
To cool a gipsy's lust.

Flourish. Enter ANTONY, CLEOPATRA, *her Ladies, the Train, with Eunuchs fanning her.* 10

Look where they come.
Take but good note, and you shall see in him
The triple pillar of the world transformed 15

Into a strumpet's fool. Behold and see.
CLEOPATRA: If it be love indeed, tell me how much.
ANTONY: There's beggary in the love that can be reckoned.
CLEOPATRA: I'll set a bourn how far to be beloved.
ANTONY: Then must thou needs find out new heaven, new earth. 20

Enter an ATTENDANT

ATTENDANT: News, my good lord, from Rome.
ANTONY: Grates me, the sum.

We might suspect that:

(i) Demetrius and Philo would be towards the front of the stage and to one side and that they would have quite an intimate relationship with the audience;
(ii) they would remain on stage, even when the centre of interest had moved to Antony and Cleopatra, but would remain separate from them;
(iii) the entrance of Antony and Cleopatra would be a dramatic spectacle, using the full extent of the acting area as they made their progress. 'Look where they come' and the following three lines would be pointless if they had only a short distance to cover;
(iv) the location of the scene and the contrast between Romans and Egyptians would be suggested by means of costumes and a few props;
(v) the arrival of the attendant rapidly ushers in another focus of interest for both the audience and the characters on stage.

It goes without saying that in such a very short extract as this not all the potential of the Elizabethan stage can be illustrated. It is a stage that allows a dramatist to stress the loneliness and isolation of a character like Hamlet or King Lear, by placing the actor alone in a vast empty space; it allows a dramatist to create the hurly-burly of a tavern scene (as in *Henry IV Part I*) or the battlefields of the Wars of the Roses; it allows him the freedom to change mood and location from a jealousy-ridden and doom-laden royal court in Sicily to an idyllic, pastoral, rural Bohemia within one play (*The Winter's Tale*) without undue strain. Flexibility was the hallmark of Elizabethan staging.

We suggest that you examine (either individually or in groups) the following scenes from Shakespeare (though you could choose any from his plays for yourself) and try to visualise how they might have been staged in the Elizabethan theatre. Where would they have been played? (Main-stage, inner-stage, upper-stage or a combination of all these three?) Do the lines contain any implied stage-directions, giving hints to actors about moves or exits and entrances? How close (or distant) a relationship would there have been between actor and audience?

(i) *Twelfth Night*: Act II.v (Malvolio finds the letter forged by Maria.)

(ii) *Macbeth*: Act III.iv (The banquet at which the ghost of the murdered Banquo appears.)
(iii) *Richard III*: Act III.ii (The king is confronted by the successful invader, his cousin, Bolingbroke.)
(iv) *King Lear*: Act I.i (Read the whole of this great opening scene.)

If you are interested in reading a more detailed account of the Shakespearean stage and its influence on his plays you might like to consult Andrew Gurr's book, *The Shakespearean Stage*.

Our response to the question we set earlier is as follows: you will probably have come to the conclusion, following your discussions, that the consequences we have listed as numbers 1, 3, 5, 6, 9, 11, 12 and 14 were most likely to result from Elizabethan stage conditions.

THE VICTORIAN THEATRE

We should like to consider one further example of how conditions in the theatre affected the nature of the plays written and the way they were acted. In Victorian England there was a vast explosion of interest in the theatre—many new ones were opened, the size of audiences increased, as did the number of new plays written, but whereas in the Elizabethan theatre the audiences were drawn from all classes of society, in the Victorian the audiences were predominantly working class. Their 'betters' did not attend and, of course, this had an effect on the type of plays that were written. The theatres themselves were mainly of the 'Proscenium arch' type and the stage managers now had an amazing array of 'special effects' at their command, being able to create spectacles ranging from royal palaces and Gothic castles to haunted houses and country hovels. The combination of these two elements—the very large and relatively unsophisticated audiences, together with the potential for extremely spectacular stage effects and scenery—led to a very different type of theatre from that of earlier ages. Amongst these were:

(i) plays in which subtlety of characterisation became unimportant;
(ii) characters were one-dimensional stereotypes, such as the moustache-twirling villain and the virtuous, but impoverished virgin;
(iii) the moral 'status' of characters was marked by the costumes they wore or the settings in which they were found;
(iv) the working-class audience demanded that vice be found amongst their oppressors and betters (the upper-class and those in authority) and that virtue, ever triumphant, had its natural home amongst the poor and oppressed;
(v) the huge audiences in large theatres meant that acting styles had to be very exaggerated and 'theatrical', both in speech and in the poses that actors struck to express particular emotions;
(vi) there was much audience participation and response to what they saw on stage. For instance, villains were roundly booed and

Drury Lane Theatre

In the 'flies' at Drury Lane

Stage effect for Isaac Pocock's The Miller and His Men

hissed, whilst actors played to the gallery for all they were worth;

(vii) spectacular scenery and stunning stage effects were highly popular;

(viii) the proscenium arch design, together with the elaborate sets, meant that actors played their parts mainly in front of the 'scenic area'.

Thus, the writer of the typical Victorian melodrama wrote plays that owe their nature and style to a combination of theatre architecture, the type of audience, technical advances and the manner of acting.

Clearly, the proscenium arch or 'picture-frame' theatre lacks flexibility and though such theatres continued to be built in the twentieth century, as with the Shakespeare Memorial Theatre at Stratford-upon-Avon, modern theatre design has offered playwrights, actors and directors the opportunity of rediscovering much of this freedom and flexibility that was associated with, for example, the Elizabethan theatre. Despite technological advances in such areas as sound and lighting, the theatre will never be able to rival the cinema in creating realistic effects, so the days of the train crashes and naval battles of the Victorian theatre are gone. The best of modern theatre designs now combine the strengths of the past with the opportunities offered by modern technical devices.

We would like you to study the plans on p. 169 of modern theatres and to discuss what advantages they offer to directors, actors and writers. You might like to consider some of these questions in your discussion:

(i) What sort of relationship with the audience does the theatre design offer an actor?
(ii) Is any particular style of acting encouraged?
(iii) Is any particular type of play more suited to one theatre than another (for instance, pageants, intimate psychological dramas, farces, social comedies, etc.)?
(iv) What opportunities for setting are offered?

SOME STUDIES IN MODERN STAGING

We would like now to move on and consider how particular playwrights have used these opportunities provided by modern staging, design and technical advances to create the effects that they wanted in their plays. Our first two examples are designed to show how two modern American playwrights have used the resources of the theatre to extend its ability to speak to an audience by moving away from what they saw as the rigid restrictions of the earlier conventions that demanded naturalistic staging. In the published version of *Death of a Salesman* (1949), Arthur Miller gives an account of his requirements for the set and staging of his play. It is obviously a 'reading' rather than an 'acting' version of the text (i.e. a text not for use by actors 'working' on the play in rehearsal, but one designed to be 'read' by the general theatre-going public) with its references to the flute music 'telling of grass and trees and the horizon' and to the house having 'the air of a dream . . . a dream rising out of reality'. We would like you to consider the questions that follow and then perhaps to compare your answers with the notes we have made. You might find it helpful to make a rough sketch of the setting.

A melody is heard, played upon a flute. It is small and fine, telling of grass and trees and the horizon. The curtain rises.

Before us is the Salesman's house. We are aware of towering, angular shapes behind it, surrounding it on all sides. Only the blue light of the sky falls upon the house and forestage; the surrounding area shows an angry glow of orange. As more light appears we see a solid vault of apartment houses around the small, fragile-seeming home. An air of the dream clings to the place, a dream rising out of reality. The kitchen at centre seems actual enough, for there is a kitchen table with three chairs, and a refrigerator. But no other fixtures are seen. At the back of the kitchen there is a draped entrance, which leads to the living-room. To the right of the kitchen, on a level raised two feet, is a bedroom furnished only with a brass bedstead and a straight chair. On a shelf over the bed a silver athletic trophy stands. A window opens on to the apartment house at the side.

Behind the kitchen, on a level raised six and a half feet, is the boy's bedroom, at present barely visible. Two beds are dimly seen, and at the back of the room a dormer window. (This bedroom is above the unseen living-room.) At the left a stairway curves up to it from the kitchen.

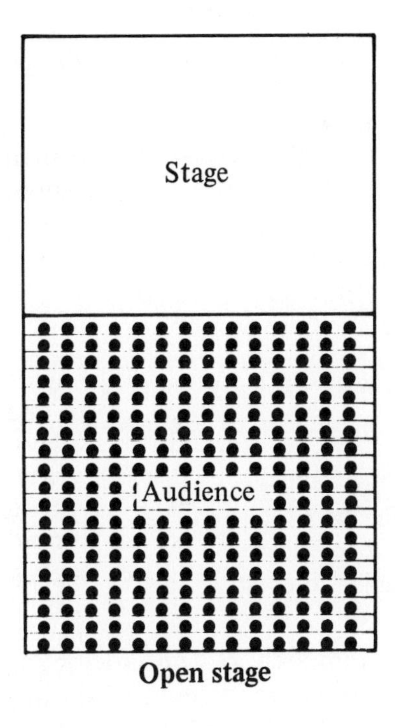

Open stage

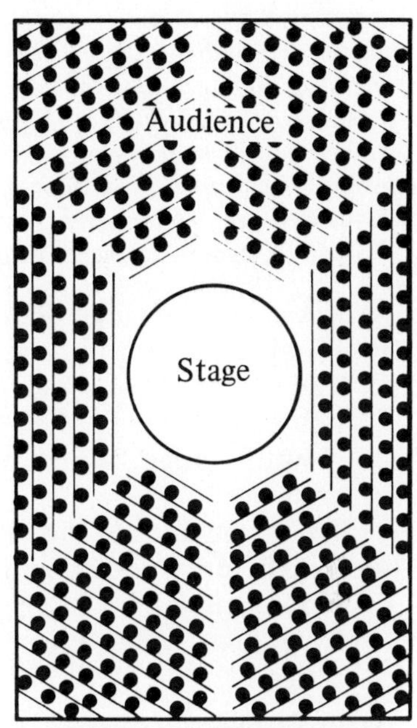

Theatre in the Round

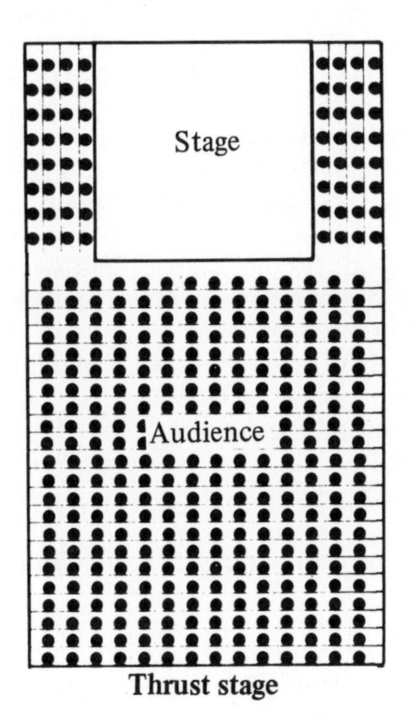

Thrust stage

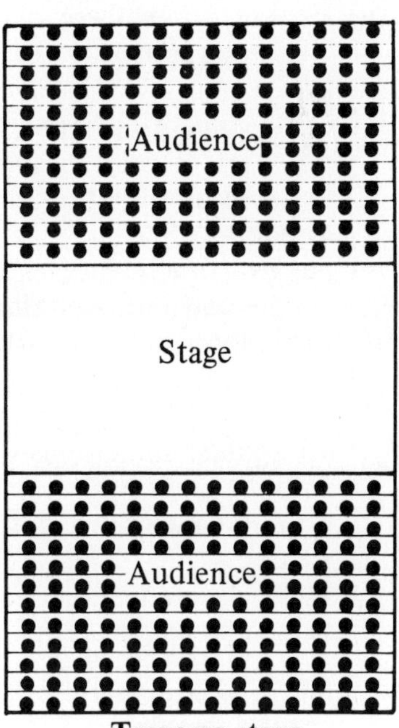

Traverse stage

The entire setting is wholly or, in some places, partially transparent. The roof-line of the house is one-dimensional; under and over it we see the apartment buildings. Before the house lies an apron, curving beyond the forestage into the orchestra. This forward area serves as the back yard as well as the locale of all Willy's imaginings and of his city scenes. Whenever the action is in the present the actors observe the imaginary wall-lines, entering the house only through its door at the left. But in the scenes of the past these boundaries are broken, and characters enter or leave a room by stepping 'through' a wall on to the forestage.

(i) What kind of stage does Arthur Miller have in mind?
(ii) What is the atmospheric effect of the flute music?
(iii) The setting stresses the 'towering, angular shapes' of 'apartment houses' and the lighting 'the blue light of the sky' and 'an angry glow of orange'. What impression is intended to be conveyed to an audience?
(iv) What function do the various props on stage have?
(v) Are there any indications, from the set Miller requires, about the kind of play the audience is about to witness?
(vi) How does Miller ensure a visually interesting setting for his action?

(i) Probably a variant on the proscenium arch, but not attempting realism of setting, traditionally associated with it; projecting apron stage allows for flexibility in portraying action in different times and places than the house alone.
(ii) Evokes atmosphere of wide open spaces, the great American outdoors; contrasts with ugly cityscape that surrounds Salesman's house.
(iii) Tiny, vulnerable house, surrounded by antagonistic forces; house not part of real harsh world, but an escape from it; contrast between blue light on house and (angry) orange on neighbouring buildings.
(iv) Suggest function of each room (bed, fridge); background kept simple and unfussy, allowing for dramatic action to be highlighted; sport likely to play an important part later.
(v) Suggestion of a 'documentary' study of some aspect of urban life in America (emphasising its oppressive, monolithic quality?) set against something more lyrical and elusive which has to do with the great American outdoors; it seems likely to be a 'memory play' in which the action will move fluidly from the present to the past.
(vi) Three different levels; four different acting areas; use of colour; suggestive use of props.

You might find it a useful exercise to draw set designs for *Death of a Salesman* for different types of theatre, such as theatre-in-the-round or an open-stage theatre.

We can look at a short scene from *Death of a Salesman* to see how Arthur Miller uses the facilities the theatre offers him. In this extract, at the end of the first act, Biff and Happy, Willy Loman's sons, have decided to go into business together and the next day Biff plans to see his former employer, Bill Oliver, to try to borrow some money from him. They go to say goodnight to their parents, and Willy remembers Biff's triumphs as a High School football star. At the close of the scene, Biff finds evidence of Willy's suicidal depression.

BIFF *and* HAPPY *enter the bedroom. Slight pause.*

WILLY (*stops short, looking at Biff*): Glad to hear it, boy.
HAPPY: He wanted to say good night to you, sport.
WILLY (*to Biff*). Yeah. Knock him dead, boy. What'd you want to tell me?
BIFF: Just take it easy, Pop. Good night. (*He turns to go.*) 5
WILLY (*unable to resist*): And if anything falls off the desk while you're talking to him—like a package or something—don't you pick it up. They have office boys for that.
LINDA: I'll make a big breakfast—
WILLY: Will you let me finish? (*To Biff.*) Tell him you were in the business 10 in the West. Not farm work.
BIFF: All right, Dad.
LINDA: I think everything—
WILLY (*going right through her speech*): And don't undersell yourself. No less than fifteen thousand dollars. 15
BIFF (*unable to bear him*): Okay. Good night, Mom. (*He starts moving.*)
WILLY: Because you got a greatness in you, Biff, remember that. You got all kinds a greatness . . . (*He lies back, exhausted.* BIFF *walks out.*)
LINDA (*calling after Biff*): Sleep well, darling!
HAPPY: I'm gonna get married, Mom. I wanted to tell you. 20
LINDA: Go to sleep, dear.
HAPPY (*going*): I just wanted to tell you.
WILLY: Keep up the good work (HAPPY *exits.*) God . . . remember that Ebbets Field game? The championship of the city?
LINDA: Just rest. Should I sing to you? 25
WILLY: Yeah. Sing to me. (LINDA *hums a soft lullaby.*) When that team came out—he was the tallest, remember?
LINDA: Oh, yes. And in gold.

BIFF *enters the darkened kitchen, takes a cigarette, and leaves the house. He comes downstage into a golden pool of light. He smokes, staring at the* 30 *night.*

WILLY: Like a young god. Hercules—something like that. And the sun, the sun all around him. Remember how he waved to me? Right up from the field, with the representatives of three colleges standing by? And the buyers I brought, and the cheers when he came out—Loman, Loman, 35 Loman! God Almighty, he'll be great yet. A star like that, magnificent, can never really fade away!

The light on WILLY *is fading. The gas heater begins to glow through the kitchen wall, near the stairs, a blue flame beneath red coils.*

LINDA (*timidly*): Willy dear, what has he got against you? 40
WILLY: I'm so tired. Don't talk any more.

BIFF *slowly returns to the kitchen. He stops, stares toward the heater.*
LINDA: Will you ask Howard to let you work in New York?
WILLY: First thing in the morning. Everything'll be all right.
BIFF *reaches behind the heater and draws out a length of rubber tubing. He is horrified and turns his head toward Willy's room still dimly lit, from which the strains of Linda's desperate but monotonous humming rise.* 45
WILLY (*staring through the window into the moonlight*): Gee, look at the moon moving between the buildings!
BIFF *wraps the tubing around his hand and quickly goes up the stairs.* 50

CURTAIN

(i) How does Arthur Miller use the various acting areas of the stage in this scene? (You might find it useful to give a movement plot for the excerpt.)
(ii) What do you feel is the atmosphere that this scene generates? How does Miller create this effect?

Another American play, written at almost the same time as *Death of a Salesman*, Tennessee Williams' *The Glass Menagerie* (1945), demonstrates vividly how much attention a playwright pays to what Williams calls the 'extra-literary accents' of his drama. In his production notes, he tells us that '*The Glass Menagerie* can be presented with unusual freedom from convention'. He wishes to avoid 'the straight realistic play . . . characters that speak exactly as its audience speaks. Everyone should know nowadays the unimportance of the photographic in art . . . that truth, life or reality is an organic thing which the poetic imagination can represent or suggest, in essence, only through transformation.' Williams continues and draws attention to the parts that music and lighting play in generating the particular atmosphere of *The Glass Menagerie*. 'A single recurring tune . . . . is used to give emotional emphasis to suitable passages . . . . it is the highest, most delicate music in the world and perhaps the saddest. It expresses the surface vivacity of life with the underlying strain of immutable and inexpressible sorrow, ... it serves as a thread of connection and allusion between the narrator with his separate point in time and space and the subject of his story. Between each episode it returns as reference to the emotion, nostalgia, which is the first condition of the play . . . . The lighting is not realistic. In keeping with the atmosphere of memory, the stage is dim. Shafts of light are focussed on selected areas or actors, sometimes in contradistinction to what is the apparent centre . . . the light upon Laura should be distinct from the others, having a peculiar pristine clarity such as light used in early religious portraits of female saints or madonnas . . . . a free imaginative use of light can be of enormous value in giving a mobile plastic quality to plays of a more or less static nature.'

In the opening scene of the play, Tom, the narrator, himself draws attention to the part played by music and lighting. We would like you to:

(i) comment on the part played by the set design in creating atmosphere;
(ii) consider how successful this whole scene would be in arousing the interest of an audience at a performance; and
(iii) discuss to what extent you think the scene is likely to convey in the theatre the kind of abstract effect Tennessee Williams wrote about above.

The Wingfield apartment is in the rear of the building, one of those vast hive-like conglomerations of cellular living-units that flower as warty growths in overcrowded urban centres of lower-middle-class population and are symptomatic of the impulse of this largest and fundamentally enslaved section of American society to avoid fluidity and differentiation and to exist and function as one interfused mass of automatism. 5

The apartment faces an alley and is entered by a fire-escape, a structure whose name is a touch of accidental poetic truth, for all of these huge buildings are always burning with the slow and implacable fires of human desperation. The fire-escape is included in the set – that is, the landing of it and steps descending from it. 10

The scene is memory and is therefore non-realistic. Memory takes a lot of poetic licence. It omits some details; others are exaggerated, according to the emotional value of the articles it touches, for memory is seated predominantly in the heart. The interior is therefore rather dim and poetic. 15

[At the rise of the curtain, the audience is faced with the dark, grim rear wall of the Wingfield tenement. This building, which runs parallel to the footlights, is flanked on both sides by dark, narrow alleys which run into murky canyons of tangled clothes-lines, garbage cans, and the sinister lattice-work of neighbouring fire-escapes. It is up and down these side alleys that exterior entrances and exits are made, during the play. At the end of TOM'S *opening commentary, the dark tenement wall slowly reveals (by means of a transparency) the interior of the ground floor Wingfield apartment.* 20

Downstage is the living-room, which also serves as a sleeping-room for LAURA, *the sofa unfolding to make her bed. Upstage, centre, and divided by a wide arch or second proscenium with transparent faded portières (or second curtain), is the dining-room. In an old-fashioned what-not in the living-room are seen scores of transparent glass animals. A blown-up photograph of the father hangs on the wall of the living-room, facing the audience, to the left of the archway. It is the face of a very handsome young man in a doughboy's First World War cap. He is gallantly smiling, ineluctably smiling, as if to say 'I will be smiling for ever'.* 25 30

The audience hears and sees the opening scene in the dining-room through both the transparent fourth wall of the building and the transparent gauze portières of the dining-room arch. It is during this revealing scene that the fourth wall slowly ascends out of sight. This transparent exterior wall is not brought down again until the very end of the play, during TOM'S *final speech.* 35

The narrator is an undisguised convention of the play. He takes whatever licence with dramatic convention is convenient to his purposes.

TOM *enters dressed as a merchant sailor from alley, stage left, and strolls* 40 *across the front of the stage to the fire-escape. There he stops and lights a cigarette. He addresses the audience.*]

TOM: Yes, I have tricks in my pocket, I have things up my sleeve. But I am the opposite of a stage magician. He gives you illusion that has the appearance of truth. I give you truth in the pleasant disguise of illusion. 45
To begin with, I turn back time. I reverse it to that quaint period, the thirties, when the huge middle class of America was matriculating in a school for the blind. Their eyes had failed them, or they had failed their eyes, and so they were having their fingers pressed forcibly down on the fiery Braille alphabet of a dissolving economy. 50
In Spain there was revolution. Here there was only shouting and confusion.
In Spain there was Guernica. Here there were disturbances of labour, sometimes pretty violent, in otherwise peaceful cities such as Chicago, Cleveland, Saint Louis. . . . 55
This is the social background of the play.

[MUSIC]

The play is memory.
Being a memory play, it is dimly lighted, it is sentimental, it is not 60 realistic.
In memory everything seems to happen to music. That explains the fiddle in the wings.
I am the narrator of the play, and also a character in it. The other characters are my mother Amanda, my sister Laura, and a gentleman 65 caller who appears in the final scenes.
He is the most realistic character in the play, being an emissary from a world of reality that we were somehow set apart from.
But since I have a poet's weakness for symbols, I am using this character also as a symbol; he is the long-delayed but always expected something that we live for. 70
There is a fifth character in the play who doesn't appear except in this larger-than-life-size photograph over the mantel.
This is our father who left us a long time ago.
He was a telephone man who fell in love with long distances; he gave up his job with the telephone company and skipped the light fantastic out 75 of town. . . . .
The last we heard of him was a picture postcard from Mazatlan, on the Pacific coast of Mexico, containing a message of two words—
'Hello—Good-bye!' and no address.
I think the rest of the play will explain itself. . . . 80

[AMANDA'S *voice becomes audible through the portières.* LEGEND ON SCREEN: OÙ SONT LES NEIGES'. *He divides the portières and enters the upstage area.*]

We have already made reference on pages 94–7 to Samuel Beckett's *Waiting for Godot* and you will remember the very austere dialogue that the two tramps, Vladimir and Estragon, utter. The staging and setting are of a piece with this dialogue. Not for Beckett the elaborateness of a Tennessee Williams; rather the only indication he gives as to setting is 'a country road'; as to time 'evening'; and as to scenery, 'a tree'. This is theatre stripped bare, with almost the maximum of simplicity. The effect is to concentrate the audience's attention on the dialogue and action of the tramps, with scant danger of its being deflected elsewhere; the deliberately unspecified locale means that the universality of their situation is emphasised; its emptiness a powerful symbol of the wasteland of civilization. With such a setting, naturally any change, however small, is going to have a great impact. Thus, though Act II opens with the directions 'Next day. Same Time. Same Place', there has been, in the context of the play, a startling change: 'The tree has four or five leaves.' Beckett makes a similarly dramatic lighting change in each act. No subtle fading of lights to indicate the gradual passage of time, but rather the 'light suddenly fails. In a moment it is night. The moon rises at back, mounts in the sky, stands still, shedding a pale light on the scene.'

It will be clear to you from your work in this chapter that very few dramatists have tried to make their plays photographic replicas of everyday life, though this idea of drama still persists in many people's minds as we suggested at the beginning of this chapter. To conclude, therefore, we would like to look at the work of two men whose writings about drama, theatre and the nature of acting have exercised a very great influence on twentieth-century drama and whose work was designed as an antidote to then current ideas about naturalistic drama—Bertolt Brecht and Antonin Artaud. A third major influence on twentieth-century theatre was the Russian, Konstantin Stanislavsky (1863–1938) whose theories on the nature of acting we have already referred to on pages 36–41.

BRECHT AND 'ALIENATION'

Bertolt Brecht (1898–1956) was the major German dramatist of his age and produced more writings on the nature and theory of the theatre than probably any other playwright. Much of what he wrote was in rebellious reaction to the concept of the stage as a naturalistic representation of the world peopled with actors, in the Stanislavsky mould, whose aim was to identify totally with the characters that they were playing. Brecht reacted strongly to what he thought was the dangerous illusion that such theatre produces in an audience who 'stare at the stage as if spell bound' and who seem to want to identify with the characters on stage—'those dream figures up there on the rostrum'. This, in Brecht's eyes, was dangerous because it prevented his audience from thinking critically about what they were witnessing and it was this critical thinking on the part of the audience that he most wanted to encourage because, for him, the theatre ought to be a place where moral and social instruction and improvement took place. He believed that audiences would not see the social and moral significance of the actions on stage if both the style of acting and the nature of the theatre itself were designed to make them *identify* with the characters, their situations and their emotions. If we are so enthralled with the character of say, Othello, that we see the action entirely from his point of view and if we are so caught up in the action that we mistake it for reality for the duration of the performance, then we would have no chance of achieving this necessary critical detachment. The aim of the Brechtian theatre was, as he put it, 'to induce an enquiring critical attitude on the part of the spectators towards the events shown.' Brecht's theatre was a place where moral and social truths were to be demonstrated to an audience in the hope that they would come to share some of his Marxist principles and sympathies. To achieve this, it was necessary for the dramatist to destroy the theatre of illusion. The audience should not think it is watching real people and real events, but should be made to realise that it is witnessing an account of things that, as Martin Esslin has written, 'have happened in the past at a certain time, in a certain place . . . [Brecht's theatre] constantly reminds the audience that it is merely getting a report of past events'.

The word that Brecht uses to describe this liberation of the audience's critical faculties that he felt was so vital for his socially committed theatre was '*Verfremdungseffekt*' or 'alienation'. In fact, *Verfremdungseffekt* is often wrongly translated as 'alienation effect', whereas it really means something like 'strange-making effect', a reference to the way in which Brecht wished to keep the spectator emotionally detached from the play's action. It was by means of *Verfremdungseffekt* that he hoped to create in his audiences a new and clearer understanding of the human situation.

We need now to look at some of the main methods Brecht uses to achieve this 'strange-making effect'. Read the following extract which forms the Prologue to *The Resistible Rise of Arturo Ui* (1941), Brecht's reworking of the rise of Hitler in terms of a Chicago gangster's take-over of the greengrocery trade in the city and neighbouring towns. See if you can identify some of the ways in which *Verfremdungseffekt* is achieved.

The Announcer steps before the curtain. Large notices are attached to the curtain: 'New developments in dock subsidy scandal' . . . 'The true facts about Dogsborough's will and confession' . . . 'Sensation at warehouse fire trial' . . . 'Friends murder gangster Ernesto Roma' . . . 'Ignatius Dullfeet blackmailed and murdered' . . . 'Cicero taken over by gangsters'. Behind the 5
curtain popular dance music.

THE ANNOUNCER:

Friends, tonight we're going to show—
Pipe down, you boys in the back row!
And, lady, your hat is in the way!— 10
The great historical gangster play
Containing, for the first time, as you'll see
The truth about the scandalous dock subsidy.
Further we give you, for your betterment

Dogsborough's confession and testament. 15
Arturo Ui's rise while the stock market fell.
The notorious warehouse fire trial. What a sell!
The Dullfeet murder! Justice in a coma!
Gang warfare: the killing of Ernesto Roma!
All culminating in our stunning last tableau: 20
Gangsters take over the town of Cicero!
Brilliant performers will portray
The most eminent gangsters of our day.
You'll see some dead and some alive
Some by-gone and others that survive 25
Some born, some made—for instance, here we show
The good old honest Dogsborough!

Old Dogsborough steps before the curtain.

His hair is white, his heart is black.
Corrupt old man, you may step back. 30

Dogsborough bows and steps back.

The next exhibit on our list
Is Givola—

Givola has stepped before the curtain.

—the horticulturist. 35
His tongue's so slippery he'd know how
To sell you a billy-goat for a cow!
Short, says the proverb, are the legs of lies.
Look at his legs, just use your eyes.

Givola steps back limping. 40

Now to Emanuele Giri, the super-clown.
Come out, let's look you up and down!

Giri steps before the curtain and waves his hand at the audience.

One of the greatest killers ever known!
Okay, beat it. 45

Giri steps back with an angry look.

And lastly Public Enemy Number One
Arturo Ui. Now you'll see
The biggest gangster of all times
Whom heaven sent us for our crimes 50
Our weakness and stupidity!

Arturo Ui steps before the curtain and walks out along the footlights.

Doesn't he make you think of Richard the Third?
Has anybody ever heard
Of blood so ghoulishly and lavishly shed 55
Since wars were fought for roses white and red?

In view of this the management
Has spared no cost in its intent
To picture his spectacularly vile
Manoeuvres in the grandest style. 60
But everything you'll see tonight is true.
Nothing's invented, nothing's new
Or made to order just for you.
The gangster play that we present
Is known to the whole continent. 65

While the music swells and the sound of a machine-gun mingles with it, the Announcer retires with an air of bustling self-importance.

You may in discussion have arrived at a list similar to this:

(i) use of an announcer (almost like a circus ringmaster bringing on star turns);
(ii) use of placards/headlines/notices;
(iii) events of play already summarised for audience by both placard and ringmaster. No surprise as to how events will turn out;
(iv) use of notices with main events of play on them suggests play will be an episodic history;
(v) popular dance music acts as a counterpoint to horrific events described;
(vi) sense that events are to be demonstrated for the audience's enlightenment ('Friends, tonight we're going to show'; 'our stunning last tableau');
(vii) direct address to the audience ('Lady, your hat is in the way');
(viii) deals with *historical* events whose significance will be interpreted for spectators;
(ix) jogging rhythm and heavy rhyme;
(x) main characters introduced and appear before main action commences (avoids necessity of it having to be done during main action);
(xi) reference to earlier *theatrical* villains (Richard III);
(xii) feeling that the actors are not attempting at all to *be* the characters but are there to present them to spectators and to interpret them.

Obviously in a short extract such as this, all the techniques of 'alienation' cannot be illustrated and you would need to read (or much better, watch!) some of his plays such as *Mother Courage*, *The Life of Galileo*, *The Caucasian Chalk Circle* or *The Good Person Of Szechwan* to gain a much fuller impression of the success (or failure) of Brecht's methods.

Some of the contemporary British dramatists who have been influenced by Brecht and have utilized some of his ideas have included John Arden (*Live Like Pigs* and *Sergeant Musgrave's Dance*), John Osborne (*Luther* and *The Entertainer*) and Robert Bolt (*A Man for all Seasons*).

Doubtless, as you read more widely and watch more performances, you will be able to identify many other writers who have been influenced by Brecht.

ANTONIN ARTAUD AND 'THE THEATRE OF CRUELTY'

Antonin Artaud (1896–1948) was a Frenchman who was a member of the theatrical avant-garde between the two World Wars and like his contemporary, Brecht, expressed considerable dissatisfaction with the theatre, calling the popular version fit only 'for idiots, madmen, inverts, grammarians, grocers, antipoets and positivists' and condemning the great dramatists of an earlier age, such as Shakespeare, for their lack of relevance to present-day audiences. However, unlike Brecht, Artaud was an indifferent dramatist and his importance to twentieth-century theatre lies not in any plays that he wrote but in the pervasive influence of his ideas which he summed up as 'The Theatre of Cruelty'. Artaud loathed Western civilization and he wished intently for a total alteration of its structure which he believed, almost with religious fervour, could be begun in the theatre—'I do believe that the theatre . . . has the power to influence the aspect and formation of things,' he wrote. He used the metaphor of the theatre as a plague to explain what he meant—'the action of the theatre, like that of the plague, is beneficial, for, pushing men into seeing themselves as they are; it causes the mask to fall and reveals the lie, and moral inertia, baseness and hypocrisy of our world'. As Jacques Guicharnaud says of Artaud in his book *Modern French Theatre*: 'just as during the plagues of the Western world men were rid of their Western character (order, reason, morality) and restored to their true powers, great theatre not only presents the spectacle of individuals restored to those powers but awakens them in the spectator'.

So, the type of theatre that Artaud visualises is one that purges man of the violent impulses that he believes are most manifest when man claims to be motivated by such things as love of one's country, love of God and love for another person. 'The theatre will never find itself again—i.e. constitute a means of true illusion—except by furnishing the spectator with the truthful precipitates of his dreams, in which his taste for crime, his erotic obsessions, his savagery, his chimaeras . . . even his cannibalism, pour out, on a level not counterfeit and illusory, but interior.' (Artaud)

So what is an audience to expect when it attends a piece of Artaud theatre? As is clear from his synopsis of a play he planned for the 'Theatre of Cruelty', *The Conquest of Mexico*, it is primarily a visual spectacle; everything is subordinated to the visual impact of the *mise-en-scène*. Spectacle for him was more important than character, than plot, than language, and he wished to use 'all the means of expression utilisable on stage, such as music, dance, plastic art, pantomime, mimicry, gesticulation, intonation, architecture, scenery and lighting . . . . manikins, enormous masks, objects of strange proportions'. Clearly, it is not surprising that Artaud's specific ideas for magical, mystical theatre have not been followed in their entirety, but it is nonetheless true that he remains an important influence on contemporary theatre. Many modern playwrights have incorporated violence, cruelty and madness into their works so as to make the audience aware of what it means to be human in a world stripped of the veneer of 'civilization' and as the French critic Jacques Guiharnaud has indicated 'almost all the great modern playwrights try to prevent the spectator from drowsing in a peaceful definition of man. While few, of course, go as far as Artaud in rejecting Western thought as a whole, all question the basic values of our world, its conception of good and evil, and the satisfactions of rationalism'. Artaud's influence can be traced in the work of many modern French dramatists, such as Camus, Genet, Sartre and Ionesco, and perhaps in the British theatre to a writer such as David Rudkin (*Afore Night Come*). The most striking example in post-war British theatre is Peter Brooks' production of Peter Weiss' *Marat/Sade* in which the audience is asked to take the part of spectators at a performance at Charenton lunatic asylum in 1808 in which the inmates act out under the direction of the Marquis de Sade the events leading up to the assassination of the French revolutionary leader, Jean-Paul Marat, in his bath by Charlotte Corday.

13

Style

By the 'style' of a writer we mean the kind of language he uses to express what he has to say: an author's distinctive style, therefore, may be seen as a product of such elements as diction (choice of words), the shifting rhythms of syntax, sentence construction and the sound quality of words, and the use and type of metaphorical language. In *Considering Prose* we discuss at length the ways in which prose style may be analysed, and in this book, in connection with our study of dramatic dialogue, we have already underlined the importance of the language and patterning of dialogue as the main stylistic indicator in a play. However, when we are considering the style of *drama*—i.e. the various means by which meaning is to be communicated in the theatre—it will be immediately apparent that more is involved here than just the nature of the words that appear in a script. The preceding chapter, for instance, will have given you some indication of how different methods of staging affect the channels of communication between the acting area and an audience. And when we refer to the style of a production, many specifically theatrical elements are involved—acting technique, the use of costume and lighting and so on—as well as the linguistic components of style noted above. What we wish to do in this section is to make a general kind of statement about how we should approach questions of dramatic style.

While students who are beginning to study drama—or any branch of literature for that matter—usually find it relatively easy to enter into a discussion of matters such as a work's 'themes' or 'characters', they often encounter problems in considering 'style'. This is often because many students tend to regard the style of a work as a kind of literary cosmetic which the author has smeared over the surface of his writing in order to give it a pleasing appearance. It is, however, only when we see an author's style as integral to the content of his subject matter—i.e. recognise the organic relationship between what is said and how it is said—that we will be able to discuss style in any meaningful way. This is why, for instance, when we were discussing the linguistic manoeuvres of dialogue, we stressed the direct link between the kind of language involved and its likely impact on an audience. We have also considered in some detail how a playwright uses language to create the particular 'voicing' for a character (see pages 118–22). So, to study the style of a dramatist's text is not to become obsessed with arcane matters of pure technique; what is really involved is an appreciation of how the dramatist makes his language and the conventions of the theatre embody the vision he wishes to share with an audience. And in performance, too, the style of a production is not some extraneous matter; rather it concerns all the expressive and theatrical methods by which a text is brought to life on the stage.

What we want to stress at this point is that it is through the style of a play that a playwright gives both actor and audience a sense of how the play is to be interpreted. From our chapter on dialogue you will already be familiar with some of the levels of language in drama which can produce quite different effects: these can range from elevated and stylised language, suggesting the formality of a rather rarefied world which is at some remove from quotidian reality, to rhythms clearly based on colloquial speech which will require an entirely different, more naturalistic, acting technique. As an example of the way in which the language of dialogue signals a definite range of tone, movement, gesture (and even dress) on the actor's part, turn back to the extract from *Billy Liar* on page 28. It is evident that the language used in this passage rises out of an everyday, domestic situation. If Billy, hunched over the breakfast table in his old raincoat, were to cough loudly, take out a cigarette butt and light up—or start picking his nose—we would hardly raise an eyebrow. On the other hand, imagine an audience's reaction if Hamlet, in the scene with Ophelia which we examined earlier (see page 146), were to act in a similar way—or if a simpering Ophelia appeared in hair-curlers. The audience would be struck by a ludicrous sense of incongruity between what the language of the scene seemed to be telling them and the crude intrusion of a highly idiosyncratic (and anachronistic) interpretation.

This is not to suggest that *Hamlet* cannot be successfully presented in a certain kind of modern dress or to rule out a whole range of various movements and gestures which would blend with the nature and suggestiveness of Shakespeare's dramatic verse. We also need to recognise that a director, in quite a calculated fashion, may wish to set off the dramatist's apparent original intention (as expressed in the play's style) against the director's own novel, or even iconoclastic, way of staging the drama—in the hope of making an audience see the play with fresh eyes. Yet, in the first place, the director of any effective production must address himself very carefully to what the style of the text indicates about such matters as the appropriate methods of acting and staging a play. Many productions fail because either the director has not tuned in properly to the style of the text (and what this suggests and demands) or has been unable to match his awareness with its realisation through the appropriate theatrical presentation.

So to summarise an essential point: the style of a play will suggest a certain interpretative range which includes possible techniques of acting and corresponding methods of staging and using costume, lighting and so on. All these elements need to be made to work, in performance, in a harmonious way with the language of the play. The style of drama is the key to a discovery of the kind of emotional and intellectual impact which the play has been designed to have on the members of an ideal audience. For instance, it is through the play's style that we will be able to appreciate the kind of atmosphere a dramatist wishes to create, the nature of the vision he wishes to share with the members of the audience and the degree of emotional involvement he requires from them.

With this awareness of the importance of style in mind, we would recommend a re-examination of the following extracts:

Macbeth (page 20)
The Cherry Orchard (page 53)
St Joan (page 60)
Oedipus Rex (page 65)
The School for Scandal (page 71)

Answer the following questions in connection with each of the passages listed above.

(i) Describe the general nature of the style of the extract. (For example, to think in terms of extremes, is the language elevated or colloquial, rhetorically patterned or apparently unpremeditated? And does the style suggest the conventions of a naturalistic or of a stylized mode of presentation?)
(ii) By what means is this style created – both through the language and any specifically theatrical devices?
(iii) What does the particular style of the scene suggest about the effect it is designed to have on an audience?
(iv) Imagine that you are directing this scene. Write down some notes, to actors and to technical staff, on the style of acting you wish to employ (include also specific points about the use of voice, movement and gesture) and the kind of effects of staging, set, scenery, costume and lighting, etc.—some sketches or diagrams might be useful here—that you will require. The essential point is to describe how you intend to realise in theatrical terms the effect you have defined in response to the previous question.

VARIATIONS IN STYLE

In the previous exercise you were, of course, considering style in relation to short extracts, but even within the space of a single scene you probably discovered that dramatic style can shift into quite a number of different keys. (Which of the passages that you examined showed most evidence of this—and why?) When we are studying a play as a whole we will generally find that the play quickly defines its stylistic compass—the range of upper and lower notes through which it will move. The span of this range depends on the nature and breadth of experience which the playwright wishes to encompass in his drama. A play such as Edward Bond's *Saved* (1966) remains fairly consistently on the level of a crude 'proletarian' discourse, the threadbare, imprecise quality of which is always to the fore. At the other extreme, in Wilde's *The Importance of Being Earnest* (1895), even a relatively minor character such as the butler, Lane, is endowed with the ability to polish epigrams with the urbanity of his 'betters'; while in a tragedy written in the French neo-classical tradition in the seventeenth century—Corneille's *Le Cid* (1637), for example—the style of the play will be consistently elevated and in accordance with exacting metrical conventions. (As we have said before, these contrasting modes of language will each virtually dictate its own distinctive style of acting and theatrical presentation.)

During its course, however, a play may range through quite a rich variety of registers and tones. We have already examined one example of Hamlet's discourse (see page 146), but equally characteristic of him is his clear-headed advice on acting technique to the players who visit Elsinore or the soliloquy full of the passionate pent-up feeling of a deeply introspective, sensitive nature. To follow in detail the tonal variations of a drama is one of the delights of dramatic criticism: it reveals the creation of the light and shade, and the varying tones in between, which is an essential element in most plays. In this book we have to work on fairly small canvases; however, the following scene from Shakespeare's *Henry IV, Part 1* (1597) should provide you with the opportunity of considering some of the contrasts and juxtapositions of different dramatic styles that can be achieved within a relatively short space.

(i) Identify the variations of style and the way they are created in this scene. (Consider, for instance, the different uses to which prose and verse are put and the contrast between Falstaff's speeches and the language used in the exchanges between Prince Hal and Hotspur.)
(ii) Comment on the dramatic impact of these variations of style within the scene as a whole.

After associating for some time with riotous drinking companions, of whom Falstaff is the dissolute leader, Prince Hal has joined his father, Henry IV, who faces an armed rebellion led by the Percys. Hal sees Henry Percy (known as Hotspur) as a personal rival. The Percys also have in their army, among other rebels, the Earl of Douglas.

The scene is the battlefield at Shrewsbury. Douglas has just killed one of the King's followers, Sir Walter Blunt. Falstaff is (nominally) fighting on the King's side.

Alarum. Enter FALSTAFF *solus.*

FALSTAFF: Though I could scape shot-free[1] at London, I fear the shot here, here's no scoring[2] but upon the pate. Soft! who are you? Sir Walter Blunt—there's honour for you! Here's no vanity[3]! I am as hot as molten lead, and as heavy too: God keep lead out of me, I need no more weight than mine own bowels. I have led my ragamuffins where they are 5

[1] two senses: (i) without paying the bill; (ii) unwounded.
[2] two senses: (i) charging a bill; (ii) striking a blow.
[3] spoken ironically—i.e. 'Here is vanity—something futile'.

peppered,[4] there's not three of my hundred and fifty left alive, and they are for the town's end, to beg during life. But who comes here?

Enter the PRINCE.

PRINCE: What, stands thou idle here? Lend me thy sword:
Many a nobleman lies stark and stiff 10
Under the hoofs of vaunting enemies,
Whose deaths are yet unrevenged. I prithee lend me thy sword.
FALSTAFF: O Hal, I prithee give me leave to breathe awhile—
Turk Gregory[5] never did such deeds in arms as I have done this day; I have paid[6] Percy, I have made him sure. 15
PRINCE: He is indeed, and living to kill thee:
I prithee lend me thy sword.
FALSTAFF: Nay, before God, Hal, if Percy be alive thou gets not my sword, but take my pistol if thou wilt.
PRINCE: Give it me: what, is it in the case? 20
FALSTAFF: Ay, Hal, 'tis hot,[7] 'tis hot; there's that will sack a city.
The Prince draws it out, and finds it to be a bottle of sack[8].
PRINCE: What, is it a time to jest and dally now?
He throws the bottle at him. Exit.
FALSTAFF: Well, if Percy be alive, I'll pierce him. If he do come in my way, 25 so: if he do not, if I come in his willingly, let him make a carbonado[9] of me. I like not such grinning honour as Sir Walter hath. Give me life, which if I can save, so: if not, honour comes unlooked for, and there's an end. *Exit.*

Some time later 30

. . . *Enter* DOUGLAS.

DOUGLAS: Another king! They grow like Hydra's heads[10]:
I am the Douglas, fatal to all those
That wear those colours on them. What art thou
That counterfeit'st the person of a king? 35
KING: The King himself, who, Douglas, grieves at heart
So many of his shadows thou hast met,
And not the very King. I have two boys
Seek Percy and thyself about the field,
But seeing thou fall'st on me so luckily 40
I will assay thee, and defend thyself.
DOUGLAS: I fear thou art another counterfeit,
And yet, in faith, thou bearest thee like a king;
But mine I am sure thou art, whoe'er thou be,
And thus I win thee. *They fight, the King being in danger.* 45

---

[4] come under heavy attack.
[5] i.e. the type of a fiery, cruel opponent.
[6] killed.
[7] Falstaff pretends he has put his pistol in its case to cool after much use.
[8] Spanish white wine.
[9] meat scored across for broiling.
[10] several of Henry's followers are wearing the King's colours in order to confuse the enemy. The Hydra = a many-headed monster which grew two heads for each one cut off.

Re-enter PRINCE OF WALES.

PRINCE: Hold up thy head, vile Scot, or thou art like
Never to hold it up again! The spirits
Of valiant Shirley, Stafford, Blunt are in my arms.
It is the Prince of Wales that threatens thee, 50
Who never promiseth but he means to pay.
They fight: Douglas flieth.
Cheerly, my lord, how fares your grace?
Sir Nicholas Gawsey hath for succour sent,
And so hath Clifton—I'll to Clifton straight. 55
KING: Stay and breathe a while:
Thou hast redeem'd thy lost opinion[11],
And show'd thou mak'st some tender[12] of my life,
In this fair rescue thou hast brought to me.
PRINCE: O God, they did me too much injury 60
That ever said I hearken'd for your death.
If it were so, I might have let alone
The insulting hand of Douglas over you,
Which would have been as speedy in your end
As all the poisonous potions in the world, 65
And sav'd the treacherous labour of your son.
KING: Make up to Clifton, I'll to Sir Nicholas Gawsey. *Exit.*

Enter HOTSPUR.

HOTSPUR: If I mistake not, thou art Harry Monmouth.
PRINCE: Thou speak'st as if I would deny my name. 70
HOTSPUR: My name is Harry Percy.
PRINCE: Why then I see
A very valiant rebel of the name.
I am the Prince of Wales, and think not, Percy,
To share with me in glory any more: 75
Two stars keep not their motion in one sphere[13],
Nor can one England brook[14] a double reign
Of Harry Percy and the Prince of Wales.
HOTSPUR: Nor shall it, Harry, for the hour is come
To end the one of us, and would to God 80
Thy name in arms were now as great as mine!
PRINCE: I'll make it greater ere I part from thee,
And all the budding honours on thy crest
I'll crop to make a garland for my head.
HOTSPUR: I can no longer brook thy vanities. *They fight.* 85

Enter FALSTAFF.

FALSTAFF: Well said, Hal! To it, Hal! Nay, you shall find no boy's play here, I can tell you.

[11] reputation.
[12] value (for).
[13] orbit.
[14] bear, put up with.

Re-enter DOUGLAS; *he fighteth with Falstaff, who falls down as if he were dead.* [*Exit Douglas.*] *The Prince mortally wounds Hotspur.* 90

HOTSPUR: O Harry, thou hast robb'd me of my youth!
I better brook the loss of brittle life
Than those proud titles thou hast won of me;
They wound my thoughts worse than thy sword my flesh:
But thoughts, the slaves of life, and life, time's fool, 95
And time, that takes survey of all the world,
Must have a stop. O, I could prophesy,
But that the earthy and cold hand of death
Lies on my tongue: no, Percy, thou art dust,
And food for— [*Dies.*] 100

PRINCE: For worms, brave Percy. Fare thee well, great heart!
Ill-weav'd ambition, how much art thou shrunk!
When that this body did contain a spirit,
A kingdom for it was too small a bound;
But now two paces of the vilest earth 105
Is room enough. This earth that bears thee dead
Bears not alive so stout[15] a gentleman.
If thou wert sensible of courtesy
I should not make so dear[16] a show of zeal;
But let my favours[17] hide thy mangled face, 110
And even in thy behalf I'll thank myself
For doing these fair rites of tenderness.
Adieu, and take thy praise with thee to heaven!
Thy ignominy sleep with thee in the grave,
But not remember'd in thy epitaph! 115
He spieth Falstaff on the ground.
What, old acquaintance, could not all this flesh
Keep in a little life? Poor Jack, farewell!
I could have better spar'd a better man:
O, I should have a heavy miss of thee 120
If I were much in love with vanity:
Death hath not struck so fat a deer today,
Though many dearer, in this bloody fray.
Embowell'd[18] will I see thee by and by,
Till then in blood by noble Percy lie. *Exit.* 125

FALSTAFF *riseth up.*

FALSTAFF: Embowelled? If thou embowel me today, I'll give you leave to powder[19] me and eat me too tomorrow. 'Sblood, 'twas time to counterfeit, or that hot termagant Scot had paid me, scot and lot[20] too.

---

[15] valiant.
[16] heartfelt.
[17] probably the plumes from Hal's helmet.
[18] disembowelled for embalming his corpse.
[19] pickle in salt.
[20] killed me—literally 'paid me in full'.

Counterfeit? I lie, I am no counterfeit: to die is to be a counterfeit, for he 130
is but the counterfeit of a man, who hath not the life of a man: but to
counterfeit dying, when a man thereby liveth, is to be no counterfeit, but
the true and perfect image of life indeed. The better part of valour is
discretion, in the which better part I have saved my life. 'Zounds, I am
afraid of this gunpowder Percy, though he be dead; how if he should 135
counterfeit too and rise? By my faith, I am afraid he would prove the
better counterfeit; therefore I'll make him sure, yea, and I'll swear I killed
him. Why may not he rise as well as I? Nothing confutes me but eyes, and
nobody sees me: therefore, sirrah [*stabbing him*], with a new wound in
your thigh, come you along with me. 140

He takes up Hotspur on his back.

Finally, it is important to emphasise that dramatic style in the theatre involves an integration of the text with the full range of theatrical resources. One of the most critical factors is the matching of the language and feelings the actors have to communicate with the appropriate movements and gestures. One lesson we hope you learnt from the very basic exercise on page 41 is the extent to which the physical relation between the participants in a dialogue may embody a definition of the nature of their interaction. Sometimes a playwright will make this explicit in a stage direction: for instance, in the extracts by Robert Bolt (page 83) or Shaw (page 101), note the very simple movement made by one character in order to exert dominance over another. More often than not, however, it will be left to the director or actor to decide these essential, interpretative questions. So, at a particular moment in *Othello*, as Iago plants the seeds of jealousy in Othello's mind, does Iago stand over Othello, whispering in his ear, or circle him like some spider weaving a web, or show his power to galvanise his prey by speaking almost casually from some distance? And so on.

In the last extract, from *Henry IV, Part I*, certain obvious stage directions are included, but generally the movement and positioning of one character relative to the other are left open to individual interpretation. Consider, for instance, two key moments from the scene—involving the King and his son, Hal (ll. 56–66) and Hal and Hotspur (ll. 91–115). If you were directing this scene, what would be *your* visualisation of these two pieces of speech and action?

To practise further the discovery of the 'spatial embodiment' of meaning in drama, we suggest that you select one passage you have already studied and, having decided on the type of staging you wish to use, block out the exact movements around the stage that you feel the characters should make. Perhaps notes to individual actors, sketches and diagrams might be useful. Another approach would be to take the viewpoint of one single character in a scene and to describe, in the form of a running commentary, the moves he or she should make. Be prepared to *justify* your 'choreography'!

14

Genre

In the extract from *Henry IV, Part 1*, the serious business of the King's battle against the rebels is juxtaposed with the humour of Falstaff's cowardly behaviour. The resulting contrast between the ideals of honour and military glory and the Falstaffian priority of self-preservation at all costs creates a strong dramatic tension. *Henry IV, Part 1* is, of course, one of Shakespeare's history plays, based on the old chronicles of English history, but even in Shakespeare's tragedies, as the famous examples of the Porter Scene in *Macbeth* and the Gravediggers' Scene in *Hamlet* demonstrate, we find that a world of intense suffering and anguish is made to lie down side by side with comedy—or even buffoonery. It will not do to say that such scenes are simply 'light relief': they are integral to the plays of which they form a part. So when Shakespeare's Porter in *Macbeth* drunkenly imagines that he is the keeper of the gate of hell, he speaks, ironically, more truly than he can imagine: after the murder of Duncan, Macbeth's castle *has* become a kind of living hell. In *Hamlet,* too, the gravediggers' bumbling talk and jests about human mortality bear on and intensify some of the play's central issues. Scenes of this kind have a clear thematic and structural unity with the more serious and sombre tragic tone that predominates elsewhere in the world of tragedy.

The other side of the coin is that in many of Shakespeare's comedies—*Measure for Measure* would be an extreme example—darker elements intrude which for a time threaten the lighter tone and conventional 'happy ending' of comedy. And in the Romances, the plays of Shakespeare's final period (see *The Winter's Tale*), we find portrayed situations of tragic potential, the pain and apparent human loss of which are finally short-circuited by the process of reconciliation.

When we speak of 'tragedy' and 'comedy' we are referring to two of the most essential *genres* of drama—a 'genre' being a term originally taken from French to denote a 'species', or as we would more usually say, a literary *form*. Shakespeare's inclusion of comic elements in the world of tragedy—and *vice versa*—is characteristic of English drama; it is a tradition that goes right back to the mediaeval Mystery Plays, from which we gave you a sample earlier (see page 17). However, this 'blending of genres' has in the past puzzled, in particular, some critics and playwrights who belong to other European traditions in which the interpenetration of the tragic with the comic is viewed as a dubious, primitive practice. When the German playwright and poet Schiller (1759–1805) adapted *Macbeth*, for instance, he deleted the Porter Scene because he felt it was inappropriate to a poetic tragedy. In seventeenth-century France, comedy and tragedy exist virtually in watertight compartments; so in a tragedy by Corneille or Racine the intensity of the dramatic action is never 'lowered' by what would have been viewed as the heterogeneous elements of comedy. Voltaire (1694–1778), an influential French critic, was bewildered by Shakespeare's hybrid tragedies and lamented his influence on English drama. In his *Lettres Philosophiques* (1734) Voltaire concedes that Shakespeare possessed a 'strong and fertile genius'; yet he states that Shakespeare wrote 'without the slightest spark of good taste or the least knowledge of the rules'. With evident distaste Voltaire tells his French readers: 'You are not unaware that in Hamlet gravediggers dig a grave, swallowing drinks and singing popular songs, cracking jokes typical of men of their calling about the skulls they come across'.

Whereas the 'rules' Voltaire endorsed required that tragedy and comedy must exist as pure strains, it is likely that the vision of life Shakespeare expresses in his plays is profounder than Voltaire realises. Shakespeare knows, for instance, that suffering and pain co-exist with the most grotesque kinds of humour and that the inclusion of these wider perspectives intensifies our sense of the tragic. The mingling of elements of tragedy and comedy is true to our experience of life: while we celebrate moving into our new house, somebody next door is dying of cancer. In fact, the pedantic itch of some critics to classify plays according to the fixed, qualifying 'rules' of genres is a tendency Shakespeare playfully sends up when in *Hamlet* he makes the laughably tedious Polonius comment on the actors who have recently arrived at Elsinore in terms of the following catalogue:

> The best actors in the world, either for tragedy, comedy, history, pastoral, pastoral-comical, historical-pastoral, tragical-comical-historical-pastoral, scene individable, or poem unlimited.
>
> (*Hamlet*, II.ii)

While avoiding such absurd pigeon-holing, it will be useful, however, to make certain rough distinctions between the two great dramatic genres of tragedy and comedy. The process of definition has been carried on in virtually every age and such theoretical discussion has had its impact on the writing of plays, though we must bear in mind that definitions have varied greatly and, because we are dealing with abstract concepts, 'real plays' tend not to correspond obligingly with them. What we will offer, as a useful starting point for considering the nature of tragedy, is an abbreviated set of definitions taken from—or derived from—the classic discussion of tragedy by Aristotle (384–22 BC) in the *Poetics*. This view of the form was based on Aristotle's observation and analysis of the plays of the great Ancient Greek tragedians. It needs to be emphasised that there is no absolute consensus among critics about the nature of tragedy and that to define our modern sense of the 'tragic' as it applies to the plays of our time and tradition must entail substantial modifications of Aristotle's definition. Nearly every statement below would need, therefore, to be followed by 'generally', 'often' or 'in many periods'—qualifications which for reasons of brevity we have usually omitted. Nevertheless, virtually every serious attempt to define the nature of tragedy begins with some consideration of the following issues.

TRAGEDY

1. The action moves towards catastrophe, involving a sudden reversal of the hero's fortunes from happiness to misery and culminating almost invariably in his death.
2. The hero will be an individual of some high rank or status—a king or prince whose fall involves the fate of a whole nation. (Though in England in the eighteenth-century a tradition of 'bourgeois' or 'domestic' tragedy emerges. And compare in our own period the appearance of the tragic 'anti-hero'.)
3. The hero is neither pre-eminently virtuous nor completely evil: the reversal of his fortune is brought about by some 'tragic flaw' in his character or 'error of judgement'.
4. The hero is therefore involved in a struggle against fate or the hostility/indifference of the gods or a malign set of circumstances which exposes the hero's vulnerability, and his suffering moves us because it is incommensurate with his faults.
5. Because of the stature and nature of the hero, he compels our attention—and probably our identification with his plight.
6. Courage and endurance in the face of inevitable defeat are the predominant notes. It may be that through the agency of suffering the hero is brought to some measure of self-knowledge; often on the very brink of death he will see his situation as it really is.
7. The play finally arouses in an audience 'pity and fear, wherewith to accomplish the *catharsis* of such emotions'—the famous Aristotlean formulation. *Catharsis* suggests a purging or a purification of feeling. Certainly we experience a sense of waste at the end of a tragedy, though this will probably be combined with a feeling of elevation at having witnessed a sublime struggle, mediated to us in the form of a profound aesthetic experience, from which we derive insights transcending our mundane experience.
8. The style is in keeping with the intensity and grandeur of the action. The characteristic medium is dramatic poetry.

General discussion topics

1. How does the preceding set of definitions square with the tragedies you have read or seen performed?

2. 'The sudden death of any man or woman in the prime of life is 'tragic' in one sense—but not inherently so if we are considering the material which goes to make up tragedy as a dramatic form.' What distinction is being made here? Do you agree with the statement?
3. 'The traditional genre of tragedy seems to impose a pre-ordained pattern on experience—and on the shape of a play. As all art should seek to interpret the varied experience of life in a fresh way and to discover new patterns which will help to explain why things are as they are, the dramatist should break out of the straitjacket of a conventional view of the nature of tragedy.' Give your own opinion.
4. How would you define our modern sense of what constitutes a tragedy—in the light of reading a play such as Arthur Miller's *Death of a Salesman* (1949)?
5. What kind of subjects in modern experience might make fit material for tragedy? (Make clear first whether you are following the essentially Aristotlean view or providing your own definition of tragedy.) For instance, would it be possible to write a tragedy about somebody who was on the dole? Could a tragedy effectively be set in a concentration camp or in a city devastated by bombing in time of war?
6. 'Tragedy ought to be a great kick at misery.' (D. H. Lawrence)
   'Tragedy is one long lament. Not restrained or elegaic but plangent and full-throated, it speaks of all the pity of life and the terror.' (Eric Bentley)
   What does the first statement mean? Is it possible to reconcile it with the second statement?
7. Taking up the point listed (7) in our set of definitions, in what sense can we be said to 'enjoy' a tragedy?
8. In the light of your previous discussion, write the plot outline of a tragedy you think would make a successful piece of drama.

COMEDY

Comedy is a more amorphous form than tragedy and therefore more difficult to define. We shall attempt some kind of definition by boiling down the 574 romantic comedies we have seen or read. What we shall give you is the general outline of a comedy of classic shape—an archetype. It looks something like this.

The action of our comedy will move through a series of complications and confusions—perhaps involving disguise, mistaken identity, errors of judgement and all kinds of strategems (successful and unsuccessful)—yet though disaster may threaten, a happy ending is assured because of the quick-wittedness of some of the characters, but mainly as a result of our manipulation (as dramatists) of a highly artificial plot. In fact, plot will tend to predominate over character in our comedy, and it will be a plot, exhibiting strong elements of both contrivance and symmetry, which follows a virtually predetermined general pattern—though with subtle variations. Here is our basic story coming up.

Take two pairs of lovers—or three pairs if you like; we will make the third pair servants so they can echo in a minor key the romantic preoccupations of their masters and mistresses. For at the end of the play the lovers are all going to end up married to the 'right' partner, but initially they face some barrier to matrimony that has to be surmounted. Perhaps the difficulty they confront takes the shape of parental opposition—usually it will be the girl's father who objects—or it could be that the partners who are so obviously meant for each other are apparently separated by social class or convention. Maybe at the outset the lovers themselves think they are in love with somebody else or refuse to be in love, blindly failing to recognise the partners for whom the comic fates have destined them. Anyway, the barrier that separates them *will* be surmounted, and the means by which this is achieved will form one of the major elements of the plot. Hence the predominance of the devices of tricks and deceptions that we noted at the outset.

Let our setting be metropolitan; but whether we choose instead some exotic-sounding Italian town or some location of apparent retreat or escape from the everyday world, such as a suitably idyllic forest, our play will be concerned primarily with the social relations of the 'here and now'. In its preoccupation with the surface of contemporary social life, manners and conventions, comedy's world is much more 'secular' than that of tragedy. Our characters will tend to be drawn from a wider social range than those of tragedy—we will include some 'below-stairs' activity and perhaps even some vulgar characters taken from 'low life'—and they will fall into fairly recognisable types. Let us have, along with our sighing or cynical lovers, at least one jealous husband, a rake, a clown or trickster, a braggart and an outsider who fails to conform to the prevailing social values and will therefore provide a useful comic butt. Human weaknesses and foibles will be gently mocked, or perhaps subjected to some fairly bitter satire on occasions—our comedy may even have a certain didactic function—but by the end of the play the more harmful consequences of our fallen natures will be checked and differences generally smoothed over by reconciliation and compromise. Although the situation may contain some of the seeds of tragedy, they will not grow into the destructive upheavals of the tragic universe. For comedy recognises that ultimately people have to learn to live together within the constraints of a given social context, even if this may mean 'making the best of things'. Yet at the end of our comedy we will aim at evoking an atmosphere of joyfulness and harmony, and perhaps the festive note that sounds in the inevitable wedding bells—along with, maybe, a holiday mood of dance, song and celebration—asserts the value of stabilising social continuities. From this we may gather comedy will be essentially conservative: the values of the society for which the play is written may have been questioned (or even temporarily undermined), but in the last analysis—at the final curtain—the *status quo* is tacitly accepted or openly endorsed.

We will not require the total emotional absorption of our audience in the action of the comedy. As they watch the pieces of our archetypal pattern come together, they will smile (we hope) at the absurdities, affectations and hypocrisies that are revealed to them, and they may even recognise that a mirror is being held up to some of their own follies. As for the style of our comedy, it will be more closely related to everyday speech and the preoccupations of social life than that of tragedy, though we will set off the dialogue of our 'low-life' characters against a more polished kind of discourse which, in the verbal battles that run throughout the main action of the play, manifests epigrammatic poise and urbanity.

SPOTTING THE GENRE

We have provided merely a platform for an initial study of tragedy and comedy. For the next stage, we suggest you begin by reading two books in *The Critical Idiom* series published by Methuen: they are *Tragedy* by Clifford Leech and *Comedy* by Moelwyn Merchant, both of which explore a number of theories in connection with their respective genres and contain useful bibliographies. There are, of course, many other dramatic genres—and sub-divisions of genres. You need to get to know the various members of the Comedy Family—*Comedy of Humours, Romantic Comedy, Satiric Comedy, Comedy of Manners, Black Comedy* and *Farce*—and the offspring of the marriage of Comedy and Tragedy, *Tragicomedy*, and Tragedy's noisy little brother, *Melodrama*. Look up these genres in a good reference book, such as *A Glossary of Literary Terms* by M. H. Abrams, and read some of the wide variety of plays that will be suggested as examples of these genres. This should enable you to discover for yourself the relation between the theory of genres and the nature of living plays.

Particularly during the nineteenth century, under the pressure of a number of forces, not least the impact of the Romantic Movement, the traditional genres were stretched into novel shapes and some new dramatic forms came into being. In many quarters the structure of a play came to be seen not as something which was imposed from without—a shape partially determined by the conventional pattern of a given genre—but rather as an organic development which would be formed as a result of the particular nature of the dramatic materials with which a dramatist was working. To discover what variations on old genres occur (and what new forms emerge) as a part of the large-scale movements in the history of the theatre of our own century, we would recommend you consult the three volumes by J. L. Styan: *Modern Drama in Theory and Practice* (Cambridge University Press): 1. *Realism and Naturalism;* 2. *Symbolism, Surrealism and the Absurd;* 3. *Expressionism and Epic Theatre.*

A study of genre is valuable in that, not only does it direct our attention to the aesthetics and structure of drama, it is also a matter which has the most practical bearing on the way a play is to be performed. For instance, each of the various varieties of comedy–from farce to the comedy of manners–requires its distinctive techniques of acting and direction. The question of a play's genre, therefore, must be included with the other factors we discussed earlier (see page 182–4) which influence any judgement on the appropriate style in which a play is to be presented in order to achieve its desired impact on an audience. In connection with an example we have referred to before, Chekhov's *The Cherry Orchard*, the playwright himself declared: 'I call the play comedy'; his director Stanislavsky did not agree: 'This is not a comedy or a farce . . . it is a tragedy, whatever the solution you may have found for a better life in the last act'. What dramatist and director are disagreeing about here is not some mere hair-splitting piece of classification; it rather concerns the most central questions of all: 'What is the essential vision of the play?' and 'What is the effect the play should achieve in the theatre?'.

In the light of the research you have done into the genres of drama (see our suggestions on page 194), read the following four extracts carefully. We want you to:

(i) state what you think is likely to be the genre of the play from which each extract is taken;
(ii) suggest what it is in the subject matter and style of each passage that has led you to your conclusion.

In a way the second question is probably more important than the first. It might be possible to 'get the genre wrong', but for the very best of reasons. You are forming a judgement on the basis of a mere extract, and certainly in relation to at least one of the passages we have not played quite fair and you may be deceived. Read the plays in question for yourself to find out how accurate you were in your 'genre spotting.'

A. *The ageing Lear wishes to surrender the responsibilities of kingship; he determines to divide his kingdom among his daughters—Goneril, Regan and Cordelia—according to their love for him which he asks them to declare publicly.*

GONERIL: Sir, I love you more than word can wield the matter[1];
Dearer than eyesight, space, and liberty;
Beyond what can be valued[2], rich or rare;
No less than life, with grace, health, beauty, honour;
As much as child e'er lov'd, or father found; 5
A love that makes breath poor and speech unable[3]:
Beyond all manner of so much[4] I love you.

---

[1] more than words can express, handle.
[2] estimated.
[3] inadequate.
[4] beyond all these comparisons.

CORDELIA [*Aside*]: What shall Cordelia speak? Love, and be silent.
LEAR: Of all these bounds, even from this line to this[5],
With shadowy forests and with champains rich'd[6], 10
With plenteous rivers and wide-skirted meads[7],
We make thee lady: to thine and Albany's issues[8]
Be this perpetual.—What says our second daughter,
Our dearest Regan, wife of Cornwall? Speak.
REGAN: I am made of that self[9] metal as my sister, 15
And prize me at her worth. In my true heart
I find she names my very deed of love;
Only she comes too short, that I profess
Myself an enemy to all other joys
Which the most precious square of sense possesses[10], 20
And find I am alone felicitate[11]
In your dear Highness' love.
CORDELIA [*Aside*]: Then poor Cordelia!
And yet not so; since I am sure my love's
More ponderous than my tongue. 25
LEAR: To thee and thine hereditary ever
Remain this ample third of our fair kingdom;
No less in space, validity[12], and pleasure,
Than that conferr'd on Goneril.—Now, our joy,
Although our last and least[13]; to whose young love 30
The vines of France and milk of Burgundy
Strive to be interess'd[14]; what can you say to draw
A third more opulent than your sisters? Speak.
CORDELIA: Nothing, my lord.
LEAR: Nothing! 35
CORDELIA: Nothing.
LEAR: Nothing will come of nothing. Speak again.
CORDELIA: Unhappy that I am, I cannot heave
My heart into my mouth. I love your Majesty
According to my bond[15]; no more nor less. 40
LEAR: How, how, Cordelia! Mend your speech a little,
Lest you may mar your fortunes.
CORDELIA: Good my lord,
You have begot me, bred me, lov'd me; I
Return those duties back as are right fit, 45
Obey you, love you, and most honour you.
Why have my sisters husbands, if they say

[5] Lear is indicating on a map the part of the country he will give to Goneril.
[6] plains without woods.
[7] extensive grasslands.
[8] descendants (Albany is Goneril's husband).
[9] same.
[10] the most sensitive part of my nature claims and judges as joys.
[11] made happy.
[12] value.
[13] youngest.
[14] closely connected (Cordelia's hand in marriage is sought by the rulers of France and Burgundy).
[15] duty, obligation as a daughter.

They love you all? Haply, when I shall wed,
That lord whose hand must take my plight[16] shall carry
Half my love with him, half my care and duty. 50
Sure I shall never marry like my sisters,
To love my father all.

LEAR: But goes thy heart with this?

CORDELIA: Ay, my good lord.

LEAR: So young and so untender? 55

CORDELIA: So young, my lord, and true.

LEAR: Let it be so! Thy truth, then, be thy dower!
For, by the scared radiance of the sun,
The mysteries of Hecat[17] and the night;
By all the operation of the orbs[18] 60
From whom we do exist and cease to be;
Here I disclaim all my paternal care,
Propinquity[19] and property of blood,
And as a stranger to my heart and me
Hold thee from this for ever. The barbarous Scythian[20], 65
Or he that makes his generation messes[21]
To gorge his appetite, shall to my bosom
Be as well neighbour'd, pitied, and reliev'd,
As thou my sometime[22] daughter.

Shakespeare: *King Lear* (1604–5)

B. *Jack Worthing (Known as Ernest to Gwendolen) and Gwendolen Fairfax take the opportunity for a tête-à-tête while Gwendolen's mother, Lady Bracknell, is out of the room.*

JACK: Gwendolen, . . . We must get married at once. There is no time to be lost.

GWENDOLEN: Married, Mr Worthing?

JACK (*astounded*): Well . . . surely. You know that I love you, and you led me to believe, Miss Fairfax, that you were not absolutely indifferent 5 to me.

GWENDOLEN: I adore you. But you haven't proposed to me yet. Nothing has been said at all about marriage. The subject has not even been touched on.

JACK: Well . . . may I propose to you now? 10

GWENDOLEN: I think it would be an admirable opportunity. And to spare you any possible disappointment, Mr Worthing, I think it only fair to tell you quite frankly beforehand that I am fully determined to accept you.

JACK: Gwendolen!

---

[16] plighted troth, vows.
[17] goddess of the infernal world, associated with magic and witchcraft.
[18] astrological influence.
[19] close relationship.
[20] a type of the savage who eats his own offspring.
[21] portions of food.
[22] former.

GWENDOLEN: Yes, Mr Worthing, what have you got to say to me? 15
JACK: You know what I have got to say to you.
GWENDOLEN: Yes, but you don't say it.
JACK: Gwendolen, will you marry me? (*Goes on his knees.*)
GWENDOLEN: Of course I will, darling. How long you have been about it! I am afraid you have had very little experience in how to propose. 20
JACK: My own one, I have never loved any one in the world but you.
GWENDOLEN: Yes, but men often propose for practice. I know my brother Gerald does. All my girl-friends tell me so. What wonderfully blue eyes you have, Ernest! They are quite, quite, blue. I hope you will always look at me just like that, especially when there are other people present. 25

Enter LADY BRACKNELL.

LADY BRACKNELL: Mr Worthing! Rise, sir, from this semi-recumbent posture. It is most indecorous.
GWENDOLEN: Mamma! (*He tries to rise; she restrains him.*) I must beg you to retire. This is no place for you. Besides, Mr Worthing has not quite finished yet. 30
LADY BRACKNELL: Finished what, may I ask?
GWENDOLEN: I am engaged to Mr. Worthing, mamma. (*They rise together*).
LADY BRACKNELL: Pardon me, you are not engaged to any one. When you do become engaged to some one, I, or your father, should his health permit him, will inform you of the fact. An engagement should come on a young girl as a surprise, pleasant or unpleasant, as the case may be. It is hardly a matter that she could be allowed to arrange for herself. . . . 35

Oscar Wilde: *The Importance of Being Earnest* (1895)

C. *The scene is a church where the Friar is about to conduct the marriage ceremony which will unite Claudio and Hero; but Claudio and his friend Don Pedro, Prince of Aragon, have recently been deceived into believing that the chaste Hero is licentious. Among others also present are Hero's father, Leonato, and Benedick.*

LEONATO: Come, Friar Francis, be brief: only to the plain form of marriage, and you shall recount their particular[1] duties afterwards.
FRIAR: You come hither, my lord, to marry this lady?
CLAUDIO: No.
LEONATO: To be married to her, friar: you come to marry her. 5
FRIAR: Lady, you come hither to be married to this Count?
HERO: I do.
FRIAR: If either of you know any inward impediment why you should not be conjoined, I charge you on your souls to utter it.
CLAUDIO: Know you any, Hero? 10
HERO: None, my lord.
FRIAR: Know you any, Count?

---

[1] personal.

LEONATO: I dare make his answer, None.
CLAUDIO: O, what men dare do! What men may do! What men daily do,
not knowing what they do! 15
BENEDICK: How now? Interjections? Why then, some be of[2] laughing, as
ah, ha, he![3]
CLAUDIO: Stand thee by[4], friar. Father, by your leave:
Will you with free and unconstrained soul
Give me this maid, your daughter? 20
LEONATO: As freely, son, as God did give her me.
CLAUDIO: And what have I to give you back whose worth
May counterpoise[5] this rich and precious gift?
DON PEDRO: Nothing, unless you render her again.
CLAUDIO: Sweet Prince, you learn me noble thankfulness. 25
There, Leonato, take her back again.
Give not this rotten orange to your friend;
She's but the sign and semblance[6] of her honour.
Behold how like a maid[7] she blushes here!
O, what authority and show of truth 30
Can cunning sin cover itself withal!
Comes not that blood as modest evidence
To witness simple virtue? Would you not swear,
All you that see her, that she were a maid,
By these exterior shows? But she is none: 35
She knows the heat of a luxurious[8] bed:
Her blush is guiltiness, not modesty.
LEONATO: What do you mean, my lord?
CLAUDIO: Not to be married, not to knit my soul
To an approved wanton[9]. 40
LEONATO: Dear my lord, if you, in your own proof[10],
Have vanquish'd the resistance of her youth,
And made defeat of her virginity—
CLAUDIO: I know what you would say: if I have know her[11],
You will say she did embrace me as a husband, 45
And so extenuate the 'forehand sin.
No, Leonato.
I never tempted her with word too large,
But, as a brother to his sister, show'd
Bashful sincerity and comely love. 50
HERO: And seem'd I ever otherwise to you?
CLAUDIO: Out on thee, seeming! I will write against it.

---

[2] some are concerned with.
[3] examples of interjections.
[4] stand aside.
[5] equal, balance.
[6] outward show, seeming.
[7] chaste woman, virgin.
[8] lustful.
[9] prostitute, lecherous woman.
[10] experience.
[11] had sexual relations with her.

You seem to me as Dian[12] in her orb,
As chaste as is the bud ere it be blown;
But you are more intemperate in your blood[13] 55
Than Venus, or those pamper'd animals
That rage in savage sensuality.

HERO: Is my lord well that he doth speak so wide[14]?

LEONATO: Sweet Prince, why speak not you?

DON PEDRO: What should I speak? 60
I stand dishonour'd, that have gone about
To link my dear friend to a common stale[15].

LEONATO: Are these things spoken, or do I but dream?

DON JOHN: Sir, they are spoken, and these things are true.

BENEDICK: This looks not like a nuptial! 65

Shakespeare: *Much Ado About Nothing* (1598–9)

D. *After Hal and his friend have robbed a bank, they remove the corpse of Hal's mother from her coffin—it is the day of her funeral—hide the body in a cupboard and stash the loot in the coffin. Hal now enlists the assistance of Fay, a nurse, to help undress the corpse so it can be dumped in the countryside.*

FAY: I need help to get her out of the cupboard.

HAL *goes behind the screen.*

I'm not taking the head end.

HAL: She won't bite. You have your gloves on.

They lift the corpse from the wardrobe and lay it on the bed . . . 5
FAY *goes behind the screen.* HAL *takes a sheet from off the screen and spreads it on the floor.*

FAY (*from behind the screen*): Lovely-shaped feet your mother had. For a woman of her age.

She hands a pair of shoes across the screen. HAL *places them, in the centre* 10 *of the sheet.*

What will you do with the money?

She hands a pair of stockings over the screen.

HAL: I'd like to run a brothel. (*He pushes the stockings into the shoes.*) I'd run a two-star brothel. And if I prospered I'd graduate to a three-star 15 brothel. I'd advertise 'By Appointment'. Like jam.

FAY *hands a* W.V.S. *uniform across the screen.* HAL *folds it up and puts it into the sheet.*

[12] virginal goddess of the moon.
[13] passion, sexual desire.
[14] so far from the truth.
[15] prostitute.

I'd have a spade bird. I don't agree with the colour bar. And a Finnish bird. I'd make them kip together. To bring out the contrast. 20

FAY *hands a slip across the screen.* HAL *puts it into the pile.*

I'd have two Irish birds. A decent Catholic. And a Protestant. I'd make the Protestant take Catholics. And the Catholic take Protestants. Teach them how the other half lives. I'd have a blonde bird who'd dyed her hair dark. And a dark bird who'd dyed her hair blonde. I'd have a midget. 25 And a tall bird with big tits.

FAY *hands across the screen in quick succession, a pair of corsets, a brassiere and a pair of knickers.* HAL *puts them into the pile.*

FAY: Are you committed to having her teeth removed?
HAL: Yes 30

Pause.

I'd have a French bird, a Dutch bird, a Belgian bird, an Italian bird—

FAY *hands a pair of false teeth across the screen.*

—and a bird that spoke fluent Spanish and performed the dances of her native country to perfection. (*He clicks the teeth like castanets.*) I'd call it 35 the Consummatum Est. And it'd be the most famous house of ill-fame in the whole of England.

Joe Orton: *Loot* (1966)

IT MAKES ME LAUGH

As was the case with our generalisations about tragedy, our outline of a 'typical comedy' (see page 192) is too schematic to correspond with *all* the varied plays written in this form, and we need to guard against basing a view of a genre on one of its principal schools. For instance, our outline of a comedy would not do at all if we were considering the kind of satiric comedy written by Ben Jonson—see plays such as *Volpone* (1605–6) and *The Alchemist* (1610). Our summary does, however, give some idea of a tradition of romantic comedy which runs directly from Shakespeare, through Restoration Comedy to Oscar Wilde. You will also find the blueprint of this kind of plot visible in many other forms of writing, such as the novel.

You may have been struck by one point so far in our discussion of comedy: there has not been much reference to *laughter*, has there? And that is where most people's definition of comedy would begin. In fact, it is perfectly legitimate to think of the genre of comedy in terms of the shaping of a certain kind of plot and dramatic conventions, rather than as a trigger for instant laughter. If tragedy shows us the turning through its upper half-revolution of the Wheel of Fortune, the shape of comedy follows its contrary, more optimistic movement. However, humour is certainly a natural concomitant of the comic view of existence, though it can take many forms.

What makes me laugh (or smile) will probably be different from what amuses you. We must all have had the experience of telling a joke in public which we think is hilarious, only to be greeted at the punch line by an unsmiling circle of faces or a measured, polite response. It is an odd physical trait, laughter: an almost instinctive human response, it seems, yet open to wide subjective variation; erratic and unreliable. Humour often does not transfer well from one age to the next—hence the potentially ephemeral nature of some sorts of comedy—and it is difficult to study in a strictly academic fashion, though literary critics, among others, have a long record of having made the attempt. When we analyse this thing we call 'humour' it is liable to slip through our fingers, and there is, indeed, something inherently ludicrous about a group of people sitting around in a room and seriously discussing the subject of humour—or trying to write a chapter in a book on the subject.

And what different varieties of humour there are! Humour can have an audience 'rolling in the aisles'; but there is also 'thoughtful laughter' and the smile which is close to tears. There is humour which soothes us into accepting things as they are and humour of an iconoclastic kind which subverts our cosy expectations. There is humour which is primarily a matter of verbal wit and depends on such devices as the pun and the epigram. And there is humour of the banana-skin variety which is essentially visual: we need to see it enacted for us. For instance, in Molière's *Le Bourgeois Gentilhomme* (1660), the description on the page of Monsieur Jourdain's naive and ungainly attempts to learn the arts of fencing and dancing may look very thin; in the theatre, these scenes, depending on the skill of the actor, can produce a hilarious kind of physical comedy.

What lies behind humour? Many theories have been advanced, but can one single definition of the springs of humour account for all its varied manifestations? Is the source of laughter fundamentally malicious? Does laughter confirm our sense of superiority over somebody who has been shown to be absurd or is in a position we are glad we are not in ourselves? Laughter would then combine elements of relief and detachment. But is there not often a kind of fellow feeling produced by humour—a link forged between the mocker and the mocked? We can laugh *with* somebody at well as *at* him or her. Laughter can entail sympathy: 'There but for the grace of God go I.' Yet humour can have its exclusive side, confirming our sense of identity with a certain group: 'My kind of people find this very amusing, but you won't see the point.' What is it, however, that produces the laughter in the first place? Is it the result of our surprised sense of incongruity at some occurence or statement? Laughter might then derive from the disparity between what we expect or feel ought to be the case and things as they really are. Can laughter be used as a way of unmasking affectation and hypocrisy—and possibly of making us recognise our own follies? But surely humour does not have to be an instrument for instruction? Can it not be irresponsible—a joyous return to the lack of inhibitions of our childhood? The liberation of playtime? A safety valve? But then jokes also release aggression; they can be a means of asserting ourselves in a veiled way. Yet there is self-deprecating humour. It is also through laughter that we sometimes sanitize our latent anxieties and touch on normally taboo subjects. How can we pin down this thing we call humour?

We would like you to consider the relevance of *some* of these questions and suggestions about the nature of humour in relation to a specific passage of drama which has made many people laugh. It is taken from Alan Ayckbourn's *Absurd Person Singular* (1972).

It is Christmas Eve in the kitchen of Geoffrey and Eva Jackson's flat. Geoffrey is a womanizer who has told his wife the previous evening that he intends to leave her to live with somebody else. He has just returned from work, via the pub, when he remembers at the very last minute that they have invited some people round for a party. He interprets his wife's suicidal (if self-dramatizing) depression as a kind of wilful non-cooperation.

The first guests, Jane and Sidney Hopcraft, have just arrived.

GEOFFREY: Eva, come on, love, for heaven's sake.
[GEOFFREY *goes out, closing the door.*]
[EVA *opens the window. She inhales the cold fresh air. After a second, she climbs uncertainly on to the window ledge. She stands giddily, staring down and clutching on to the frame. The door opens, chatter,* GEOFFREY *returns, carrying a glass.*] 5
[*Calling behind him*] I'll get you a clean one, I'm terribly sorry. I'm afraid the cook's on holiday. [*He laughs.*]
[*The Hopcrofts' laughter is heard.* GEOFFREY *closes the door.*] Don't think we can have washed these glasses since the last party. This one 10 certainly didn't pass the Jane Hopcroft Good Housekeeping Test, anyway. [*He takes a dish cloth from the sink and wipes the glass rather casually.*] I sometimes think that woman must spend . . . Eva! What are you doing?
[EVA, *who is now feeling sick with vertigo, moans.*] 15
Eva! Eva – that's a good girl. Down. Come down – come down – that's a good girl – down. Come on . . . [*He reaches Eva.*] That's it. Easy. Come on, I've got you. Down you come. That's it.
[*He eases* EVA *gently back into the room. She stands limply. He guides her inert body to a chair.*] 20
Come on, sit down here. That's it. Darling, darling, what were you trying to do? What on earth made you want to . . .? What was the point of that, what were you trying to prove? I mean . . . [*He sees the note and the knife for the first time.*] What on earth's this? [*He reads it.*] Oh, no. Eva, you mustn't think of . . . I mean, what do you mean, a burden to 25 everyone? Who said you were a burden? I never said you were a burden . . .
[*During the above,* EVA *picks up the bread-knife, looks at it, then at one of the kitchen drawers. She rises, unseen by* GEOFFREY, *crosses to the drawer and, half opening it, wedges the knife inside so the point sticks out.* 30

She measures out a run and turns to face the knife. GEOFFREY, *still talking, is now watching her absently.* EVA *works up speed and then takes a desperate run at the point of the knife.* GEOFFREY, *belatedly realizing what she's up to, rushes forward, intercepts her and re-seats her.*]
Eva, now, for heaven's sake! Come on . . . [*He studies her nervously.*] 35
Look, I'm going to phone the doctor. I'll tell him you're very upset and overwrought. [*He backs away and nearly impales himself on the knife. He grabs it.*] He can probably give you something to calm you down a bit.
[*The doorbell rings.*]
Oh God, somebody else. Now, I'm going to phone the doctor. I'll just be 40
two minutes, all right? Now, you sit there. Don't move, just sit there like a good girl. [*Opening the door and calling off.*] Would you mind helping yourselves? I just have to make one phone call . . .
[GEOFFREY *goes out.*]
[*Silence.* EVA *finishes another note. A brief one. She tears it out and* 45
weights it down, this time with a tin of dog food which happens to be on the table. She gazes round, surveying the kitchen. She stares at the oven. She goes to it and opens it, looking inside thoughtfully. She reaches inside and removes a casserole dish, opens the lid, wrinkles her nose and carries the dish to the draining-board. Returning to the oven, she removes three shelves 50
and various other odds and ends that seem to have accumulated in there. It is a very dirty oven. She looks at her hands, now grimy, goes to the kitchen drawer and fetches a nearly clean tea towel. Folding it carefully, she lays it on the floor of the oven. She lies down and sticks her head inside, as if trying it for size. She is apparently dreadfully uncomfortable. She wriggles about 55
to find a satisfactory position.]
[*The door opens quietly and* JANE *enters.*]
[*The hubbub outside has now died down to a gentle murmur so not much noise filters through.* JANE *carries rather carefully two more glasses she considers dirty. She closes the door. She looks round the kitchen but sees no* 60
one. She crosses, rather furtively, to the sink and rinses the glasses. EVA *throws an oven tray on to the floor with a clatter.* JANE, *startled, takes a step back and gives a little squeak.* EVA, *equally startled, tries to sit up in the oven and hits her head with a clang on the remaining top shelf.*]
JANE: Mrs Jackson, are you all right? You shouldn't be on the cold floor in 65
your condition, you know. You should be in bed. Surely? Here . . .
[*She helps* EVA *to her feet and steers her back to the table.*]
Now, you sit down here. Don't you worry about that oven now. That oven can wait. You clean it later. No point in damaging your health for an oven, is there? Mind you, I know just what you feel like, though. You 70
suddenly get that urge, don't you? You say, I must clean that oven if it kills me. I shan't sleep, I shan't eat till I've cleaned that oven. It haunts you. I know just that feeling. I'll tell you what I'll do. Never say I'm not a good neighbour – shall I have a go at it for you? How would that be? Would you mind? I mean, it's no trouble for me. I quite enjoy it, 75
actually – and you'd do the same for me, wouldn't you? Right. That's settled. No point in wasting time, let's get down to it. Now then, what are we going to need? Bowl of water, got any oven cleaner, have you? Never mind, we'll find it – I hope you're not getting cold, you look very peaky.

[*Hunting under the sink.*] Now then, over cleaner? Have we got any? 80
Well, if we haven't, we'll just have to use our old friend Mr Vim, won't we? [*She rummages.*]

[*The door opens.* GEOFFREY *enters and goes to* EVA. *Conversation is heard in the background.*]

GEOFFREY: Darling, listen, it looks as if I've got . . . [*Seeing* JANE.] Oh. 85

JANE: Hallo, there.

GEOFFREY: Oh, hallo—anything you—want?

JANE: I'm just being a good neighbour, that's all. Have you by any chance got an apron I could borrow?

GEOFFREY [*rather bewildered, pointing to the chair*]: Er—yes—there. 90

JANE: Oh, yes. [*Putting it on.*] Couldn't see it for looking.

GEOFFREY: Er—what are you doing?

JANE: Getting your oven ready for tomorrow, that's what I'm doing.

GEOFFREY: For what?

JANE: For your Christmas dinner. What else do you think for what? 95

GEOFFREY: Yes, well, are you sure . . . ?

JANE: Don't worry about me. [*She bustles around singing loudly, collecting cleaning things and a bowl of water.*]

GEOFFREY [*over this, irritated*]: Oh. Darling—Eva, look I've phoned the doctor but he's not there. He's apparently out on a call somewhere and 100 the fool woman I spoke to has got the address and no number. It'll be quicker for me to try and catch him there than sitting here waiting for him to come back. Now, I'll be about ten minutes, that's all. You'll be all right, will you?

JANE: Don't you fret. I'll keep an eye on her. [*She puts on a rubber glove.*] 105

GEOFFREY: Thank you. [*He studies the immobile* EVA. *On a sudden inspiration, crosses to the kitchen drawer and starts taking out the knives. He scours the kitchen, gathering up the sharp implements.*]

[JANE *watches him, puzzled.*]

[*By way of explanation.*] People downstairs are having a big dinner party. 110 Promised to lend them some stuff.

JANE: Won't they need forks?

GEOFFREY: No. No forks. They're Muslims. [*As he goes to the door.*] Ten minutes.

[*The doorbell rings.*] 115

JANE: There's somebody.

GEOFFREY: The Brewster-Wrights, probably.

JANE: Oh . . .

[GEOFFREY *goes out, the dog barking as he does so, until the door is closed.*] 120

[*Turning to the oven.*] Now then—oh, this is going to be a big one, isn't it? Dear oh dear. Never mind. Where there's a will. [*Removing the tea towel from the oven.*] You haven't been trying to clean it with this, have you? You'll never clean it with this. Good old elbow grease—that's the way. [*She sets to work, her head almost inside the oven.*] Shall I tell you 125 something—Sidney would get so angry if he heard me saying this—but I'd far sooner be down here on the floor, on my knees in the oven—than out there, talking. Isn't that terrible? But I'm never at ease, really, at parties. I don't enjoy drinking, you see. I'd just as soon be out here, having a natter with you. [*She starts to sing cheerily as she works, her* 130 *voice booming round the oven.*]

[*During this,* EVA *rises, opens the cupboard, pulls out a tin box filled with first-aid things and searches through the contents. Eventually, she finds a white cylindrical cardboard pill box which is what she's looking for. She goes to the sink with it and runs herself a glass of water. She opens the box,* 135 *takes out a couple of small tablets and puts the box back on the draining-board. She swallows one tablet with a great deal of difficulty and water. The same with the second. She leaves the tap running, pulls the cotton-wool out of the box—and the rest of the pills rattle down the drain.* EVA *tries desperately to save some with her finger before they can disappear, turning* 140 *off the tap. This proving ineffective, she tries with a fork.*]

[*The door opens. Barking and chatting are heard.* SIDNEY *enters.*]

SIDNEY: Hallo, hallo. Where's everyone gone then . . .? [*Seeing* JANE] Dear oh dear. I just can't believe it. I just can't believe my eyes. You can't be at it again. What are you doing? 145

JANE: She's under the weather. She needs a hand.

SIDNEY: Do you realize that's your best dress?

JANE: Oh, bother my best dress.

SIDNEY: Mr and Mrs Brewster-Wright have arrived, you know. Ron and Marion. I hope they don't chance to see you down there. [*Turning to* EVA 150 *who is still fishing rather half-heartedly with the fork.*] And what's the trouble over here, eh? Can I help—since it seems to be in fashion this evening?

[SIDNEY *takes the fork from* EVA *and seats her in her chair.*]

Now. I'll give you a little tip, if you like. You'll never get a sink unblocked 155 that way. Not by wiggling a fork about in it, like that. That's not the way to unblock a sink, now, is it? All you'll do that way, is to eventually take the chrome off your fork and possibly scratch the plug hole. Not the way. Let's see now . . . [*He runs the tap for a second and watches the water running away.*] Yes. It's a little on the sluggish side. Just a little. But it'll 160 get worse. Probably a few tea-leaves, nothing more. Let's have a look, shall we? [*He opens the cupboard under the sink.*] Ten to one, this is where your troubles lie. Ah-ha. It's a good old-fashioned one, isn't it? Need the wrench for that one.

JANE: He'll soon fix that for you, won't you, Sidney? 165

SIDNEY: Brace of shakes. Shake of braces as we used to say in the Navy. I've got the tools. Down in the car. No trouble at all. [*He turns to* EVA.] Nothing serious. All it is, you see—where the pipe bends under the sink there—they call that the trap. Now then. [*He takes out a pencil.*] I'll show you. Always useful to know. Paper? [*He picks up* EVA*'s latest suicide* 170 *note.*] This is nothing vital, is it . . .? Now then [*He glances curiously at it, then turns it over and starts to draw his diagram on the back.*] Now—here's your plug hole, do you see, here—if I can draw it—and this is your pipe coming straight down and then almost doubling back on itself like that, for a second, you see? Then it runs away here, to the drain . . . 175

JANE: You want to know anything, you ask Sidney . . .

SIDNEY: And this little bit here's the actual drain trap. And all you have to do is get it open and out it all comes. Easy when you know. Now I suppose I'll have to walk down four flights for my tools. [*He screws up the paper and throws it away. At the door.*] Now, don't worry. Lottie's keeping them entertained at the moment and Dick's busy with George, so everybody's happy, aren't they? 180

[SIDNEY *opens the door and goes out. We hear* LOTTIE*'s laughter and the dog barking distantly for a moment before the door closes.*]

JANE: It's at times like this you're glad of your friends, aren't you? [*She goes at the oven with fresh vigour, singing cheerily.*] 185

(i) Read through again the string of questions in which we enumerated some of the possible general sources of humour (see page 202).
   (a) Do any of these suggestions explain why we might laugh at this scene? Which ones are relevant in connection with this passage?
   (b) How would you define the particular kind(s) of humour we find here?

(ii) 'The ingenious use of a full range of theatrical techniques and split-second timing are of the essence in comedy.' Discuss some of the principal devices Ayckbourn uses in this scene to produce humour.

(iii) What other passages in this book have you found amusing? (You might begin by considering, for instance, the extract from *The School for Scandal*—see page 71.) What are the sources of the humour?

General discussion topic

'In ordinary experience for long periods we may feel able to dispense with the metaphysical struggles and heightened awareness of tragic vision, but every morning at the bus stop we shall undoubtedly require our sense of the comic.' What are the implications of this statement? Do you agree?

15

General reading list

We hope that you will find the following list useful in guiding your reading of plays. Like all reading lists it is a personal choice, and you will finally want to make it your own selection by adding to it and subtracting from it. However, in order to give you some idea of where to start a reading course in drama, we have narrowed down our initial choice still further by asterisking 30 plays of outstanding quality which reveal the range of dramatic experience, though we hope that the round number does not suggest that this represents anything like a clear-cut 'top-thirty'!

In our full list you will find a preponderance of fairly modern drama: it is relatively easy to pick out the great plays which have endured from the past, but the process of theatrical natural selection has only just begun to operate on the plays of our own period.

We have taken the liberty of including Irish playwrights under our general heading of 'English drama'.

English Drama

C14–C15 Mystery play cycles: York, Wakefield
c.1510 *Everyman*
1552 *Ralph Roister Doister*—Nicholas Udall
1553 *Gammer Gurton's Needle*—attributed to either J. Still or William Stevenson
1562 *Gorboduc*—Thomas Norton and T. Sackville
1587 *The Spanish Tragedy*—Thomas Kyd
1589 *Friar Bacon and Friar Bungay*—Robert Greene
1592 **Doctor Faustus*—Christopher Marlowe
Edward II—Christopher Marlowe

Shakespeare

Comedies *Much Ado About Nothing* (1598)
**Twelfth Night* (1599)
As You Like It (1599)

Histories *Richard II* (1595)
**Henry IV*, Part 1 (1597)
Henry IV, Part 2 (1598)
Henry V (1598)

Tragedies *Hamlet* (1600)
Othello (1603)
**King Lear* (1605)
Macbeth (1605)
Antony and Cleopatra (1606)

Romances *The Winter's Tale* (1610)
**The Tempest* (1611)
1599 *The Shoemaker's Holiday*—Thomas Dekker
1604 *The Malcontent*—John Marston
1606 **Volpone*—Ben Jonson
The Revenger's Tragedy—Cyril Tourneur
1607 *The Knight of the Burning Pestle*—Francis Beaumont and John Fletcher
1610 *The Alchemist*—Ben Jonson
1612 *The White Devil*—John Webster
1614 **The Duchess of Malfi*—John Webster
1621 *Women Beware Women*—Thomas Middleton
1622 *The Changeling*—Thomas Middleton (and William Rowley)
1632 *'Tis Pity She's a Whore*—John Ford
1668 *She Would If She Could*—George Etherege
1671 *Samson Agonistes*—John Milton
1675 **The Country Wife*—William Wycherley
1677 *All For Love*—John Dryden
1682 *Venice Preserved*—Thomas Otway
1695 *Love For Love*—William Congreve
1697 *The Provoked Wife*—John Vanburgh
1700 **The Way of the World*—William Congreve
1706 *The Recruiting Officer*—George Farquhar
1728 *The Beggar's Opera*—John Gay
1773 **She Stoops to Conquer*—Oliver Goldsmith
1775 *The Rivals*—Richard B. Sheridan
1777 **The School for Scandal*—Richard B. Sheridan
1841 *London Assurance*—Dion Boucicault
1871 *The Bells*—Leopold Lewis
1886 *The Schoolmistress*—A. W. Pinero
1892 *Charley's Aunt*—Brandon Thomas
Lady Windemere's Fan—Oscar Wilde
1893 *The Second Mrs Tanqueray*—A. W. Pinero
1895 **The Importance of Being Earnest*—Oscar Wilde
1902 *The Admirable Crichton*—J. M. Barrie
1905 *The Voysey Inheritance*—Harley Granville Barker
Major Barbara—George Bernard Shaw
1906 *The Silver Box*—John Galsworthy
1907 **The Playboy of the Western World*—J. M. Synge
1910 *The Madras House*—Harley Granville Barker
Deirdre of the Sorrows—J. M. Synge
1912 *Pygmalion*—George Bernard Shaw
Hindle Wakes—Stanley Houghton
1915 *Hobson's Choice*—Harold Brighouse
1918 *Exiles*—James Joyce
1920 *The Skin Game*—John Galsworthy
1922 *The Shadow of a Gunman*—Sean O'Casey
Hassan—James Elroy Flecker
1923 **St Joan*—George Bernard Shaw
1924 *Juno and the Paycock*—Sean O'Casey
1926 *Rookery Nook*—Ben Travers

1928 *Journey's End*—R. C. Sheriff
**The Silver Tassie*—Sean O'Casey
1930 *Private Lives*—Noël Coward
1932 *Dangerous Corner*—J. B. Priestley
For Services Rendered—Somerset Maugham
1934 *Love on the Dole*—Walter Greenwood
1935 **Murder in the Cathedral*—T. S. Eliot
1936 *The Ascent of the F6*—W. H. Auden and Christopher Isherwood
1937 *Time and the Conways*—J. B. Priestley
1939 *Purgatory*—W. B. Yeats
1946 *The Winslow Boy*—Terence Rattigan
1948 *The Lady's Not For Burning*—Christopher Fry
1949 *The Cocktail Party*—T. S. Eliot
1951 *Penny for a Song*—John Whiting
1954 *The Quare Fellow*—Brendan Behan
1955 **Waiting for Godot*—Samuel Beckett
1956 *Look Back in Anger*—John Osborne
A Resounding Tinkle—N. F. Simpson
1957 *The Entertainer*—John Osborne
1958 *Live Like Pigs*—John Arden
Endgame—Samuel Beckett
A Taste of Honey—Shelagh Delaney
The Long, the Short and the Tall—Willis Hall
The Birthday Party—Harold Pinter
Five Finger Exercise—Peter Shaffer
Dock Brief—John Mortimer
1959 *Sergeant Musgrave's Dance*—John Arden
Roots—Arnold Wesker
1960 *A Man For All Seasons*—Robert Bolt
**The Caretaker*—Harold Pinter
1961 *The Devils*—John Whiting
1962 *Nil Carborundum*—Henry Livings
Chips With Everything—Arnold Wesker
Afore Night Come—David Rudkin
1963 *Everything in the Garden*—Giles Cooper
Oh What a Lovely War—Joan Littlewood and the Theatre Workshop
1964 *Armstrong's Last Goodnight*—John Arden
Entertaining Mr Sloane—Joe Orton
The Royal Hunt of the Sun—Peter Shaffer
1965 *Saved*—Edward Bond
A Patriot for Me—John Osborne
The Homecoming—Harold Pinter
1966 *Loot*—Joe Orton
Events while Guarding the Bofors Gun—John McGrath
1967 *Relatively Speaking*—Alan Ayckbourn
Rosencrantz and Guildenstern are Dead—Tom Stoppard
Zigger-Zagger—Peter Terson
1968 *Narrow Road to the Deep North*—Edward Bond
The Real Inspector Hound—Tom Stoppard
Forty Years On—Alan Bennett
1969 *The National Health*—Peter Nichols

1970 *Flint*—David Mercer
After Haggerty—David Mercer
1971 *Lear*—Edward Bond
Butley—Simon Gray
1972 *The Changing Room*—David Storey
Absurd Person Singular—Alan Ayckbourn
1973 *Equus*—Peter Shaffer
Habeas Corpus—Alan Bennett
1974 *Bingo*—Edward Bond
Travesties—Tom Stoppard
Savages—Christopher Hampton
1975 *The Norman Conquests*—Alan Ayckbourn
Bedroom Farce—Alan Ayckbourn
No Man's Land—Harold Pinter
City Sugar—Steven Poliakoff
Comedians—Trevor Griffiths
1976 *Treats*—Christopher Hampton
Donkey's Years—Michael Frayn
Weapons of Happiness—Howard Brenton
Destiny—David Edgar
1977 *Epsom Downs*—Howard Brenton
1978 *Plenty*—David Hare
1979 *Abigail's Party*—Mike Leigh
1981 *No End of Blame*—Howard Barker
Translations—Brian Friel

Ancient Greek
4th Century B.C.
Lysistrata and *Ecclesiazusae (Women in Power)*—Aristophanes
The Oresteia—Aeschylus
**King Oedipus*—Sophocles
The Bacchae—Euripedes

European
1637 *Le Cid*—Pierre Corneille
1640 *Horace*—Pierre Corneille
1643 *The Mayor of Zalamea*—Calderon
1660 *Le Bourgeois Gentilhomme*—Molière
1664 *Tartuffe*—Molière
1666 **The Misanthrope*—Molière
1667 *Andromaque*—Racine
1677 **Phèdre*—Racine
1750 *The Servant of Two Masters*—Carlo Goldini
1775 *The Barber of Seville*—Beaumarchais
1800 *Maria Stuart*—Friedrich Schiller
1808 *Faust I*—Goethe
1811 *The Prince of Homberg*—Kleist
1830 *Hernani*—Victor Hugo
1836 **The Government Inspector*—Nikolai Gogol
**Woyzeck*—Georg Büchner
1879 *A Doll's House*—Henrik Ibsen

1881 **Ghosts*—Henrik Ibsen
1884 *The Wild Duck*—Henrik Ibsen
1887 *The Father*—August Strinberg
1888 **Miss Julie*—August Strindberg
1890 *Hedda Gabler*—Henrik Ibsen
1896 *The Seagull*—Anton Chekhov
1897 *Uncle Vanya*—Anton Chekhov
1901 *The Three Sisters*—Anton Chekhov
1902 *The Lower Depths*—Maxim Gorky
1904 **The Cherry Orchard*—Anton Chekhov
1907 *A Flea in Her Ear*—Georges Feydeau
1908 *The Ghost Sonata*—August Strindberg
1921 **Six Characters in Search of an Author*—Luigi Pirandello
The Insect Play—Karel and Josef Čapek
1922 *Henry IV*—Luigi Pirandello
1928 *The Threepenny Opera*—Bertolt Brecht
1933 *Blood Wedding*—Frederico García Lorca
1935 *Tiger at the Gates*—Jean Giraudoux
1941 **Mother Courage*—Bertolt Brecht
1942 *Antigone*—Jean Anouilh
1943 *Galileo*—Bertolt Brecht
Les Mouches (The Flies)—Jean-Paul Sartre
1944 *Huis Clos (In Camera)*—Jean-Paul Sartre
1947 *The Maids*—Jean Genet
1950 *The Bald Prima Donna*—Eugène Ionesco
Ring Around the Moon—Jean Anouilh
1953 *The Lark*—Jean Anouilh
1954 *The Caucasian Chalk Circle*—Bertolt Brecht
1956 *The Visit*—Friedrich Dürrenmatt
The Balcony—Jean Genet
1958 *The Fire Raisers*—Max Frisch
1959 *Rhinoceros*—Eugène Ionesco
1962 *The Physicists*—Friedrich Dürrenmatt
1964 *The Representative*—Rolf Hochhuth

American
1921 *The Hairy Ape*—Eugene O'Neill
1930 *Once in a Lifetime*—Kaufman and Hart
1931 *Mourning Becomes Electra*—Eugene O'Neill
1935 *Waiting for Lefty*—Clifford Odets
1938 *Golden Boy*—Clifford Odets
Our Town—Thornton Wilder
1939 *The Little Foxes*—Lillian Hellman
1942 *The Skin of Our Teeth*—Thornton Wilder
1945 *The Glass Menagerie*—Tennessee Williams
1946 **The Iceman Cometh*—Eugene O'Neill
1947 *A Streetcar Named Desire*—Tennessee Williams
1949 **Death of a Salesman*—Arthur Miller
1953 *The Crucible*—Arthur Miller

1955 *A View from the Bridge*—Arthur Miller
Cat on a Hot Tin Roof—Tennessee Williams
1957 *Long Day's Journey into Night*—Eugene O'Neill
1959 *The Zoo Story*—Edward Albee
1961 *Who's Afraid of Virginia Woolf?*—Edward Albee
1967 *Little Murders*—Jules Feiffer
1969 *Indians*—Arthur Kopit

Index: Authors of extracts

Acknowledgments

The author and publishers would like to thank the following for their kind permission to reproduce copyright material: Reprinted by permission of William Heinemann Ltd: an extract from *The Art of the Theatre* by Edward Gordon Craig; Penguin Books Ltd for an extract from *Crito* by Plato, translated by Hugh Tredennick © Hugh Tredennick, 1954, 1959, 1969 and for an extract from *King Oedipus* by Sophocles from *The Theban Plays*, translated by E. F. Watling © E. F. Watling, 1947, 1974; J. M. Dent & Sons Ltd for an extract from 'Noah's Flood' from *Everyman and Medieval Mystery Plays* edited by A. C. Cawley; Michael Joseph Ltd for two extracts from *Billy Liar* by Keith Waterhouse; Methuen London for extracts from *An Actor Prepares* by Constantin Stanislavski, for an extract from 'Is there madness in the method?' by Tyrone Guthrie from *New Theatre Voices of the Fifties and Sixties*, for an extract from *The Cherry Orchard* by Anton Chekhov, translated by Michael Frayn, for two extracts from *The Caretaker* by Harold Pinter, for two extracts from *Loot* by Joe Orton, for an extract from *Lear* by Edward Bond, for an extract from *Playing Shakespeare* by J. Barton, for an extract from *The Fire Raisers* by Max Frisch, translated by M. Bullock, and for an extract from *The Resistible Rise of Arturo Ui* by Bertolt Brecht, translated by Ralph Manheim; Harvey Unna and Stephen Durbridge Ltd for an extract from *Unman, Wittering and Zigo* by Giles Cooper; Hamish Hamilton Ltd for an extract from *The Winslow Boy* by Terence Rattigan, and for an extract from *Huis Clos* (*In Camera*) by J.-P. Sartre, translated by S. Gilbert; The Society of Authors for two extracts from *St Joan* by Bernard Shaw, and for an extract from *Major Barbara* by Bernard Shaw; reprinted by permission of A. D. Peters & Co Ltd: an extract from *Abigail's Party* by Mike Leigh; Samuel French Ltd for an extract from *Hobson's Choice* by Harold Brighouse; Heinemann Educational for two extracts from *A Man For All Seasons* by Robert Bolt; Jonathan Cape Ltd for an extract from *Roots* by Arnold Wesker; Reprinted by permission of Faber & Faber Ltd: an extract from *Rosencrantz and Guildenstern are Dead* by Tom Stoppard, an extract from *Dirty Linen* by Tom Stoppard, an extract from *Look Back in Anger* by John Osborne, two extracts from *Waiting for Godot* by Samuel Beckett, an extract from *Habeus Corpus* by Alan Bennett, and an extract from *A Resounding Tinkle* by N. F. Simpson; Andre Deutsch Ltd for an extract from *Amadeus* by Peter Shaffer; Hodder & Stoughton Ltd for an extract from *The Admirable Crichton* by J. M. Barrie; Secker & Warburg for an extract from *Miss Julie* by Strindberg, translated by Michael Meyer; Penguin Books Ltd for an extract from *Death of A Salesman* by Arthur Miller © 1949 Arthur Miller; the Trustees of the Estate of Tennessee Williams for an extract from *The Glass Menagerie* by Tennessee Williams © Tennessee Williams; Chatto & Windus for an extract from *Absurd Person Singular* by Alan Ayckbourn.

We would also like to thank the Victoria and Albert Museum for permission to use the prints on pages 161, 166 and 167, and C. Walter Hodges for permission to reproduce the drawing on page 162.